HOW THEY MET

Also by Joey Green

HOW THEY MET

Fateful Encounters of Famous Lovers, Rivals, Partners in Crime, and Other Strange Bedfellows

Joey Green

BLACK DOG
& LEVENTHAL
PUBLISHERS
NEW YORK

Library of Congress Cataloging-in-Publication Data
on file at the offices of Black Dog & Leventhal.

Cover and interior design: Cindy LaBreacht

Book manufactured in the U.S.A.

Published by Black Dog & Leventhal Publishers, Inc.
151 West 19th Street, New York, NY 10011

Distributed by Workman Publishing Company
708 Broadway, New York, NY 10003

g f e d c b a

For Debbie,
my angel

Table of Contents

Introduction

"Dr. Livingstone, I presume?"

Having spent more than two years searching for explorer David Livingstone on the African continent, British explorer Henry Morton Stanley finally greeted Livingstone in the town of Ujiji, on Lake Tanganyika, on November 10, 1871, with what has undoubtedly become the most famous introduction in human history.

Meeting Livingstone changed Stanley's life forever. Instead of returning home immediately with the news of Livingstone's whereabouts, Stanley, inspired by Livingstone's hope of finding a source of the Nile River south of Lake Victoria, decided to stay. After Livingstone's death in 1873, Stanley carried on his friend's work, forever changing the course of world events.

What if Stanley had never found Livingstone? What if Napoleon had never met Josephine, if Matt Damon had never crossed paths with Ben Affleck, if Sonny had never bumped into Cher? Would we all be better off? Or would the beat still go on?

Kindred spirits seem magically to find each other all the time. Two complete strangers introduce themselves while sitting next to each other on an airplane, standing together in the check-out line in the grocery store, attending a church social, or after being randomly assigned to do a project together in Social Studies class. The next thing you know, they're married, they're recording hit records together, they're climbing Mount Everest, they're finding a cure for a deadly disease, they're inventing the world's first personal computer, or they're having a clandestine sexual liaison in the Oval office.

How do they find each other in the first place? What accounts for these chance encounters? Is there some cosmic plan at work behind the scenes? Is it fate? Kismet? Sheer coincidence? Perhaps novelist Doris Lessing explained these chance encounters best when she wrote: "Coincidences are God's way of remaining anonymous." The rest is up to us. All we have to do is recognize the moment and decide whether to seize the opportunity.

Here then are the stories of how dozens of famous couples, partners, and duos first met, and how seizing that moment changed their lives—and the course of human history—forever.

Bud Abbott and Lou Costello

While managing the National Theater in Detroit, Michigan, Bud Abbott performed as a straight man to several vaudeville comedians, including Harry Steepe and Harry Evanston. In 1931, the 36-year-old moved to Brooklyn, New York, where he worked as a cashier at the Casino Theater. One night, the

comedy team of Lyons and Costello were set to perform at the Brooklyn burlesque house. When straight man Lyons got sick, short, chubby, 25-year-old Lou Costello asked tall, slender Bud to substitute for his ailing straight man. The duo brought down the house, giving birth to the comedy team of Abbott and Costello.

Abbott and Costello worked burlesque, minstrel shows, and movie houses. In 1936, Abbott and Costello headlined in a burlesque show starring striptease artist Ann Corio. Corio graciously let Bud and Lou out of their burlesque contract so they could move up to vaudeville. In 1938, the comedy duo got national exposure on radio as regulars on *The Kate Smith Hour.*

On radio, they performed "Who's on First?"—a new routine written in collaboration with comedy writer John Grant, catapulting them to stardom. The following year, Universal Pictures, then a struggling movie studio, signed Abbott and Costello and put them in the 1940 movie *One Night in the Tropics,* starring Allan Jones and Nancy Kelly, as a "test run" to see how well movie audiences would respond to the comedy team. The movie became a huge success at the box office, prompting Universal to feature Abbott and Costello in the 1941 film, *Buck Privates,* with the Andrews Sisters. The film grossed ten million dollars, a company record at the time, turning Universal into a major movie studio and launching Abbott and Costello's long show business career.

STRANGE ENCOUNTERS

★ Born William Alexander Abbott on October 2, 1895, in Asbury Park, New Jersey, Bud was drugged at age fifteen and shanghaied aboard a ship bound for Norway. He began his show business career in 1918 as a treasurer of the National Theatre, a burlesque house in Washington, D.C.

★ Lou, born Louis Francis Cristillo on March 6, 1906, in Patterson, New Jersey, worked as a soda fountain clerk and a prizefighter. In 1927, he moved to Hollywood to break into movies, but could only get occasional work as a carpenter on the MGM and Warner lots. He appeared as an extra in the 1927 Laurel and Hardy film *The Battle of the Century,* and in the 1929 Delores Del Rio movie *The Trail of '98.* Frustrated, Lou worked his way back to the East Coast, stopping in St. Joseph, Missouri, where he got a job as a "Dutch comedian" in a burlesque theater.

★ Bud's mother performed as a bareback rider for the Ringling Bros. Circus.

★ Returning home to the East Coast, Lou continued pursuing burlesque jobs and worked as a dancing juvenile in *This Is Burlesque,* starring striptease artist Ann Corio. In 1933, Corio introduced Lou to his future wife, Anne Battler, who was in the show's chorus.

★ Bud and Lou remain the only two non-sportsmen honored in the Baseball Hall of Fame in Cooperstown, New York. The museum enshrined their "Who's On First?" routine on a plaque.

★ On November 4, 1943, after spending nine months recovering from rheumatic fever, Lou returned to work on *The Abbott and Costello Radio Show.* Three hours before air time, Costello received a telephone call informing him that his only son, Lou Costello, Jr., had drowned in a swimming pool—a day before his fourth birthday. Devastated, Costello went on with the show, refusing to disappoint the radio audience.

★ Lou mentions his hometown of Patterson, New Jersey, in virtually every episode of *The Abbott and Costello Show* on television and in many of the duo's films.

★ In 1991, the United States Postal Service issued a twenty-nine-cent stamp commemorating Abbott and Costello, drawn by caricaturist Al Hirschfeld.

★ At Lou's insistence, the comedy team split all their earnings with 60 percent going to Bud and 40 percent to himself. "Comics are a dime a dozen," explained Lou. "Good straight men are hard to find."

Woody Allen and Soon-Yi Previn

In November 1979, director and comedian Woody Allen began dating actress Mia Farrow. Publicity agent Robert Zarem had introduced them at Elaine's, the posh eatery in Manhattan's Yorkville neighborhood that Woody frequented.

At the time, Mia Farrow had recently divorced conductor André Previn, giving her custody of their six children: twins Matthew and Sascha, adopted Vietnamese orphans Kym Lark and Summer, adopted Korean orphan Soon-Yi, and biological son Fletcher.

While Woody dated Mia for several months, he never entered her Manhattan apartment and expressed no interest in meeting her children. He picked her up for dates by waiting downstairs in his chauffeured Rolls Royce. He met her children by accident in late September 1980. He pulled up to the apartment to pick up Mia just as she was bringing her children home from the playground. She introduced him to her kids, including Soon-Yi, believed to be around eight years old at the time.

Although they lived in separate apartments across Central Park, Woody and Mia adopted a son named Moses and a daughter named Dylan, and gave birth to a son named Satchel—prompting Woody to spend time at Mia's apartment. Eventually Soon-Yi, who had never really liked Woody, began doting on him, showing interest in basketball, asking him for help on her homework, and inviting him to her Sweet Sixteen party. Woody began taking Soon-Yi to Knicks basketball games.

In January 1990, freelance sports photographer Dominick Conde shot several photos of Woody holding hands with Soon-Yi at a Knicks game. Two weeks later, gossip columnist Cindy Adams, tipped off by another Knicks fan, reported in the *New York Post* that Woody had been seen at a game stroking the hair and kissing the cheek of a teenage girl. Confronted by Mia, Woody denied any impropriety.

In truth, Woody and Soon-Yi were having an affair. Soon-Yi, attending Marymount prep school, just a five-minute walk from Woody's apartment, would visit him during her lunch break. She also visited him on weekends by telling her mother that she was meeting a friend at Bloomingdale's. While starring with Bette Midler in the movie *Scenes from a Mall*, Woody got Soon-Yi a job as an extra in the film.

In 1992, Mia discovered Polaroid pictures of a nude Soon-Yi in Woody's apartment. She immediately ended her thirteen-year liaison with him, sued for custody of their adopted children, and accused Woody of having molested their adopted daughter, Dylan. Woody denied any improper behavior with his children and continued his romantic liaison with Soon-Yi, insisting that their relationship was normal. He claimed that the media attention and criticism brought them closer together.

STRANGE ENCOUNTERS

★ Before meeting Mia, Woody had cast her sister, Tisa, in his 1979 movie *Manhattan*. After *Manhattan*, Mia wrote Woody a fan letter. The letter, he later told her, had made his day.

★ In the 1979 movie *Manhattan*, Woody, playing the role of Isaac Davis, says: "I'm dating a girl who does homework."

★ Woody married and divorced Harlene Roses and Louise Lasser (who appeared in his earlier films), and had a long-term relationship with actress Diane Keaton (who starred in his 1977 movie *Annie Hall*).

★ Soon-Yi claims to have been born in 1970, although Mia insists that Soon-Yi was born in 1972, citing the results of a bone test performed in 1980. If Soon-Yi was born in 1972, she began having an affair with Woody when she was seventeen years old, making him at least thirty-five years her senior.

★ Soon-Yi was purportedly born to a physically abusive prostitute in Seoul, Korea, who punished her by making her kneel in a doorway and then slamming the door into her head. Abandoned by her mother, Soon-Yi scoured garbage cans for food and was eventually placed in a Catholic orphanage—unaware of her name, age, or how to speak Korean. The nuns named her Soon-Yi.

★ In her autobiography, *What Falls Away*, Mia claims that her ex-husband Frank Sinatra offered to have Woody Allen's legs broken after his affair with her adopted daughter Soon-Yi was discovered.

★ In 1993, a judge awarded Mia custody of adopted daughter Dylan, biological son Satchel, and adopted son Moses. The judge denounced Woody for his affair with Soon-Yi, and ruled that Woody could see Satchel once a week for an hour at a therapist's office. Mia changed Dylan's name to Eliza and Satchel's name to Seamus.

★ Soon-Yi received a master's degree in special education from Columbia University. Woody had been suspended from New York University.

★ Woody and Soon-Yi appeared together in the 1997 documentary *Wild Man Blues*.

★ On December 22, 1997, Woody and Soon-Yi, wearing street clothes, exchanged wedding vows in a small ceremony conducted by Mayor Massimo Cacciari at Palazzo Cavalli, the city hall in Venice, Italy—officially making Mia Woody's mother-in-law.

★ When Woody married Soon-Yi, Mia officially became his mother-in-law.

★ Woody and Soon-Yi adopted two daughters: Bechet Dumaine (named after jazz clarinetist Sidney Bechet) and Manzie Tio (named after Manzie Johnson, a drummer in Bechet's band, and Lorenzo Tio, the man who taught Bechet how to play).

Fred Astaire and Ginger Rogers

In 1906, seven-year-old Fred Astaire began touring the vaudeville circuit with his sister Adele as a dancing partner. The team eventually made their way to Broadway, starring in a string of hit musicals including *Lady, Be Good!*, *Funny Face*, *Smiles*, *The Band Wagon*, and *The Gay Divorce*. In August 1930, producer Alex Aarons brought Fred into a rehearsal for the Broadway show *Girl Crazy* to help fix a few dance routines. That afternoon Fred added a few steps to the "Embraceable You" dance number, dancing with actress Ginger Rogers for the first time. In 1932, Fred's sister Adele married Lord Charles Cavendish and quit show business. Undaunted, Fred headed to Hollywood to try his luck in motion pictures. The evaluation of his Hollywood screen test read: "Can't act. Can't sing. Balding. Can dance a little."

RKO put Fred under contract and then loaned him to MGM to appear in the 1933 movie *Dancing Lady* opposite Joan Crawford. RKO paired Fred with established comedienne Ginger Rogers as second leads in the 1933 movie *Flying Down To Rio*.

Ginger, having danced in vaudeville as a teenager, appeared in the Broadway musicals *Top Speed* and *Crazy Girl*. She began her Hollywood career with a bit part in the 1929 movie *A Night in a Dormitory*. Before being teamed with Fred, she appeared in nineteen movies, popularizing the songs "Did You Ever See A Dream Walking?" in the 1933 movie *Sitting Pretty* and "We're In the Money" in the movie *Gold Diggers of 1933*. "Rogers seldom played dewy-eyed ingénues," wrote movie critic Leonard Maltin in his *Movie Encyclopedia*. "Her characters were nearly always wisecracking, worldly dames who knew their apples."

Fred and Ginger performed one dance together in *Flying Down to Rio* and their fancy footwork in "The Carioca" stole the movie, launching the most famous dancing duo in movie history. RKO featured Fred and Ginger as the leads in the 1934 musical *The Gay Divorcée*, the first of ten Fred-and-Ginger musicals made over six years. The extravagant musicals provided escapist entertainment for movie audiences during the bleak years of the Depression.

Critics observed that Fred and Ginger seemed to make love through their dance routines. "Ginger was able to accomplish sex through dance," insisted Fred. "We told more through our movements instead of the big clinch. We did it all in the dance."

"We had fun and it shows," recalled Ginger. "True, we were never bosom buddies off the screen; we were different people with different interests. We were only a couple on film."

STRANGE ENCOUNTERS

★ Fred Astaire, born Frederick Austerlitz on May 10, 1899, in Omaha, Nebraska, was twelve years older than Ginger Rogers.

★ Ginger Rogers was born Virginia Katherine McMath in Independence, Missouri on July 16, 1911. Her younger cousin, unable to pronounce "Virginia" correctly, named her "Ginger."

★ When Ginger's parents separated, she and her mother moved into a hotel. Her father kidnapped her twice, but she was returned to her mother both times.

★ At nineteen, Ginger briefly dated *The New Yorker*'s founding editor Harold Ross, then thirty-seven.

★ Fred had very large hands, which he disguised by curling his middle two fingers while dancing.

★ Fred and Ginger starred together in eleven movies: *Flying Down to Rio, The Gay Divorcée, Top Hat, Roberta, Swing Time, Follow the Fleet, Shall We Dance?, A Damsel in Distress, Carefree, The Story of Vernon and Irene Castle,* and *The Barkleys of Broadway.*

★ After Ginger broke up the team in 1939 to concentrate on dramatic roles, Fred continued his dancing career, teaming with such partners as Lucille Bremer, Eleanor Powell, Rita Hayworth, Bing Crosby, Judy Garland, Jane Powell, Cyd Charisse, and Audrey Hepburn.

★ Ginger let her blond hair go naturally dark to play a working girl in the 1940 movie *Kitty Foyle*, winning the Academy Award for Best Actress.

★ In 1942, Ginger was Hollywood's highest-paid star.

★ As a Christian Scientist, Ginger neither smoked nor drank. She stocked the bar in her home with ice-cream sodas.

★ Ginger's mother Lela Rogers wrote the 1942 juvenile novel *Ginger Rogers and the Riddle of the Scarlet Cloak*.

★ During a temporary retirement from 1945 to 1947, Fred opened a chain of dancing schools. New York's Paramount Theater generated a petition of ten thousand names to persuade Fred to come out of retirement. He made a triumphant comeback in the 1946 movie *Easter Parade*.

★ Ginger was married and divorced five times. Her husbands were Edward Jackson Culpepper, Lew Ayres, Jack Briggs, Jacques Bergerac, and William Marshall, Jr.

★ Fred and Ginger reunited in the 1949 movie *The Barkleys of Broadway*.

★ In the 1950s, Ginger's mother, Lela Rogers, a leader of the Motion Picture Alliance for the Preservation of American Ideals, testified during the hearings of the House Committee on Un-American Activities that Ginger had turned down many films—including one based on Theodore Dreiser's *Sister Carrie*— because they were "un-American."

★ Fred was nominated for an Academy Award for best supporting actor for his role in the 1974 disaster movie *The Towering Inferno*.

★ When asked why the team was known as "Fred and Ginger" rather than "Ginger and Fred," despite Ginger's longer history in films, Ginger explained, "It's a man's world!"

★ Fred and Ginger are buried in the same cemetery—Oakwood Memorial Park in Chatsworth, California.

Lucille Ball and Desi Arnaz

In 1939, RKO Studios sent 28-year-old Lucille Ball, who had played a floozy with a heart of gold in the hit movie *Five Came Back*, to New York City to promote the film. While in New York, Lucy had instructions to go see the hit Broadway musical comedy *Too Many Girls*, written by Richard Rodgers and Lorenz Hart. RKO had bought the movie rights to the stage show, and the studio head hoped to give Lucy a starring role in the film.

While doing a pratfall on the ice-skating rink at Rockefeller Center for a publicity photo, Lucy cracked her sacroiliac—before getting a chance to see the show. Friends visiting her in the hospital told her that *Too Many Girls* featured a dynamic Cuban nightclub entertainer named Desi Arnaz who stole the show.

When Lucy finally went to see *Too Many Girls*, she couldn't take her eyes off 22-year-old Desi. "Then Desi opened his mouth and began talking in his own peculiar brand of broken English," recalled Lucy, "and a great belly laugh burst out of me." After the show, she went to La Conga, a club where Desi headlined nightly, singing and dancing the conga, a dance craze sweeping the nation. Lucy never met Desi that night. It was his night off.

Lucy returned to Hollywood to costar as a wisecracking burlesque striptease dancer in the movie *Dance, Girl, Dance*, starring Maureen O'Hara. On the day Lucy filmed the scene in which she stripteases in a burlesque house, director George Abbott, while having lunch in the RKO commissary with Desi and Eddie

Bracken (the only two members of the original Broadway cast of *Too Many Girls* hired to be in the film), called Lucy over. "I was wearing a slinky gold lamé dress slit up to my thigh, and my long reddish-gold hair fell over my bare shoulders," recalled Lucy. "I also sported a fake black eye, where my lover had supposedly socked me."

This is how she met Desi. "Desi reared back at the sight of me," recalled Lucy. "'Whatta honk of a woman!' he gasped."

"They hit it off right away," recalled Abbott. "It was love at first sight."

Maureen O'Hara attested that the two fell for each other immediately: "It was like *Wow!* A bolt of lightning. Lucille fell like a ton of bricks."

When Lucy saw Desi again later that day at a reading of the script, he didn't recognize her. No longer dressed like a battered tart, Lucy wore a yellow sweater and tight beige slacks. After being reintroduced, Desi invited Lucy out for rumba lessons and dinner at a Mexican restaurant called El Zarape, where they spent the night talking. "It was *not* love at first sight," recalled Lucy. "It took five minutes."

STRANGE ENCOUNTERS

★ Born Desiderio Alberto Arnaz y De Acha III in Santiago, Cuba, on March 2, 1917, Desi Arnaz was engaged to dancer Renée de Marco when he met Lucy. Within a few days, Desi called off the engagement.

★ Desi's father served as mayor of Santiago, Cuba, for ten years. His mother Delores was an heir to the Bacardi rum fortune. The 1933 Batista revolution landed his father in jail and stripped the Arnaz family of its wealth, property, and power.

★ In 1933, for the filming of the movie *Roman Scandals*, the makeup people at RKO shaved off Lucy's eyebrows. They never grew back.

★ In 1934, after Batista's Cuban revolution, seventeen-year-old Desi fled to Miami, where he lived with his father in a rat-infested warehouse and worked at a pet store cleaning canary cages.

★ On March 19, 1936, Lucy registered as a voter for the Communist Party solely to please her maternal grandfather, Fred Hunt. In 1952, the House Un-American Activities Committee (HUAC) summoned Lucy to appear before a closed session to explain herself. Since she had never voted in any Communist primaries, the committee let her go. In 1953, HUAC reopened its investigation of Lucy's alleged communist activities, questioned her again behind closed doors for several hours, but ultimately cleared the redhead of all charges.

★ The initial five-year contract Desi signed with RKO prohibited him from getting married during that time.

★ Besides Lucy and Desi, the 1940 movie *Too Many Girls* starred Eddie Bracken, Hal LeRoy, Van Johnson, and Ann Miller. In the film, prestigious Pottawatomie College in Stopgap, New Mexico, hires four boys to keep an eye on footloose Lucy. The movie marked the film debuts of Arnaz, Bracken, and Johnson.

★ Before dawn on November 30, 1940, Desi and Lucy eloped by driving from the Pierre Hotel in New York City to Greenwich, Connecticut, with Desi's agent and business manager to act as witnesses. Just across the state line in Connecticut, the eager couple could avoid New York's required waiting period and return to Manhattan, according to Desi's calculations, in time for his noon performance at the Roxy Theatre. The blood tests, however, took longer than anticipated. Then Desi had to send his business manager into Woolworth's to buy a brass ring for Lucy. The justice of the peace also slowed things down by insisting upon marrying the couple in a more romantic environment than his office, bringing them to the Bryam River Beagle Country Club to conduct the ceremony before a roaring fireplace. The couple then returned to New York City where Desi, having missed the first of his five performances, carried Lucy over the threshold of the Roxy Theater. When Desi and Lucy walked onto the stage, the audience, having been told why the show would be starting late, gave the newlywed couple a standing ovation.

★ On their wedding night, Desi woke Lucy out of a sound sleep in the Pierre Hotel to get him a glass of water, which she obligingly did.

★ For many years during their marriage, Lucy and Desi hid the fact that she was six years older than he by splitting the difference in their ages. They said they were both born in 1914.

★ Lucy, born a brunette, first became a redhead in 1943 at the hands of MGM's image makers.

★ *I Love Lucy* was based on the radio show *My Favorite Husband*, based on the 1940 best-selling novel *Mr. and Mrs. Cugat: The Record of a Happy Marriage* by Isabel Scott Rorick. Coincidentally, Desi had performed in 1938 with big band leader Xavier Cugat, who had no connection to the main character in the novel.

★ With *I Love Lucy*, Lucy and Desi pioneered the three-camera technique which became the standard in filming television sitcoms and developed the concept of syndicating television programs.

★ Lucy became the first woman to own her own film studio as the head of Desilu.

★ The cover of the first issue of *TV Guide*, published in 1953, featured a photograph of Lucy and her newborn son Desi Arnaz, Jr.

★ Lucy divorced Desi in 1960 and bought out his share of Desilu Productions, selling the company to Paramount in 1968.

★ During an interview with Barbara Walters, Jane Fonda claimed that her father Henry Fonda was deeply in love with Lucy and that the two were "very close" during the filming of the 1968 movie *Yours, Mine, and Ours*.

★ Lucy died on April 26, 1989—the fifty-sixth birthday of her close friend, Carol Burnett.

Antonio Banderas and Melanie Griffith

In January 1995, actress Melanie Griffith met actor Antonio Banderas on the set of the movie *Two Much*. Melanie called it love at first sight. Unfortunately, at the time, both Melanie and Antonio were married to other people. In fact, Melanie was on her third marriage.

In 1976, nineteen-year-old Melanie married actor Don Johnson. They divorced a few months later. After appearing in several unmemorable movies (*Night Moves*, *Smile*, *The Drowning Pool*), and struggling with substance abuse in the wake of a car accident, Melanie married actor Steven Bauer in 1980. After achieving critical acclaim for her roles in the movies *Body Double* and *Something Wild*, Melanie divorced Bauer in 1987. She was nominated for an Academy Award as best actress for the 1988 movie *Working Girl*, and the following year remarried her first husband Don Johnson, who starred as Detective Sonny Crockett on the hit television series *Miami Vice* from 1984 to 1989. The couple co-starred in the 1991 movie *Paradise* and the 1993 remake of *Born Yesterday*. Melanie divorced Johnson again in 1996 to marry Antonio Banderas in London on May 14, 1996.

Born in Málaga, Spain, to a police officer and a teacher, José Antonio Dominguez Banderas began his acting career in theater and television in Madrid, where he became a regular in

movies by director Pedro Almodóvar, most notably the 1988 film *Women on the Verge of a Nervous Breakdown.* That same year he married actress Ana Leza, who had appeared in the film with him. He crossed into American films with the 1992 movie *The Mambo Kings.* In 1996, Banderas divorced Ana Leza to marry Melanie.

S T R A N G E   E N C O U N T E R S

★ While Melanie is three years older than Antonio, their birth dates are one day apart. She was born on August 9, 1957. He was born on August 10, 1960.

★ Melanie met Don Johnson while he was costarring with her mother, actress Tippi Hedren, in the 1973 movie *The Harrad Experiment.*

★ During the filming of the 1963 movie *The Birds,* starring Tippi Hedren, director Alfred Hitchcock gave Tippi's daughter Melanie a doll that looked exactly like her mother. The doll came in an ornate wooden box, which Melanie misconstrued to be a coffin, frightening her.

★ As a teenager, Antonio aspired to a career as a professional soccer player—until he broke his foot.

★ Melanie auditioned for the title role in the 1976 movie *Carrie,* but lost the part to Sissy Spacek.

★ During filming of the 1977 movie *Roar,* produced by her mother Tippi, Melanie was mauled by a lion and required plastic surgery.

★ While walking through a crosswalk on Sunset Boulevard in 1978, Melanie was hit by a car and flung onto the curb.

★ Unable to speak English, Antonio learned his lines for the 1992 movie *The Mambo Kings* phonetically.

★ Antonio refers to his first wife Ana Leza as Anita. She appeared with him in the 1993 movie *Philadelphia.*

★ Melanie has children from three different husbands: Alexander Bauer (with Steven Bauer), Dakota Johnson (with Don Johnson), and Stella Banderas (with Antonio Banderas).

★ Melanie's daughters Dakota and Stella played her daughters in the 1999 movie *Crazy in Alabama,* directed by husband Antonio.

★ Melanie declared her love for Antonio by having a large heart inscribed with his name tattooed on her arm.

Roseanne Barr and Tom Arnold

In 1988, Scott Hanson, the owner of the Comedy Club in Minneapolis, Minnesota, booked comedienne Roseanne Barr to be his headline act. He scheduled a meeting to introduce her to the male comedian he had booked as her opening act. Roseanne hated sexist male comedians. When 29-year-old Tom Arnold, who had recently won first place in the Minneapolis Comedy Competition, arrived late for the meeting, 37-year-old Roseanne said, "Listen, you don't do any pig-type shit, do ya?"

"Oh, no, no," replied Tom. "I don't do any kind of sexist stuff. Not at all. Well, I call women cum dumpsters and hose-bags and stuff like that. Is that okay?"

Roseanne cracked up, instantly warming to Tom's irreverence. He offered her some cocaine. Roseanne says it was one of the first times she had used the drug. That night at the club, Roseanne was awed by Tom's act. He was equally impressed by hers. After the show, Tom invited Roseanne to a party at the house where he was staying. "Up in this room that wasn't his, we slept side by side, huddled on top of a sleeping bag," recalls Roseanne. "There was nothing sexual at all between us. It was like meeting your doppelganger." At the time, Roseanne had been married to Bill Pentland for fourteen years. Bill was back home in Denver, Colorado, with their three kids. Tom was engaged.

Tom began writing material for Roseanne, who took him on tour as her middle act. When Roseanne was offered the opportunity to create and star in her own television series, she convinced Tom to move to Los Angeles with his fiancée to work on her television show, *Roseanne*. Unable to get Tom a job as a writer for the first season of the show, Roseanne got him hired as the comedian who warms up the audience during the tapings. He stunk. When the producers fired him, Roseanne got him a job as a writer on her HBO special.

On February 12, 1989, Tom took Roseanne to a Grateful Dead concert at the Forum in Los Angeles, where, under the influence of marijuana, he confessed his love for her. She drove him back to his apartment in Van Nuys where, after pouring their hearts out to each other, Tom asked Roseanne to divorce her husband. Two nights later, Roseanne spent Valentine's Day with Tom, getting stoned at his apartment. A reporter from the *National Enquirer,* apparently tipped off by Roseanne's husband Bill, knocked at the door and asked Roseanne when she was planning to leave her husband to marry Tom Arnold.

With the cat out of the bag, Rosie threatened to leave her smash hit sitcom unless the production company fired producer Matt Williams and hired Tom as a writer. Tom was made a writer on the show. In March, Roseanne and her sister Steph drove to Tom's apartment, unannounced. Roseanne sent Steph to get Tom, who got into the car. Roseanne told him that she wanted to consummate their relationship.

"I glared at Tom," she recalled, "and just for effect hit the automatic door locks." They drove to a motel in Encino. Steph paid the twenty-seven dollars for the room with her credit card, and Roseanne and Tom went up to the room. Steph waited. "We went into the room and came out about thirteen minutes later," recalls Roseanne. "Tom swears it was sixteen."

Shortly afterwards, Tom broke off his engagement to his fiancée Denise, and Roseanne divorced her husband Bill after nearly twenty years of marriage.

STRANGE ENCOUNTERS

★ Roseanne, born Roseanne Cherrie Barr on November 3, 1952, in Salt Lake City, Utah, dropped out of Salt Lake High School East, and worked as a dishwasher, cook, and waitress.

★ Tom Arnold was born on March 6, 1959, in Ottumwa, Iowa.

★ At age seventeen, Roseanne, having been confined to a state mental hospital, left Utah and moved to Denver, Colorado, where she gave birth to a daughter named Brandi, who she put up for adoption.

★ After graduating from the University of Iowa, Tom moved to Minneapolis and worked as a meat packer, box stacker, bartender, and bouncer—to support himself as a stand-up comedian.

★ Roseanne based the character Dan Conner, her husband on *Roseanne,* on Tom Arnold.

★ Tom converted to Judaism to marry Roseanne. Despite their divorce, he remains committed to Judaism.

★ Roseanne is six years older than Tom.

★ At the 1989 World Series, Roseanne and Tom dropped their pants and mooned the crowd to show off their tattoos of each other's names.

★ Roseanne had a tattoo on the inside of her thigh that read "Property of Tom Arnold."

★ After featuring Tom as a semi-regular on *Roseanne* and making him a producer, Roseanne convinced the network to give him his own sitcom, the short-lived *Jackie Thomas Show*.

★ In her book *My Lives*, Roseanne claims that she was sexually abused as a child. She also claims that she suffered from Multiple Personality Disorder. In a 1991 *People* magazine interview, she accused both parents of having abused her physically and sexually, charges they publicly denied.

★ After filing for divorce from Tom on April 18, 1994, Roseanne began a two-month vacation touring Europe. When Tom heard rumors that 41-year-old Roseanne was having an affair with her 29-year-old bodyguard and chauffeur Ben Thomas, he flew to the Mediterranean island of Sardinia to confront her, only to be shooed away.

★ After Roseanne divorced Tom, critics predicted the demise of Tom's career, but his excellent performance in the 1994 movie *True Lies*, starring Arnold Schwarzenegger, revitalized his career. Tom also gave an outstanding performance in the 1995 movie *Nine Months*, starring Hugh Grant. Subsequently, Tom starred in the 1997 movie *McHale's Navy*, which bombed at the box office.

★ In 1995, Roseanne married her former bodyguard Ben Thomas and had a tubal ligation reversed to get pregnant with their son, Buck. The couple divorced in 2002.

★ Roseanne has five children: Brandi (whom she put up for adoption); Jennifer, Jessica, and Jacob (with first husband Bill Pentland); and Buck (with third husband Ben Thomas).

★ Roseanne played the role of the Wicked Witch of the West in the Broadway production of *The Wizard of Oz*.

★ In 2000, Tom announced in the *National Enquirer* that he wanted to marry again and that he was accepting applications through his web site, www.marrytom.com.

★ Tom has been married three times, to Roseanne, hairdresser Julie Champnella, and political consultant Shelby Roos.

Burt Baskin and Irv Robbins

As a teenager in the 1930s, Irv Robbins managed an ice cream shop in Tacoma, Washington. Bored with serving traditional flavors like chocolate and vanilla, Irv began experimenting, mixing fruit and candies into the ice cream. In 1945, after serving in World War II, Irv moved to Glendale, California, and opened an ice cream parlor called Snowbird, featuring twenty-one exotic flavors.

Irv's brother-in-law, Burt Baskin, shared his entrepreneurial dream and opened his own ice cream shop called Burton's. In 1946, the two brothers-in-law decided to team up and open an ice cream store together. They flipped a coin to see whose name would go first on the sign. Burt won. By 1948, Burt and Irv had opened six successful Baskin-Robbins ice cream stores. Realizing that the proper care of each store required a manager with a vested interest in its success, the brothers-in-law began licensing the operation of Baskin-Robbins stores, pioneering the concept of franchising in the ice cream industry. In 1953, they added the number "31" to the logo at all Baskin-Robbins stores, offering customers thirty-one different flavors of ice cream—one for each day of the month.

STRANGE ENCOUNTERS

★ Baskin-Robbins, the world's largest chain of ice cream specialty stores, has more than 4,500 locations around the world.

★ In the United States alone, Baskin-Robbins stores serve more than 150 million ice cream cones each year.

★ Baskin-Robbins has created nearly one thousand ice cream flavors, with such whimsical names as Beatle Nut (in honor of Beatlemania), Lunar Cheesecake (in honor of the Apollo 11 moon landing), Winter White Chocolate, Love Potion #31, and Trick-Oreo-Treat.

★ The best-selling flavors at Baskin-Robbins are Vanilla, Chocolate, Mint Chocolate Chip, Pralines 'n Cream, and Chocolate Chip.

★ Baskin-Robbins popularized the practice of offering free tastes on miniature pink spoons to help customers decide which flavor to choose.

★ In 1957, when the Brooklyn Dodgers moved to Los Angeles, Baskin-Robbins introduced "Baseball Nut" ice cream—complete with a raspberry for the umpire.

★ In 1965, Baskin-Robbins introduced "0031 Secret Bonded Flavor" ice cream in honor of James Bond.

★ In 1968, as Americans tuned into the television comedy *Laugh-In*, Baskin-Robbins introduced "Here Comes The Fudge" ice cream.

★ Burt Baskin and Irv Robbins' idea to franchise their stores inspired the company's former milk shake machine salesman, Ray Kroc, to adopt the technique in expanding his new chain of McDonald's hamburger outlets.

★ Baskin-Robbins rotates nearly 100 flavors through its stores every year.

★ In his book, *The Food Revolution*, John Robbins, son of Irv, tells that his family had "an ice cream cone-shaped swimming pool, our cats were named after ice cream flavors, and I sometimes ate ice cream for breakfast."

Carl Bernstein and Bob Woodward

On the morning of Saturday, June 17, 1972, Barry Sussman, the city editor of the *Washington Post*, telephoned reporter Bob Woodward, who had been working at the newspaper for nine months, and asked him to come in to the office to cover a burglary at the headquarters of the Democratic National Committee in the Watergate complex. The ambitious Woodward began making phone calls, and noticed that fellow reporter Carl Bernstein, whose desk sat a few rows away, was also working on the burglary story. The two reporters had never worked together. Woodward had heard rumors that Bernstein frequently weaseled his way into working on important stories to get his byline on them. He intended to steer clear of the parasitic Bernstein.

Bernstein, who had been calling waiters, maids, and desk clerks at the Watergate for any information they might have, soon realized that Woodward was also working on the burglary story. Bernstein, a college dropout who had worked himself up from a copy boy to full reporter at the *Washington Star* by age nineteen, figured that Woodward, a Yale graduate who couldn't write very well, had landed his job at the *Washington Post* based on his credentials, not talent.

Alfred E. Lewis, the *Washington Post*'s police reporter, phoned in the first details of the burglary to Woodward and told him that the five suspects were scheduled to appear in court that afternoon for a preliminary hearing. Woodward went. He discovered that one of the five burglars, James W. McCord, Jr., claimed to be a former employee of the CIA, and that the group, including three Cuban-Americans, had plotted to bug the offices of the Democratic National Committee. The story made the front page of the Sunday paper, which also carried a story by Bernstein on the suspects, all of whom seemed to have connections to the CIA.

City editor Barry Sussman asked both Woodward and Bernstein to return to work on Sunday morning to follow up on the burglary story. That morning they learned from an item on the Associated Press wire service that James McCord was the security coordinator for President Richard M. Nixon's reelection committee. Astonished, Woodward and Bernstein suddenly found themselves working together to track down McCord or people who knew him.

Woodward began typing up the profile and turned in the first page to an editor on the city desk. "A minute later, Bernstein was looking over the editor's shoulder, Woodward noticed," according to the reporters' account in *All the President's Men*. "Then Bernstein was walking back to his desk with the first page of the story; soon he was typing. Woodward finished the second page and passed it to the editor. Bernstein had soon relieved him of it and was back at his typewriter. Woodward decided to walk over and find out what was happening. Bernstein was rewriting the story. Woodward read the rewritten version. It was better."

An investigative partnership was born.

STRANGE ENCOUNTERS

★ *Washington Post* editor Ben Bradlee referred to Woodward and Bernstein collectively as "Woodstein."

★ Carl Bernstein, born on February 14, 1944, in Washington, D.C., dropped out of the University of Maryland. In 1966, he joined the *Washington Post*.

★ Robert Upshur Woodward, born on March 26, 1943, in Geneva, Illinois, graduated from Yale in 1965 and spent five years in the Navy as a communications officer. He began his newspaper career with the Montgomery County *Sentinel* in 1970, and joined the *Washington Post* in September 1971.

★ On May 26, 1972, a group of seven members of President Richard M. Nixon's reelection committee tried to break into the headquarters of the Democratic National Committee (DNC) in the Watergate Building and bug the offices. Nicknamed the "plumbers," the group waited in a rented banquet hall in the Watergate building until DNC staffers went home. The plumbers accidentally got locked in the banquet hall and hid for the night in a liquor cabinet, where former CIA operative E. Howard Hunt relieved himself by urinating into a bottle of Johnny Walker Red.

★ On the night of May 28, the plumbers broke into the Democratic headquarters and planted their electronic bugs. The main bug, however, wasn't working properly, so they planned to return on June 17. James McCord put a strip of electrical tape over the lock of an entry door from the garage so they could enter the building later. Before the team arrived, the tape was removed. McCord stuck a new piece of tape over the lock. That second piece of tape prompted a security guard to call the police, who arrested the plumbers for trying to break into DNC headquarters, eventually leading to Nixon's resignation.

★ Bernstein and Woodward abbreviated Richard Nixon's Committee to Re-Elect the President to the acronym CREEP.

★ While investigating the Watergate scandal, Woodward and Bernstein referred to an anonymous Nixon administration source as Deep Throat. To this day, Deep Throat's true identity remains a mystery.

★ Bernstein and Woodward wrote *All the President's Men* and *The Final Days*. The 1974 movie version of *All the President's Men* starred Robert Redford as Woodward and Dustin Hoffman as Bernstein.

★ The 1986 movie *Heartburn,* written by Nora Ephron and based on her novel of the same name, stars Jack Nicholson and Meryl Streep as a mismatched married couple—based on Ephron and her ex-husband, Carl Bernstein.

Edwin Binney and C. Harold Smith

I n 1864, Joseph W. Binney founded the Peekskill Chemical Works in Peekskill, New York, producing hardwood charcoal and a black pigment called lamp-black. In 1880, he opened a New York office and invited his son, Edwin Binney, and his nephew, C. Harold Smith, to join the company. The cousins renamed the company Binney & Smith and expanded the product line to include shoe polish, printing ink, and black crayons.

In 1900, Binney & Smith bought a water-powered stone mill along Bushkill Creek near Easton, Pennsylvania, to make slate pencils for schools using slate and other materials from nearby quarries. The success of the pencils led Binney & Smith to develop chalk for teachers. Binney & Smith chalk was dustless, made by a process called extrusion, still used to this day. Binney & Smith chalk won a Gold Medal for excellence at the 1902 St. Louis Exposition.

In 1903, Binney & Smith made the first box of Crayola crayons, costing a nickel and containing eight colors: red, orange, yellow, green, blue, violet, brown, and black. In 1958, the company introduced the now-classic box of sixty-four crayons, complete with built-in sharpener. In 1993, Binney & Smith celebrated Crayola brand's ninetieth birthday by introducing the biggest crayon box ever with ninety-six colors.

STRANGE ENCOUNTERS

★ Alice Binney, wife of company co-owner Edwin Binney, coined the word Crayola by joining *craie*, from the French word meaning chalk, with *ola*, from oleaginous, meaning oily.

★ In 1949, Binney & Smith introduced another forty colors: Apricot, Bittersweet, Blue Green, Blue Violet, Brick Red, Burnt Sienna, Carnation Pink, Cornflower, Flesh (renamed Peach in 1962, partly as a result of the civil rights movement), Gold, Gray, Green Blue, Green Yellow, Lemon Yellow, Magenta, Mahogany, Maize, Maroon, Melon, Olive Green, Orange Red, Orange Yellow, Orchid, Periwinkle, Pine Green, Prussian Blue (renamed

Midnight Blue in 1958 in response to teachers' requests), Red Orange, Red Violet, Salmon, Sea Green, Silver, Spring Green, Tan, Thistle, Turquoise Blue, Violet Blue, Violet Red, White, Yellow Green, and Yellow Orange.

★ In 1958, Binney & Smith brought the total number of colors to sixty-four by adding sixteen new colors: Aquamarine, Blue Gray, Burnt Orange, Cadet Blue, Copper, Forest Green, Goldenrod, Indian Red, Lavender, Mulberry, Navy Blue, Plum, Raw Sienna, Raw Umber, Sepia, and Sky Blue.

★ In 1972, Binney & Smith introduced eight fluorescent colors: Atomic Tangerine, Blizzard Blue, Hot Magenta, Laser Lemon, Outrageous Orange, Screamin' Green, Shocking Pink, and Wild Watermelon. In 1990, the company introduced eight more fluorescent colors: Electric Lime, Magic Mint, Purple Pizzazz, Radical Red, Razzle Dazzle Rose, Sunglow, Unmellow Yellow, and Neon Carrot.

★ In 1990, Binney & Smith retired eight of its traditional colors from the box of sixty-four crayons (Green Blue, Orange Red, Orange Yellow, Violet Blue, Maize, Lemon Yellow, Blue Gray, and Raw Umber) and replaced them with such New Age hues as Cerulean, Vivid Tangerine, Jungle Green, Fuchsia, Dandelion, Teal Blue, Royal Purple, and Wild Strawberry. Retired colors were enshrined in the Crayola Hall of Fame. Protests from groups such as RUMPS (The Raw Umber and Maize Preservation Society) and CRAYON (The Committee to Reestablish All Your Old Norms) convinced Binney & Smith

to release one million boxes of the classic Crayola Eight in October 1991.

★ In 1993, Binney & Smith introduced sixteen more colors, all named by consumers: Asparagus, Cerise, Denim, Granny Smith Apple, Macaroni and Cheese, Mauvelous, Pacific Blue, Purple Mountain's Majesty, Razzmatazz, Robin's Egg Blue, Shamrock, Tickle Me Pink, Timber Wolf, Tropical Rain Forest, Tumbleweed, and Wisteria.

★ On average, children between the ages of two and seven color twenty-eight minutes a day.

★ The average child in the United States wears down 730 crayons by his or her tenth birthday.

★ The scent of Crayola crayons is among the twenty most recognizable to American adults.

★ Red barns and black tires got their colors due in part to two of Binney & Smith's earliest products: red pigment and carbon black. Red and black are also the most popular crayon colors, mostly because children tend to use them for outlining.

★ Binney & Smith produces two billion Crayola crayons a year, which, if placed end to end, would circle the earth 4.5 times.

★ Crayola crayon boxes are printed in eleven languages: Danish, Dutch, English, Finnish, French, German, Italian, Norwegian, Portuguese, Spanish, and Swedish.

Humphrey Bogart and Lauren Bacall

In 1943, Director Howard Hawks, determined to make a movie version of Ernest Hemingway's novel *To Have and Have Not*, brought his wife's discovery, nineteen-year-old model Lauren Bacall, to the sound stage where 44-year-old Humphrey Bogart was making the film *Passage to Marseille*. Hawks instructed Bacall to wait on the set, and he returned shortly with Bogart and introduced them. "There was no clap of thunder, no lightning bolt, just a simple how-do-you-do," recalled Bacall in her autobiography *By Myself*. "Bogart was slighter than I imagined—five feet ten and a half, wearing his costume of no-shape trousers, cotton shirt, and scarf around neck. Nothing of import was said—we didn't stay long—but he seemed a friendly man."

After seeing Bacall's screen test, Bogart agreed to costar with the little-known model. A couple of weeks before filming began, Bacall and Bogart met again outside Hawks' office. Bogart was leaving, Bacall was walking in. "I just saw your test," Bogart told her. "We'll have fun together."

In February 1944, during the filming of *To Have and Have Not*, Bogart took Bacall under his wing, became her mentor, and helped the nervous newcomer relax by making her laugh during rehearsals. Three weeks into shooting, Bogart stepped into Bacall's dressing room one evening to say good night, put his hand on her chin, gently kissed her on the lips, and asked her to write her phone number on the back of a matchbook. At the time, Bogart was married to his third wife, the alcoholic and frequently violent Mayo Methot, with whom he was having severe marital difficulties. He called Bacall later that evening, beginning a courtship they agreed to keep secret to avoid his wife's jealous rage. They met frequently and discreetly, exchanged passionate love letters, and called each other Steve and Slim, after the characters they played in *To Have and Have Not.*

In the fall of 1944, during the filming of *The Big Sleep,* Mayo discovered the affair and turned Bogie's life at home into sheer hell. Ultimately, Bogie moved out, and on January 29, 1945, he announced his engagement to Bacall. His divorce came through on May 10, and on May 21, Bogie married Bacall on a farm in Malabar, Ohio, owned by his best man, Louis Bromfield. For a wedding gift, Jack Warner, head of Warner Bros., gave Bacall the Buick from *The Big Sleep.*

STRANGE ENCOUNTERS

★ Lauren Bacall was born Betty Joan Perske on September 16, 1924, in New York City. She changed her last name to Bacal, her mother's maiden name. Director Howard Hawks added a second "l" and came up with the name Lauren by dropping the "ce" from Laurence.

★ Bogie, born Humphrey DeForest Bogart on December 25, 1899, in New York City, was 25 years older than Bacall.

★ A persistent rumor holds that Bogie was the model for the Gerber Baby. The actual baby, sketched by Dorothy Hope Smith, was Ann Turner. Bogie's mother, Maud Bogart, drew a picture of her baby Humphrey that appeared in a national advertising campaign for Mellin's baby food.

★ While serving in the United States Navy, Bogie was wounded in the shelling of the Leviathan. The resulting partial paralysis caused his signature snarl and lisp.

★ Nancy Hawks spotted a picture of Bacall modeling on the cover of *Harper's Bazaar* and told her husband, director Howard Hawks, to give her a screen test.

★ Slim, Bacall's character in *To Have and Have Not,* was named after Nancy Hawks, nicknamed Slim.

★ In their first movie together, *To Have and Have Not,* Bacall uttered the famous line to Bogie: "You know how to whistle, don't you, Steve? You just put your lips together and blow." For Christmas in 1944,

Bogart gave Bacall a small, gold whistle. At Bogie's funeral, Bacall placed the whistle in the coffin.

★ Before marrying Bacall, Bogie was married and divorced three times, to actresses Helen Menken, Mary Philips, and Mayo Methot. He had children only with Bacall: Leslie and Stephen.

★ Bogart and Bacall starred together in four movies: *To Have and Have Not*, *The Big Sleep*, *Dark Passage*, and *Key Largo*.

★ Shortly after Bogart's death in 1957, Bacall announced her engagement to Frank Sinatra, who promptly backed out.

★ Bacall and former Israeli Prime Minister Shimon Peres are cousins. They share the same original last name—Perske.

★ In 1961, Lauren Bacall married actor Jason Robards. Together, they had a son: Jason. Bacall and Robards were divorced in 1969.

Napoleon Bonaparte and Josephine de Beauharnais

On October 15, 1795, 26-year-old Napoleon Bonaparte, an ambitious Major-General in the French Army seeking a rich wife, made his first visit to the Parisian home of 32-year-old Rose de Beauharnais. Napoleon had seen Rose on several occasions at aristocrat Thérésia Tallien's mansion home La Chaumiére.

Rose, whose husband Alexandre had been guillotined five days before the French Revolution, had become the mistress of men able to help support her two children. Seeing Napoleon as a possible patron, Rose cultivated his friendship.

Napoleon began visiting Rose every evening at her home. On the November morning after they consummated their relationship, Napoleon wrote a love letter to Rose, renaming her Josephine for all time: "The memory of yesterday's intoxicating evening has left no rest of my sense ... Sweet and incomparable Josephine, I draw from your lips, from your heart, a flame which consumes me."

Napoleon continued to spend every night with Josephine, proposing in January 1796; until they wed on March 9, 1796. As a wedding present, Napoleon gave Josephine a gold medallion inscribed with the words "To Destiny."

STRANGE ENCOUNTERS

★ Josephine, born Marie-Josèphe-Rose Tascher on June 23, 1763, on the French island of Martinique in the Caribbean, had bad teeth.

★ Josephine's Aunt Edmée, who lived in France as the mistress of aristocrat Francois de Beauharnais, arranged a marriage between Francois' son Alexandre and Josephine's twelve-year-old sister Catherine. Before Josephine's father could bring Catherine to France, she died, so instead he brought sixteen-year-old Josephine to France to wed Alexandre.

★ Josephine had two children with her first husband Alexandre de Beauharnais: Eugène and Hortense.

★ While Josephine was pregnant with her second child, her husband Alexandre de Beauharnais went to Martinique with his former mistress, Laure de Longpré, who convinced him that Josephine had led a promiscuous early life. When Alexandre returned to France, he kidnapped their first child, Eugène, but was forced to return him to Josephine.

★ In 1794, the French government imprisoned Josephine in the notorious Les Carmes prison for petitioning for the release of her estranged husband Alexandre from the very same prison. While jailed, Josephine had an affair with fellow inmate General Lazare Hoche.

★ After the Thermidorian coup on July 27, 1794, the new French government freed all political prisoners—including Josephine—from Les Carmes prison. Unfortunately, her husband Alexandre, also imprisoned in Les Carmes, had been guillotined five days earlier.

★ After being freed from prison, Josephine became mistress to former commissar Paul Comte de Barras.

★ Days after Napoleon married Josephine, he left to command the French army near Italy. Over the following months, he wrote her deeply passionate love letters, begging her to join him in Milan for a honeymoon. In March 1798, plagued by rumors that Josephine was having an affair with officer Hippolyte Charles, Napoleon confronted Josephine. She denied his accusations, but, fearing a divorce, became more willing to accompany him on his

campaigns. Napoleon's love turned to resentment, and he took a mistress, Pauline Bellisle Foures, the wife of a junior officer.

★ In a love letter to his Empress, Napoleon wrote, "See you next Thursday. Please don't bathe in the meantime!"

★ After Napoleon returned to France in October 1799, Josephine stopped having adulterous affairs, but Napoleon felt free to have as many mistresses as he pleased.

★ Napoleon and Josephine were crowned Emperor and Empress of France in 1804, but the couple failed to conceive an heir to the throne. Since Josephine already had two children, Napoleon remained convinced that he was infertile, until his mistress, Eleonore Denuelle, became pregnant with his child.

★ In 1807, Josephine's grandson Napoleon, who had been declared Napoleon's heir, died. Two years later, Napoleon told Josephine that he wanted to find a new wife who could produce an heir. The following day servants moved Josephine and all her possessions to Malmaison castle, which became her home.

★ In 1810, Napoleon married Archduchess Marie Louise of Austria, the daughter of his old enemy, Emperor Francis I of Austria, aligning France with one of the oldest ruling families in Europe.

★ In March 1811, Marie Louise gave birth to a son. Two years later Napoleon arranged for Josephine to meet the young prince.

★ In 1814, Napoleon, exiled on the island of Elba, learned of Josephine's death through a French journal. He locked himself in his room for two days.

★ After returning to France from exile on Elba, Napoleon visited Malmaison and collected violets from Josephine's garden. He wore them in a locket until his death.

Mel Brooks and Anne Bancroft

In 1961, comedian Mel Brooks stopped by the set of *The Perry Como Show*, where he discovered actress Anne Bancroft rehearsing a song-and-dance number. At the time, Anne had been playing the part of Anne Sullivan in the Broadway play *The Miracle Worker* for more than a year, and had won a Tony Award for her performance.

Mel had started as an irreverent comedian at the resort hotels in the Catskill Mountains, writing for Sid Caesar on television's *Admiral Broadway Revue, Your Show of Shows,* and *Caeasar's Hour.* He had worked alongside such gifted writers as Woody Allen, Selma Diamond, Larry Gelbart, Carl Reiner, Neil Simon, and Mel Tolkin. In 1960, Mel and Carl Reiner created the 2,000-Year-Old Man (performed by Mel and interviewed by Carl), and over the years recorded four popular albums.

After meeting Anne on the set, Mel later paid a woman who worked on the show to tell him which restaurant Anne was going to eat at that night so he could accidentally bump into her again and strike up a conversation.

"After that he followed me everywhere I went for three days," recalled Anne. At the time, Mel was divorced from his wife, Florence Baum, with whom he had three children.

"I was a Catholic girl who had been divorced and living alone for a long time," recalled Anne, whose first marriage, to builder Martin May, had ended four years earlier. "My mother was so happy, she didn't even care if he was Mel Brooks, Jewish, or what. She was just happy he was a man."

On August 5, 1964, Mel married Anne at City Hall in Manhattan, where a passerby served as their witness.

★ Mel Brooks, born Melvin Kaminsky on June 28, 1926, in Brooklyn, New York, graduated from Boston College and adapted his stage name from his mother's maiden name, Brookman.

★ Anne Bancroft was born Anna Maria Louisa Italiano on September 17, 1931, in the Bronx, New York.

★ Mel, a corporal in the United Sates Army during World War II, defused landmines and fought in the Battle of the Bulge.

★ Mel was the first guest on the premiere of *The Tonight Show with Johnny Carson*.

★ Mel created the television comedy series *Get Smart* with Buck Henry. (Buck cowrote the screenplay to the movie *The Graduate,* which starred Anne Bancroft as Mrs. Robinson, a sexually frustrated housewife who seduces a college graduate, played by Dustin Hoffman.)

★ Mel and Anne starred together in the movie *To Be or Not to Be*. Anne made cameo appearances in Mel's movies *Blazing Saddles, Silent Movie,* and *Dracula: Dead and Loving It.* She also appeared in several pictures made by Mel's production company, Brooksfilms, including *The Elephant Man* and *84 Charing Cross Road*.

★ In a 1975 interview with *Playboy* magazine, Mel revealed that his favorite candy was Raisinets.

★ In the 2000 movie *Keeping the Faith*, Anne plays a Jewish mother who refuses to speak to her son because he married a gentile.

★ Mel calls Anne his "Obi-Wan Kenobi" for advising him to turn his movie *The Producers* into a Broadway musical.

★ When asked if he was nervous at the opening of the Broadway production of *The Producers*, Mel replied, "If it flops, I'll take the other sixty million and fly to Rio."

★ Mel is one of the few people to have won an Academy Award, Emmy Award, Grammy Award, and Tony Award.

★ Mel has four children: Stephanie, Nicholas, and Edward (with Florence Baum) and Max (with Anne Bancroft).

Jerry Brown and Linda Ronstadt

In 1971, singer Linda Ronstadt sat alone eating enchiladas in the second booth from the front door of El Adobe Café, across the street from Paramount Studios in Hollywood. When California Secretary of State Jerry Brown, the son of former California governor Pat Brown, entered the café all by himself, proprietor Lucy Casada, egged on by her husband Frank, introduced Jerry to Linda. The singer invited Jerry to join her for lunch. They hit it off immediately.

The singer and the politician quickly discovered that they had a great deal in common. They were both raised Roman Catholic, both loved ethnic food, and both enjoyed eclectic music. On their first official date, Jerry took Linda to see the movie *American Graffiti*. They began seeing each other frequently—walking along the beach in Malibu, attending midnight screenings of Japanese movies in West Los Angeles, going to the Palomino night club in the San Fernando Valley to listen to country music, and frequenting El Adobe, where they first met. "They talk, eat together and kid around," Frank Casada told *Newsweek*. "She gives him a little kiss on the cheek. He gives her a kiss on the cheek. Jerry's kind of an inward guy."

Aside from sharing mutual interests, Jerry and Linda also shared enormous determination. Linda wanted her songs to reach the Top Ten charts, a goal she soon accomplished with the hit songs "Desperado," "Love Is a Rose," and "When Will I Be Loved?" Jerry planned to run for governor of California. Two years after meeting Linda, he was elected head of the most populous state in the union at age thirty-four, succeeding Ronald Reagan.

★ Jerry, born Edmund Gerald Brown, Jr., on April 7, 1938, in San Francisco, became the youngest person to climb Yosemite's Ledge Trail at age three.

★ Linda, born on July 15, 1946, in Tucson, Arizona, is eight years younger than Jerry.

★ Jerry studied at the Jesuit Seminary, received degrees in Latin and Greek from the University of California at Berkeley, and earned a law degree from Yale University.

★ When she started dating Jerry, Linda took out subscriptions to the *New York Times* and the *Wall Street Journal* so she could discuss current events with her new boyfriend—prompting Jerry to do something he had never done before: read the *Wall Street Journal* regularly.

★ As governor of California, Jerry refused to live in the luxurious new governor's mansion or be chauffeured around in the governor's limousine. Instead, he rented a modest apartment for 250 dollars a month and drove a state-issued baby-blue Plymouth Satellite.

★ As governor, Jerry called California "the meeting place of the inner and the outer universe," earning himself the nickname "Governor Moonbeam."

★ Jerry Brown ran for the Democratic presidential nomination in 1976, upsetting frontrunner Jimmy Carter in several primaries. He called Carter "a political hemophiliac." The press, aware that Jerry was dating Linda, who had confessed to using marijuana and cocaine (requiring that her nose be cauterized twice), questioned whether the singer would make a good First Lady.

★ In 1977, Linda stated her sexual philosophy: "I used to think you could only go to bed with a man out of pure love. I still think that's the best reason to, but I don't fall in love very often…. I've now included pure lust as the second reason to go to bed with someone, and a perfectly acceptable third reason is curiosity. It's a good way to get to know someone."

★ In 1979, Linda and Jerry traveled to Africa together for a ten-day safari, prompting the media to wonder whether the singer and the presidential hopeful were getting ready to tie the knot or whether the relationship was purely a publicity stunt.

★ Linda has had romantic liaisons with journalist Pete Hamill, director George Lucas, singer Mick Jagger, and comedian Steve Martin.

★ After serving as governor and breaking up with Linda, Jerry traveled to Japan to study Zen Buddhism and to Calcuttta, India, to work with Mother Teresa.

★ In 1992, Jerry ran for the Democratic presidential nomination on a platform advocating campaign finance reform and attacking special interest groups. He urged his supporters to call his toll-free telephone number to make individual campaign contributions, limiting the donations to a maximum of one hundred dollars.

George Burns and Gracie Allen

In 1922, the vaudeville comedy duo of George Burns and Billy Lorraine decided to break up the act and go their separate ways. Twenty-year-old Gracie Allen, who had worked in vaudeville as a child and was now attending secretarial school, was invited by her roommate to Union Hill, New Jersey, to see if she was interested in teaming up with either George Burns or Billy Lorraine. After watching the duo perform, Gracie picked George. At the time, Gracie was engaged to another man.

George and Gracie performed together for the first time at the Hillstreet Theatre in Newark, New Jersey. They were paid five dollars a day. Initially George delivered the jokes, but he soon noticed that audiences loved Gracie's scatterbrained character, so he gave her all the jokes and became her straight man. They quickly rose to stardom and George fell in love with his new partner.

They were married on January 7, 1926. "Gracie didn't marry me because I was a sex symbol," insisted George. "We were in show business and we made each other laugh. That's why it lasted 38 years. We slept together, ate together, dressed together, and worked together and never had a fight. It was a partnership and a friendship, too. And she knew everything."

★ George Burns was born Nathan Birnbaum on January 20, 1896, in New York City.

★ Gracie Allen was born Grace Ethel Cecile Rosalie Allen on July 26, 1902, in San Francisco.

★ As a child, George dropped out of P.S. 22 after the fourth grade for economic reasons.

★ Gracie's father abandoned her family when she was five years old. Gracie never spoke of him again.

★ Gracie started out in an Irish dancing group called "The Allen Sisters" with her three older sisters, Bessie, Hazel, and Pearl.

★ Gracie accidentally spilled boiling water on her arm as a child, leaving a bad scar that she concealed for the rest of her life.

★ George called Gracie "Googie." She called him "Natty."

★ Gracie had one blue eye and one green.

★ George and Gracie recreated their popular stage routines in such short subject featurettes as *Lamb Chops.*

★ George and Gracie appeared together in the movies *The Big Broadcast, International House, College Humor, We're Not Dressing, Six of a Kind, Many Happy Returns, Love in Bloom, The Big Broadcast of 1936, College Holiday, The Big Broadcast of 1937, College Swing, A Damsel in Distress,* and *Honolulu.*

★ Gracie appeared without George in the movies *The Gracie Allen Murder Case, Mr. and Mrs. North,* and *Two Girls and a Sailor.*

★ *The George Burns and Gracie Allen Show* ran for eight years on CBS—until Gracie decided to retire from show biz in 1958. At the time, Gracie stood five feet tall and weighed a mere one hundred pounds.

★ Gracie and George adopted two children: Sandra and Ronald.

★ George won an Academy Award for his role in the movie *The Sunshine Boys* as a crotchety vaudeville star reunited with his partner, played by Walter Matthau.

★ George starred as God in the movies *Oh, God!, Oh God! Book II,* and *Oh, God! You Devil.*

★ George was booked to play the London Palladium on his one hundredth birthday.

★ Gracie and George are buried together at Forest Lawn cemetery in Los Angeles under a headstone engraved with the words "Together Again." Gracie is buried above George because he "wanted her to have top billing."

Richard Burton and Elizabeth Taylor

In 1952, actress Elizabeth Taylor and her first husband, Michael Wilding, attended a Sunday brunch at the home of Stewart Granger and Jean Simmons, whose houseguests were Welsh actor Richard Burton and his wife Sybil Williams. Dick and Sybil had just arrived in Hollywood. Liz, sitting in a chair by the pool with her face buried in a book, caught glimpses of Dick quoting Shakespeare and reciting Dylan Thomas. She considered him to be "rather full of himself."

In 1957, their paths crossed again when Liz, dining in a London restaurant with her third husband, Michael Todd, spotted Dick across the room and waved. Months later on New Year's Eve, Dick and Liz were both guests at a party in Manhattan hosted by Tyrone Power. By then, Dick had garnered a reputation as a notorious womanizer.

On September 19, 1959, Liz and her fourth husband, Eddie Fisher, attended a Twentieth Century-Fox luncheon with more than four hundred Hollywood stars (including Richard Burton) to honor Soviet premier Nikita Khrushchev. When Khrushchev debated studio head Spyros Skouras on the merits of communism and capitalism, Dick, outraged by Khrushchev's inflammatory comments, had to be physically restrained from leaping out of his chair and yelling at the Soviet leader. Liz, standing on her table at the back of the room to get a better view of the heated debate, noticed the incensed Dick and told her husband that the actor seemed to be "foaming at the mouth."

Two years later, Liz and Dick, cast to star as Cleopatra and Mark Antony in *Cleopatra,* moved with their respective spouses (and Dick's two children) to villas outside Rome. The cast celebrated Christmas at Bricktop's jazz club in Rome, where Liz and Dick danced together. When Dick showed up drunk to their first rehearsal together, Liz helped hold a cup of coffee to his lips, forging a bond between them. At a New Year's Eve party to usher in 1962 at the Burtons' villa, Liz and Dick, clearly smitten with each other, "were off on their own," recalled actor John Valva, "laughing and smooching."

Soon after shooting began, Liz and Dick consummated their relationship. One night in late January, Dick burst uninvited into a dinner party at Liz's villa and, in front of Eddie Fisher and a dozen dinner guests, pointed to Liz and announced, "I'm in love with that girl over there." He demanded to know if Liz felt the same way. When she said yes, he ordered her to kiss him passionately. She did.

In February, Eddie informed Sybil that their spouses were having an affair. Sybil already knew. Dick, determined to keep both Liz and Sybil devoted to him, played the two women against each other. Several weeks later, while traveling with Dick, Liz, tormented by jealousy over Sybil and desperate to win Dick's loyalty, attempted suicide by swallowing more than two dozen sleeping pills. Doctors pumped her stomach and hospitalized her for two days.

In March, Eddie left Liz, flew to New York, and checked into the Pierre Hotel. Sybil and her two daughters flew to London, leaving Liz and Dick free to have their adulterous love affair in the open.

STRANGE ENCOUNTERS

★ Richard Burton was born Richard Walter Jenkins, Jr., on November 10, 1925, in Pontrydyfen, Wales. He took his professional name from his former schoolmaster, Philip Burton, who became his foster father.

★ Elizabeth Rosemond Taylor was born on February 27, 1932, in London, England.

★ The twelfth of thirteen children, Dick decided to escape his impoverished Welsh childhood by reading a book each day.

★ Dick won a scholarship to attend prestigious Oxford University, but dropped out after one year of academic study to pursue a professional acting career.

★ Dick met his first wife, Sybil Williams, in 1948 on the set of his first movie, *The Last Days of Dolwyn*. She was eighteen. He was twenty-two. They had two daughters together: Kate and Jessica. Diagnosed as profoundly autistic, Jessica was institutionalized.

★ Liz converted to Judaism to marry Eddie Fisher.

★ In 1962, Liz, cast to star in *Cleopatra*, became the first actress to earn one million dollars for a movie role.

★ In 1962, when *Stern* magazine published photographs of Liz in a revealing bikini and Dick in a bathing suit smooching on the deck of a boat, the Pope denounced Elizabeth Taylor as "a woman of loose morals."

★ Liz and Dick married in 1964, divorced in 1974, reconciled and separated several times, remarried in 1975, and divorced again four months later in 1976.

★ Liz and Dick appeared together in ten movies: *Cleopatra, The V.I.P.s, Who's Afraid of Virginia Woolf?, Doctor Faustus, The Sandpiper, The Taming of the Shrew, The Comedians, Boom!, Hammersmith Is Out*, and *Divorce His, Divorce Hers*.

★ Dick gave Liz some of the world's most magnificent jewelry, including the Krupp Diamond and the LaPeregina Pearl.

★ Dick was married five times, to Sybil Williams, Elizabeth Taylor (twice), Susan Hunt, and Sally Hay.

★ Liz has been married eight times, to Conrad Hilton, Michael Wilding, Mike Todd, Eddie Fisher, Richard Burton (twice), Senator John Warner, and Larry Fortensky.

★ Liz has four children: Chris Wilding, Michael Wilding, Jr., Liza Todd, and adopted daughter Maria Carson.

★ Liz and Dick reunited on stage in a 1983 revival of *Private Lives*.

★ When Dick died in 1984, his last wife Sally Hay barred Liz from attending the funeral.

★ In 2000, Queen Elizabeth II declared Elizabeth Taylor a Dame of the British Empire.

★ Liz considers Michael Jackson among her closest friends.

George W. Bush and Laura Welch

In August 1977, Laura Welch, a librarian at Dawson Elementary School in Austin, Texas, was home visiting her parents in Midland, Texas, during her summer vacation. Her friend Jan O'Neill tried to set her up on a blind date with George Bush, a friend of her husband Joey. When she learned that George intended to run for Congress, Laura, a Democrat having no interest in Republican politics, turned down the offer. When the O'Neills persisted, Laura agreed to meet George at a barbecue in their backyard. Although George and Laura had both grown up in Midland, Texas, attended San Jacinto Junior High School, and lived in the same apartment complex in Houston at the same time, they had never met. At the barbecue, they connected at once, talking until midnight.

"If it wasn't love at first sight," wrote George, "it happened shortly thereafter. My wife is gorgeous, good-humored, quick to laugh, down-to-earth, and very smart. I recognized those attributes right away, in roughly that order, the night our friends Joey and Jan O'Neill conspired to introduce us at a dinner at their house."

Laura felt the same way about George. The following night, George and Laura went out on a double date with the O'Neills—to play miniature golf. George telephoned Laura the next day and every day after that—until the following weekend, when he visited her in Austin. He then traveled to Kennebunkport, Maine, to see his parents, but after one day, he telephoned Laura and, upon learning that another young man was visiting her, flew back to Austin to see her.

"A few months after we met, I asked Laura to marry me, the best decision I have ever made," recalls George. "I joke that I am not sure it was the best decision she has ever made to say yes, but she did." On November 5, 1977, less than four months after meeting at the O'Neills barbecue, George and Laura, both 31 years old, were married in a small ceremony at the First United Methodist Church in Midland, Texas—the same church where Laura had been baptized as a baby.

STRANGE ENCOUNTERS

★ George Walker Bush was born on July 6, 1946, in New Haven, Connecticut, to George Herbert Walker Bush, a thirteenth cousin of Queen Elizabeth II of England, and Barbara Pierce Bush, a direct descendent of United States President Franklin Pierce.

★ Laura Welch, born on November 4, 1946, in Midland, Texas, graduated from Southern Methodist University in Dallas, Texas, worked as an elementary school teacher, and received her master's degree in library science from the University of Texas at Austin.

★ As a fourth-grade student at Sam Houston Elementary School in Midland, Texas, George painted sideburns on his face to imitate Elvis Presley during music class. The music teacher sent him to the principal, who paddled George with a board.

★ As a student at Philips Academy preparatory school, George played in a rock 'n' roll band called the Torqueys and was the head cheerleader.

★ In 1965, George, a junior at Yale University, got engaged to Cathryn Wolfman, a student at Rice University. The couple called off the engagement a few months later.

★ In 1967, the *New York Times* reported on allegations of fraternity hazing at Yale University and claimed that one fraternity had branded its pledges with a hot iron during an initiation ceremony. The article quoted Yale student George W. Bush, then president of Delta Kappa Epsilon, as saying the resulting wound was "only a cigarette burn," which left no scar.

★ In 1976, police in Maine arrested George for drunk driving. He pleaded guilty.

★ At George and Laura's wedding reception at the Racquet Club of Midland, Texas, the groom's father, former CIA director George H. W. Bush, borrowed a barbershop quartet from the party next door to entertain the guests.

★ George and Laura postponed their honeymoon so George could run for Congress in the Republican primary. He won the election and the couple went to Mexico for their honeymoon. Upon their return,

George lost the Congressional election to his Democratic opponent.

★ George and Laura have twin daughters: Barbara and Jenna.

★ In his 1999 book *Fortunate Son*, author J.H. Hatfield claimed that George W. Bush had been arrested in 1972 for possession of cocaine, but that Bush's father had used his influence to have charges dropped. The *Dallas Morning News* investigated the story and discovered that Hatfield was a convicted felon who had no evidence to back up his claims. The publishing house recalled seventy thousand copies of the book and had them destroyed.

★ On November 2, 1999, Andy Hiller, the political correspondent for WHDH-TV in Boston, asked presidential candidate George W. Bush to name the leaders of Chechnya, Pakistan, India, and Taiwan. George could only identify the president of Taiwan as "Lee," then retorted, "Can you name the foreign minister of Mexico?" Hiller replied that he was not the one running for president. After the interview, Bush spokesperson Karen Hughes attempted to defend George by admitting that neither his senior foreign policy advisor Josh Bolton nor foreign policy advisor Joel Shinn could name all four of those world leaders.

★ In August 2000, George, running on a platform of returning honor and integrity to the White House, stood before a crowd and, unaware that his microphone was on, turned to his vice presidential candidate, Dick Cheney, and said "There's Adam Clymer from the *New York Times*...A major-league asshole."

★ In November 2000, Republican presidential candidate George W. Bush stated that Social Security is not a federal program. It is.

★ In 2001, police cited nineteen-year-old Jenna Bush for attempting to buy alcohol at Chuy's Mexican restaurant in Austin, Texas, with someone else's identification. Her twin sister Barbara was cited for possession of alcohol by a minor.

Nicolas Cage and Lisa Marie Presley

In October 2000, actor Nicolas Cage met Lisa Marie Presley, the daughter of rock legend Elvis Presley, at the Los Angeles home of Ramones guitarist Johnny Ramone, during a party to celebrate the punk rocker's fifty-third birthday.

Lisa Marie Presley had shown up with her fiancé, Hawaiian-born musician John Oszajca. She started talking with Nic, who, separated from his wife Patricia Arquette and reportedly dating Penelope Cruz, his costar in the movie *Captain Corelli's Mandolin*, was attending the party alone. They took a deep interest in each other.

In April, Lisa Marie broke off her engagement to Oszajca. A month later, she and Nic were seen holding hands at a Tom Jones concert in Las Vegas. In July, Lisa Marie joined Nic in Washington, D.C., for a ceremony honoring the Navajo Indians who used their language to encode top-secret messages during World War II, and the couple spoke with President George W. Bush. A few weeks later, Nic stood by Lisa Marie's side as she cut the ribbon on a twelve-unit apartment building in Memphis, constructed through her charitable foundation for homeless families. In September, Nic and Lisa Marie threw a party (in honor of Ramone) at New York City's Hudson Hotel after the MTV Music Awards.

In February, the couple broke up, but four months later they were holding hands at the Hollywood premiere of Nic's movie *Windtalkers*. On August 10, 2002, Lisa Marie married Nic at a resort on the big island of Hawaii. The wedding, attended by close family members (including the bride's mother, Priscilla), took place during the week marking the twenty-fifth anniversary of Elvis Presley's death. Lisa Marie's daughter Danielle was a flower girl. Her son Benjamin and Nic's son Weston were ring bearers.

Less than four months later, the couple filed for divorce.

★ Nicolas Cage was born Nicolas Kim Coppola on January 7, 1964, in Long Beach, California, to comparative literature professor August Coppola (a brother of director Francis Ford Coppola) and dancer/choreographer Joy Vogelsang.

★ Lisa Marie Presley was born on February 1, 1968, in Memphis, Tennessee, to rock legend Elvis Presley and Priscilla Presley.

★ Nic changed his last name to Cage early in his career, determined to succeed on his own merits. He took the name "Cage" from comic book character Luke Cage, the "first black superhero."

★ Nic dropped out of Beverly Hills High School at seventeen and landed a bit part in the 1982 movie *Fast Times at Ridgemont High*. When the majority of his scenes were cut from the film, he took a job selling popcorn at the Fairfax Theater.

★ Nic proposed to actress Patricia Arquette the first time he met her, at Canter's Deli in Los Angeles in 1987. Arquette created a list of things Nic would have to do first to win her hand. When Nic started to work his way through the list, Arquette broke off the relationship.

★ In 1988, Lisa Marie married musician and fellow Scientologist Danny Keough. The couple had two children, Danielle and Benjamin, and divorced abruptly in 1994. Less than a month later, Lisa Marie married Michael Jackson. The marriage lasted twenty months.

★ In 1990, Nic began a long-term relationship with actress Christina Fulton. They share custody of a son, Weston.

★ In 1994, Nic was briefly engaged to model Kristen Zang.

★ In 1995, Nic again ran into Patricia Arquette at Canter's Deli. Two weeks later, they got married. They separated nine months after that.

★ Nic imitates Elvis in the 1990 movie *Wild at Heart* and skydives dressed as one of the Flying Elvises in the 1992 movie *Honeymoon in Vegas*.

★ Nic commands up to twenty million dollars per movie. Lisa Marie inherited more than 100 million dollars from her father.

★ Both Lisa Marie and Nic collect vintage cars. His collection includes a Lamborghini that once belonged to the Shah of Iran. Her collection features her father's Cadillacs.

★ Nic collects comic books and considers them a modern-day equivalent of mythology.

★ Nic, who suffers from vertigo, has a tattoo on his upper back of a monitor lizard wearing a top hat.

Johnny Carson and Ed McMahon

In 1957, Johnny Carson, having hosted the CBS show *Earn Your Vacation* and appearing as a substitute host for Jack Paar on CBS's *The Morning Show*, moved to ABC as host of a new live daytime game show, *Who Do You Trust?* He was teamed with announcer Ed McMahon. McMahon had begun his television career in Philadelphia, hosting a late-night interview show and then playing a clown on the television show *Big Top*. *Who Do You Trust?* followed Dick Clark's *American Bandstand*.

"The first day I ever worked with him, I had a script with all the sponsors," revealed Ed. "There were six sponsors. The first day, Johnny Carson set fire to my script. He took out a cigarette lighter and set fire to my script. I'm reading charcoal. I'm reading these things, I couldn't memorize every day—there were six different sponsors. So I was reading black charcoal, black typing on charcoal, and of course my fingers were burning and hurting. But that got a big laugh from the audience, so he never stopped doing it. Every day for four years. That was the beginning of our relationship, teasing one another, pulling each other's leg."

The real allure of the game show was the repartee between Johnny and Ed. In 1958 Johnny became a substitute host for Jack Paar on NBC's *The Tonight Show*. Three years later, Paar retired, and on October 1, 1962, Groucho Marx introduced Johnny Carson to the nation's late-night television audience as the new host of *The Tonight Show*. In response to the thunderous applause from the audience, Johnny said, "Boy, you would think it was Vice President Nixon." Johnny brought along his sidekick, Ed McMahon, who remained his on-air partner for a total of thirty-four years.

STRANGE ENCOUNTERS

★ Johnny Carson, born John William Carson on October 23, 1925, in Corning, Iowa, grew up in Norfolk, Nebraska.

★ Ed, born Edward Leo McMahon on March 6, 1923, in Detroit, Michigan, grew up in Lowell, Massachusetts.

★ Johnny began his career at age fourteen as a magician. "The Great Carsoni" performed at the Seven Seas lounge in Omaha, Nebraska, and also worked as a ventriloquist.

★ Ed began his career as an announcer at age fifteen as a "caller" at a bingo game in Maine and spent the next three years touring the state fair and carnival circuit.

★ In 1945, as a Navy ensign aboard the USS *Pennsylvania,* Johnny entertained enlisted men during shows on the ship.

★ Ed served with the Marine Corps as a fighter pilot during both World War II and the Korean War.

★ Ed sold vegetable slicers on Atlantic City's boardwalk to put himself through Catholic University in Washington, D.C.

★ Both Johnny and Ed worked in radio. As a student at the University of Nebraska, Johnny worked at radio station KFAB. Ed worked at WLLH in Lowell, Massachusetts.

★ In 1950 Johnny moved to Los Angeles and landed a job as staff announcer for television station KNXT (now KCBS-TV), where he soon hosted his own program, *Carson's Cellar*.

★ Johnny briefly wrote for *The Red Skelton Show*. One night, Skelton banged his head just before air time and suffered a concussion. Johnny substituted for the star, opening the show with a monologue he had written while driving to the studio. "The kid is great, just great," Jack Benny told network executives. "You better watch that Carson kid."

★ In 1960, Johnny starred as ambitious television reporter Johnny Martin in the unsuccessful sitcom pilot *Johnny Come Lately*.

★ In 1962, when Johnny became the new host of *The Tonight Show,* he cowrote "Johnny's Theme" with Paul Anka.

★ Johnny's first wife, Joan "Jody" Morrill Wolcott, was his college sweetheart. Together they had three children: Ricky, Chris, and Cory.

★ When Johnny's second wife, Joanne Copeland, divorced him, the judge awarded her nearly half a million dollars in cash and art and 100,000 dollars a year in alimony for life.

★ At *The Tonight Show*'s tenth anniversary party on September 30, 1972, Johnny announced that he had secretly married his third wife, former model Joanna Holland, that afternoon. Eleven years later, Joanna filed for divorce, ultimately receiving twenty million dollars in cash and property.

★ Johnny reportedly met his fourth wife, Alexis Mass, when he saw her strolling along the beach near his Malibu home, holding an empty wine glass. He offered to fill her glass.

★ Ed has been married three times. His wives include Alyce Ferrill, Victoria Valentine, and Pamela Hurn. He has five children: Claudia, Michael, Linda, Jeffrey, and Katherine.

Jimmy Carter and Rosalynn Smith

Jimmy Carter and Rosalynn Smith grew up together in the small farming town of Plains, Georgia. They lived three miles apart. Rosalynn lived with her family in the middle of town and Jimmy lived with his family on the outskirts of town in the nearby community of Archery. Since Jimmy was three years older than Rosalynn, they rarely spoke. They knew each other the way everyone in a small town knows everyone else. "I don't remember ever having said a word to him," recalled Rosalynn, "except when we bought ice cream cones from him one summer in the old bank building on the main street in town."

Rosalynn did, however, become close friends with Jimmy's younger sister Ruth, who was one of her classmates. While Jimmy was away at Georgia Southwestern College and the Georgia Institute of Technology for four years, Rosalynn spent a lot of time with Ruth. "I couldn't keep my eyes off the photograph of her idolized, older brother pinned up on her bedroom wall," recalled Rosalynn. "I thought he was the most handsome young man I had ever seen."

In the summer of 1945, Ruth would invite Rosalynn to her house whenever Jimmy was home in the hopes of getting her brother to take a romantic interest in her best friend. Unfortunately, whenever Rosalynn came over, Jimmy had plans to be elsewhere. Finally, at the end of the summer, Ruth invited Rosalynn to join her and Jimmy for a picnic lunch before cleaning up the Pond House, a community cabin built by their father. As they raked up the yard and swept the floor of the Pond House, twenty-year-old Jimmy finally conversed with seventeen-year-old Rosalynn.

Later that afternoon, while Rosalynn stood outside the church with some friends before a youth group meeting, Jimmy drove up, got out of the car, walked over to Rosalynn, and invited her to be his date to the movies that evening with Ruth and her boyfriend. When Jimmy took Rosalynn home that night, he kissed her. "I couldn't believe it happened," recalled Rosalynn. "I had never let any boy kiss me on a first date. My mother told me she hadn't even held hands with Daddy until they were engaged! But I was completely swept off my feet."

STRANGE ENCOUNTERS

★ Jimmy was born James Earl Carter, Jr., on October 1, 1924, in Plains, Georgia.

★ Rosalynn Smith was born Eleanor Rosalynn Smith on August 18, 1927 in Plains, Georgia, to Allie Murray Smith and Edgar Smith.

★ Rosalynn's parents named Rosalynn's sister Lillian after Jimmy Carter's mother Lillian, who worked in Plains as a registered nurse.

★ In his senior year of high school, Jimmy and a group of friends played hooky as an April Fool's Day joke and went to a movie with friends in the nearby city of Americus. The school principal, failing to see the humor in the stunt, paddled Carter and denied him the right to graduate as class valedictorian.

★ Rosalynn worked as a cleaning girl in a beauty shop to help support her family and graduated as class valedictorian.

★ The morning after his first date with Rosalynn, Jimmy told his mother that he intended to marry Rosalynn someday. That night, Ruth persuaded Rosalynn to come with her family to see Jimmy off at the train station. Jimmy, taking the midnight train back to the United States Naval Academy in Annapolis, Maryland, kissed Rosalynn goodbye and asked her to write to him. In a letter, Jimmy urged Rosalynn to date other boys rather than wait for him. Infuriated, Rosalynn "finally wrote him about all the boys at school I was seeing, even those I only played Ping-Pong with in the afternoons. It worked. He wrote me a furious letter back, asking me not to go out anymore with anybody else!"

★ While home from Annapolis for Christmas in 1945, Jimmy proposed to Rosalynn. She turned him down, insisting they wait until after she fulfilled her promise to her deceased father to get a college education.

★ When Rosalynn visited Jimmy at Annapolis over the George Washington's Birthday weekend in 1946, he proposed again. This time Rosalynn accepted, but the couple agreed to keep their plans secret.

★ Jimmy and Rosalynn were married on July 7, 1946, in the Plains Methodist Church.

★ In 1948, while Jimmy stood night watch on the bridge of the U.S.S. *Pomfret,* a huge wave swept over the ship, washed him away with it, and then returned him to the top of a gun barrel thirty feet away from where he had been standing.

★ Chosen by Admiral Hyman Rickover for the nuclear submarine program, Lieutenant Jimmy Carter did graduate work at Union College in reactor technology and nuclear physics, and served as senior officer of the nuclear submarine *Seawolf.*

★ When Jimmy's father died in 1953, Jimmy and Rosalynn moved back to Plains to run the family farm and peanut warehouse. For the first year they lived in public housing. Jimmy ran the warehouse, and Rosalynn kept the books.

★ Jimmy and Rosalynn have four children: Jack, Chip, Donnel, and Amy.

★ Jimmy Carter was elected governor of Georgia in 1970 and 39th President of the United States in 1976.

★ In 1977, when President Jimmy Carter arrived at the Warsaw airport and gave a short speech, his State Department translator, Steven Seymour, speaking a strange mixture of archaic Polish and Russian, mistranslated Carter's statement, "I have come to learn your opinions and understand your desires for the future" as "I desire the Poles carnally."

Prince Charles and Lady Diana Spencer

In November 1977, Lady Sarah Spencer, the daughter of the Viscount Althrop and Vicountess Althrop, invited her sixteen-year-old sister Diana, on weekend leave from West Heath boarding school, to join a shooting party. In the middle of a ploughed field near Nobottle Wood on the Althorp estate, Sarah introduced Diana to her boyfriend of five months—Prince Charles, the heir to the British throne. That night, Sarah's parents hosted a dinner dance for the Prince in their mansion home. After dinner, the Prince asked Diana to show him her family's 115-foot-long picture gallery—one of the finest private collections of art in Europe. When Sarah insisted upon being Charles' guide, Diana graciously stepped aside.

A year later, Charles and Sarah's romance had cooled significantly—particularly after Sarah told the press that her relationship with the Prince was "totally platonic." Still, Charles invited both Sarah and her sister Diana to his thirtieth birthday party at Buckingham Palace. Shortly after, Charles and Sarah went their separate ways.

Nearly three years later, in July 1980, Philip De Pass (a friend of Prince Philip) and his wife Philippa (a lady-in-waiting to Queen Elizabeth) invited Lady Diana Spencer to stay at their home in Petworth, West Sussex, where Prince Charles would be spending the weekend. The house party drove to nearby Cowdray Park to watch Prince Charles play polo for his team, Les Diables Blues, then returned to the house for a barbecue. Diana sat next to Charles on a bale of hay, and after exchanging pleasantries, expressed her deep sympathy over the death of his "honorary grandfather," Earl Mountbatten, who had been assassinated by the IRA eleven months earlier. Diana's heartfelt comments and big, blue eyes melted Charles' heart. They conversed

late into the evening. He invited her to drive back to Buckingham Palace the next day, but Diana, not wishing to be rude to her hosts, turned him down.

Soon after, Charles invited Diana to a performance of Verdi's *Requiem* at the Royal Albert Hall. Diana attended, chaperoned by her grandmother Lady Fermoy, who accompanied the couple back to Buckingham Palace for a cold buffet supper in the Prince's apartments. In August, Diana sailed with Charles on the royal yacht *Britannia*. In September, she joined him at Balmoral Castle for the weekend of the Braemar Games. They became frequent companions, and finally, on Friday, February 6, 1981, Charles proposed marriage in the Windsor Castle nursery.

On July 29, 1981, nineteen-year-old Lady Diana Spencer rode in a horse-drawn glass carriage to London's St. Paul's Cathedral where she married 32-year-old Prince Charles in an Anglican ceremony conducted by the Archbishop of Canterbury before more than 2,500 guests. More than 750 million people in more than seventy countries watched the event on television.

STRANGE ENCOUNTERS

★ Diana Frances Spencer was born on July 1, 1961, in Sandringham, England.

★ Charles, born on November 14, 1948, was thirteen years older than Diana.

★ Prince Charles and Princess Diana spent the first three days of their honeymoon at Broadlands, the home of Earl Mountbatten in Hampshire, followed by a cruise aboard the royal yacht *Britannia* through the Mediterranean.

★ Diana tried to send personal thank-you notes in response to the 47,000 letters of congratulation and 10,000 gifts she received for her wedding.

★ While pregnant with her first son, Prince William, in January 1982, Diana threatened to commit suicide and hurled herself down a staircase.

★ In February 1982, two tabloids published photographs of Diana, then five-months pregnant, wearing a bikini and running through the surf in the Bahamas.

★ Charles wanted to name his first son "Arthur" and his second son "Albert." Diana chose the names "William" and "Harry."

★ After the birth of his second son, Prince Harry, Charles resumed his friendship with Camilla Parker-Bowles, who became his confidante, accompanying him on his overseas visits. Smitten with love, Charles had courted Camilla for six months in 1972, but waffled in proposing to her. When Charles was summoned to sea by the Royal Navy, Camilla accepted a marriage proposal from one of Charles' friends, Andrew Parker-Bowles, whom she wed in 1973.

★ Before the royal wedding, Camilla gave Charles a pair of gold cufflinks engraved with two intertwined Cs. He wore them throughout his honeymoon.

★ While unwrapping gifts, Diana found an engraved necklace intended for Camilla Parker-Bowles. Soon after this, she discovered Camilla's photograph in Charles' wallet.

★ Charles and Camilla exchanged flowers and gifts under the nicknames Fred and Gladys, after characters from the 1950s comedy series *The Goon Show*.

★ When Diana and Andrew Parker-Bowles were away, Camilla would act as Charles' hostess at Highgrove Castle.

★ In 1992, Diana and Charles announced their separation. Diana moved into Highgrove Castle. Four years later, the royal couple finalized their divorce.

★ On August 31, 1997, Diana died along with her boyfriend, millionaire playboy Dodi Fayed, when her chauffeur-driven Mercedes Benz, being chased by paparazzi, crashed in a tunnel in Paris.

Cleopatra and Mark Antony

In 51 B.C.E., Egyptian pharaoh Ptolemy XII died, making his daughter, eighteen-year-old Cleopatra, the queen of Egypt. Her ten-year-old brother, Ptolemy XIII, became her coruler and husband. Three years later, Ptolemy's guardians, eager to seize power, drove Cleopatra from the throne. Ousted Cleopatra met Roman Emperor Julius Caesar, who happened to be in Alexandria pursuing Roman general Pompey, his rival for the throne. Caesar fell in love with Cleopatra and killed her opponents, returning her to the throne—alongside another one of her brothers, Ptolemy XIV. In 47 B.C.E., Cleopatra gave birth to a son. Insisting the child belonged to Caesar, she named the baby Caesarion. In 46 B.C.E., Caesar invited Cleopatra to stay with him in Rome. She brought Caesarion.

Sometime within the next two years, Cleopatra met Mark Antony, a calvary officer under Caesar. In 44 B.C.E., a group of Roman aristocrats led by Marcus Brutus and Gaius Cassius Longinus, assassinated Caesar. Mark Antony became the ruler of Rome. Cleopatra, devastated and heartbroken, returned to Egypt.

When Julius Caesar's son, Gaius Octavian, challenged Antony's rule, Antony agreed to share the rulership in a triumvirate with Octavian and Marcus Lepidus. In 42 B.C.E., Antony and Octavian led an army and defeated Brutus and Longinus in Macedonia. Antony then claimed Rome's eastern provinces for himself and gave Italy and the western provinces to Octavian.

In 41 B.C.E., Antony invited Cleopatra to Tarsus in Asia Minor (current day Turkey) in the hopes of obtaining her financial backing so he could become the sole ruler of Rome. Cleopatra financed him, hoping to put her son Caesarion next in line to rule Rome. In Tarsus, Antony and Cleopatra fell in love, and soon after, Cleopatra gave birth to Antony's twins, Alexander Helios and Cleopatra Selene. Later that year, Antony left Cleopatra to consolidate his political power in Rome by marrying Ocatavian's sister, Octavia. In 37 B.C.E., Antony left Octavia and married Cleopatra. Shortly after, she gave birth to another son by him, Ptolemy Philadelphos.

STRANGE ENCOUNTERS

★ Contrary to popular belief, Cleopatra lacked beauty. She was, however, known for her intelligence, charm, and wit.

★ Cleopatra was the seventh Egyptian queen of Macedonian decent with the name Cleopatra, so she is also known as Cleopatra VII.

★ In 34 B.C.E., Antony appointed Cleopatra ruler of Egypt, Cyprus, Crete, and Syria, and gave her children most of the land ruled by Alexander the Great—prompting Octavian to declare war on Antony and Cleopatra. After his naval forces defeated Antony and Cleopatra's fleets off the west coast of Greece in 31 B.C.E. in the Battle of Actium, the duo fled to Alexandria.

★ In 30 B.C.E., Octavian arrived in Alexandria in pursuit of the couple. Cleopatra spread a report that she had committed suicide. Upon hearing the report, a grief-stricken Antony stabbed himself with a knife. When he learned that Cleopatra was alive, his followers carried him to her, where he died in her arms.

★ Cleopatra, afraid that Octavian would bring her back to Rome to be publicly humiliated, killed herself by placing a poisonous snake on her body.

★ Octavian ordered his troops to kill Ceasarion to prevent him from making a claim to the Roman throne.

★ Playwright William Shakespeare dramatized the pair's story in his play *Antony and Cleopatra*, written in 1607. In his play, Shakespeare mentions billiards, centuries before the game was invented.

★ The play *All for Love*, written in 1677 by John Dryden, contains the character Mark Antony.

★ Playwright George Bernard Shaw told the story in his 1898 play *Caesar and Cleopatra*.

★ In the 1940s, workmen cleaning a Paris museum dumped the contents of a mummy case into the sewers. The case was later identified as having contained Cleopatra's mummified remains—looted from Egypt by Napoleon.

Bill Clinton and Hillary Rodham

In January 1971, Bill Clinton, a first-year law school student at Yale University, found himself in the same course on political and civil liberties with Hillary Rodham, a second-year law student and founding editorial board member of the *Yale Review*. As classmates, they were aware of each other's presence, but never spoke. One night in the library, Bill walked over to his classmate Jeffrey Gleckel and asked for his thoughts on joining the *Yale Law Journal*. Gleckel noticed that Bill wasn't really paying attention to the conversation, but was instead staring over his shoulder. Gleckel glanced around inconspicuously and spotted Hillary Rodham sitting at a desk with a stack of books and notepads.

"Finally," recalled Gleckel, "Hillary walked over to Bill and said something like, 'Look, you've been staring at me for five minutes. The least you can do is introduce yourself.'" Flabbergasted, Bill was left speechless. Gleckel politely excused himself.

Hillary soon broke up with her boyfriend and began dating Bill. She later recalled being "so struck by how he was able to be so smart and so human, at the same time. I just never had met anybody like that. It was a unique combination, particularly in a place like Yale Law School where the kind of stresses and ambitions are all very focused, and Bill was just extraordinary in his interest in other people."

In the fall, Bill and Hillary moved into an apartment together near campus. At Christmas, Hillary brought Bill home to meet her parents in Park Ridge, a suburb of Chicago. Rather than graduate with her class in 1972, Hillary stayed at Yale to study child development theory so she and Bill could remain together.

After graduation, Bill returned to Arkansas and took a job teaching a course in criminal procedure at the University of Arkansas in Fayetteville. Hillary, wanting nothing to do with Arkansas, took a job in Washington, D.C., as the staff attorney with the Children's Defense Fund. Still, she visited Bill in Arkansas and he took her on a scenic tour of Little Rock and Hot Springs. In 1974, Hillary served on a team of lawyers recruited to amass evidence so the House Judiciary Committee could conduct an impeachment inquiry of President Richard M. Nixon. Bill, running for Congress in Arkansas, stayed in touch by telephone and visited her several times in Washington.

When Nixon resigned in August 1974, Hillary accepted a job as a teacher at the University of Arkansas Law School in Fayetteville and worked for Bill's Congressional campaign. In Fayetteville, Hillary and Bill lived in separate apartments to avoid creating any political controversy. When Bill lost the election to the incumbent, Hillary went home to Chicago to visit her family. When she returned to Arkansas, Bill picked her up at the airport and drove her to a brick cottage she liked. He had bought the house while she was away, he told her, so she would marry him. He had furnished the bedroom with an antique bed made up in flowered sheets he had bought at Wal-Mart.

On Saturday, October 11, 1975, 29-year-old Bill and 27-year-old Hillary were married on the lawn of their house in Fayetteville, Arkansas, by Methodist minister Victor Nixon.

STRANGE ENCOUNTERS

★ Hillary Rodham, born in Park Ridge, Illinois, on October 26, 1947, attended Wellesley College, in Wellesley, Massachusetts, where she was elected president of the student government.

★ Bill Clinton was born William Jefferson Blythe on August 19, 1946, in Hope, Arkansas, six months after his father died in an auto accident. Raised in Hot Springs, Bill took his stepfather's last name after his mother gave to birth to his half-brother, Roger.

★ In 1969, *Life* magazine excerpted student government president Hillary Rodham's commencement speech at Wellesley University.

★ Hillary bought her wedding gown off the rack the night before she got married.

★ Hillary's father, Republican Hugh Rodham, answered telephones at Bill's Congressional campaign headquarters.

★ Bill, elected the youngest governor in Arkansas history in 1978 at age thirty-two, lost his bid for reelection in 1980. He went on to win four consecutive terms as governor.

★ On January 23, 1992, during the New Hampshire presidential primary race, former Nevada lounge singer Gennifer Flowers told *The Star*, a supermarket tabloid, that she had had a twelve-year affair with Bill while he was Arkansas governor. When Bill denied the accusations, Flowers held a news conference to play audio tapes of intimate telephone conversations between them that she claimed to have secretly recorded.

★ In 1992, Bill told the press, "When I was in England, I experimented with marijuana a time or two. I didn't like it, I didn't inhale it, and never tried it again."

★ In 1994, Arkansas state employee Paula Corbin Jones brought a lawsuit against President Bill Clinton, alleging that while governor of Arkansas in 1991, he summoned her to a Little Rock hotel room and made an unwanted sexual advance. Clinton refused to settle the case and Jones's lawyers, seeking to establish a pattern of Clinton's sexual misconduct, discovered his relationship with White House intern Monica Lewinsky—ultimately resulting in impeachment proceedings against Clinton. On November 13, 1998, Clinton settled with Jones, agreeing to pay her 850,000 dollars, but with no apology or admission of guilt. Had Clinton settled the lawsuit in 1994, he would have likely avoided the impeachment proceedings that damaged his reputation.

★ In 1996, President Bill Clinton began a clandestine sexual relationship with an unpaid intern at the White House, 21-year-old Monica Lewinsky. On January 17, 1998, during his deposition in the Paula Jones lawsuit, Clinton denied having had sexual relations with Lewinsky. On January 26, 1998, when the press began reporting on the alleged relationship, the President looked into the camera at a press conference, pointed his finger, and stated emphatically, "I did not have sexual relations with that woman, Miss Lewinsky." Unbeknownst to Clinton, Lewinsky had kept a dress stained with his semen. In August 17, 1998, Clinton admitted before a Grand Jury and later in a nationally televised address that he had had an inappropriate relationship with Lewinsky—leading to his impeachment trial in January 1999.

★ On January 27, 1998, on the *Today* show, First Lady Hillary Rodham Clinton, denying her husband's affair with Lewinsky, stated: "It's a vast right-wing conspiracy that has been conspiring against my husband since the day he announced for president."

★ In 2000, Hillary became the first First Lady ever elected to the United States Senate.

Kurt Cobain and Courtney Love

Kurt Cobain and Courtney Love first met at eleven o'clock at night on Friday, January 12, 1989, just before Kurt's band, Nirvana, took to the stage of the Satyricon nightclub in Portland, Oregon. Courtney, cofounder of the rock band Hole, in the company of a friend who was dating a member of the opening band, the Oily Bloodmen, sat in a booth. When Kurt, the lead singer of Nirvana, walked by, Courtney told him, "You look like Dave Pirner," referring to the lead singer of Soul Asylum. Kurt, having wrestled in high school, playfully grabbed Courtney, wrestled her to the floor, and pinned her down in front of the jukebox, which, Courtney recalled, "was playing my favorite song by Living Colour." Kurt lifted her back up and handed her a sticker of Chin Chin, the monkey on the animated television series *Speed Racer.*

"She looked like a classic punk rock chick," Kurt told author Michael Azerrad, for his book *Come As You Are.* "I did feel kind of attracted to her. Probably wanted to fuck her that night, but she left." At the time, Kurt was living with his girlfriend Tracy Marander, who had traveled with him to Portland. After this, Courtney followed Kurt's career, adhering the Chin Chin sticker to her guitar case, and became a huge fan of Nirvana. The two did not meet again for another two years.

In 1990, Courtney's friend Jennifer Finch became romantically involved with Nirvana drummer Dave Grohl. When Courtney told Grohl that she had a crush on Kurt, he informed her that Kurt had broken up with his girlfriend. Courtney sent Kurt a small porcelain doll inside a heart-shaped box covered in silk and lace.

In May 1991, Dave Grohl reintroduced Kurt, who was drinking from a bottle of cough syrup, to Courtney backstage during an L7 concert at the Palladium in

Los Angeles. Courtney retrieved a more potent brand of cough syrup from her purse, and once again Kurt wrestled her to the floor. After talking about the music business, Courtney handed Kurt her phone number, scrawled on a bar napkin. That night, at three o'clock in the morning, Kurt telephoned Courtney, ostensibly to find out where she got her cough syrup. Courtney, then in a long-distance relationship with Billy Corgan of the Smashing Pumpkins, talked for more than an hour.

As Nirvana rose to fame in 1991, Kurt and Courtney saw very little of each other, but kept in contact by phone, meeting as frequently as possible. At sunset on February 24, 1992, Kurt, high on heroin and dressed in blue-plaid pajamas, married Courtney, clad in an antique silk dress and three months pregnant with their child, on Waikiki Beach in Hawaii.

STRANGE ENCOUNTERS

★ Courtney Love, born Love Michelle Harrison on July 9, 1964, in San Francisco, California, to Grateful Dead devotee Hank Harrison and psychologist Linda Caroll, grew up on hippie communes and at schools in Europe and New Zealand.

★ Kurt Donald Cobain, born on February 20, 1967, in Hoquaim, Washington, was raised in Aberdeen, Washington.

★ "I just couldn't see how I was a product of my parents because they weren't artistic like I was," Kurt told author Azerrad. "I like music and they didn't. Subconsciously maybe I thought I was adopted—ever since that episode of *The Partridge Family* when Danny thought he was adopted. I really related to that."

★ Courtney, having been sent to reform school for stealing a Kiss T-shirt from Woolworth's, worked as a stripper in Los Angeles and Alaska.

★ Courtney auditioned for the role of Nancy in the 1986 movie *Sid and Nancy*, but received the small part of Gretchen.

★ Kurt frequently overdosed on heroin, only to be resuscitated by Courtney.

★ On March 4, 1994, while staying with Courtney in the five-star Excelsior Hotel in Rome, Kurt attempted suicide by taking sixty Rohypnol sedative pills. At six o'clock in the morning, Courtney discovered Kurt lying on the floor in a coma and had him rushed to the hospital, where doctors pumped his stomach. He awoke from the coma twenty-four hours later.

★ On April 8, 1994, an electrician discovered Kurt's dead body on the floor of the rock star's Seattle home, a shotgun lying on his chest pointed at his chin. Police found a suicide note written in red ink and addressed to Courtney and their daughter

Frances, closing with the words "I love you, I love you."

★ Courtney has been married twice, to James Moreland and Kurt Cobain.

★ Kurt and Courtney had one child together: Frances Bean Cobain (named after actress Frances Farmer, the subject of the Nirvana song "Frances Farmer Will Have her Revenge on Seattle"). In 2001, Courtney suffered a miscarriage, but refused to name the father.

★ After Kurt's death, Hole's second album achieved critical and popular success, elevating Courtney Love to rock star status.

Ben Cohen and Jerry Greenfield

Ben Cohen met Jerry Greenfield while running around the track in junior high school gym class in Merrick, New York. As two of the plumper and less physically adept students in the class, they became close friends. As students at Calhoun High School, Ben and Jerry double-dated in Ben's Camaro convertible.

In his senior year, Ben drove an ice cream truck for Pied Piper Distributors of Hempstead, New York, selling ice cream to children and eventually working his way up to a job in the company freezer distributing ice cream to other ice-cream truck drivers.

Jerry won a National Merit Scholarship and attended Oberlin College in Ohio as a pre-med student, where he took a job scooping ice cream in the college cafeteria. Ben attended Colgate University but dropped out in his sophomore year and returned to his job as an ice cream man. He enrolled at Skidmore College, studied pottery and jewelry making, then moved to New York City, where he continued studying pottery at the University Without Walls, supporting himself by working odd jobs.

Meanwhile, Jerry graduated from Oberlin but got rejected from medical school. He moved to New York, shared an apartment with Ben, worked as a lab technician for a year, reapplied to medical school, and got rejected again. In 1974, Ben moved to Paradox, New York, to work as a craft teacher at the Highland Community School for emotionally disturbed adolescents, on a 600-acre working farm. At the school Ben started making ice cream with his students.

Two years later, Jerry moved in with Ben in Saratoga Springs, New York, and the two childhood friends decided to start a food business together. They considered making bagels, until they discovered the high cost of the necessary machinery. After settling upon ice cream, they took a five-dollar correspondence course from Penn State University in ice cream-making. Since Saratoga Springs already had an ice cream parlor, Ben and Jerry decided to start their business in Burlington, Vermont, a college town lacking an ice cream parlor. In May 1978, with twelve thousand dollars, the chums opened Ben & Jerry's Homemade Ice Cream Parlor in a vacant gas station on a busy street corner in Burlington. Ben & Jerry's soon became famous for its super premium ice cream made with all-natural Vermont dairy products, very little air, innovative flavors, and imaginative names, and for its contributions to progressive social change in the United States.

STRANGE ENCOUNTERS

★ Jerry was born in Brooklyn, New York, in 1951, four days before Bennett Cohen, who was also born in Brooklyn, New York.

★ As a child, Ben would create his own ice cream concoctions by mushing up his favorite cookies and candies into his ice cream.

★ Ben worked as a cashier at McDonald's, Pinkerton guard at the Saratoga Raceway, night mopper at Jamesway and Friendly's, and assistant superintendent at Gaslight Square Apartments.

★ As a student at Oberlin College, Jerry took a course called "Carnival Techniques" where he learned how to swallow fire and use a sledgehammer to smash a cinder-block lying on a volunteer's belly without harming the volunteer.

★ During the summer of 1986, Ben and Jerry traveled across the country together in the Ben & Jerry's "Cowmobile," serving free samples of their ice cream to generate publicity. When a fire destroyed the Cowmobile outside Cleveland, Ohio, Ben told the press that the burning Cowmobile "looked like a giant baked Alaska."

★ When Pillsbury threatened to drop distributors from the Häagen-Dazs roster if they distributed Ben & Jerry's, the little Vermont ice cream company sued Pillsbury. The case was settled out of court, but Pillsbury's publicized fears of the new ice cream company gave Ben & Jerry's celebrity status as a down-home, extra indulgent ice cream.

★ Wavy Gravy, one of Ben & Jerry's ice cream flavors, is named in honor of the renowned Merry

Prankster and Grateful Dead disciple immortalized in Tom Wolfe's *Electric Kool-Aid Acid Test.*

★ Enlisting the help of Doonesbury cartoonist Garry Trudeau, Ben & Jerry's tried to concoct a flavor named "Zonker," but soon found themselves embroiled in an apparent trademark conflict with "Screaming Yellow Zonkers" (a glazed popcorn snack) and had to drop the idea. Ben & Jerry's ultimately named one of its sorbets "Doonesberry."

★ Since 1991, Ben & Jerry's has refused to use any dairy products containing recombinant Bovine Growth Hormone, forcing the company to pay higher prices for its ingredients.

★ Ben and Jerry originally promised never to pay anyone in the company more than ten times the salary of the company's lowest-paid employee. They broke that promise in 1994.

★ Ben & Jerry's 1995 "Do Us A Flavor" contest generated more than a half-million suggestions for ice cream inventions like "Totally Tartan Tummy Tickler," "Wadayou Nuts?," and "Jamaican Me Crazy." The winning entry was "Root Beer Float My Boat." One hundred tubs of Ben & Jerry's ice cream were donated to the winner's favorite charity.

★ In August 1995, before a crowd of forty visitors on the Ben & Jerry's Factory Tour, an announcement was made that a pint had been found on the production line and labeled with the name "Rebecca." When the tour leader retrieved the designated pint, tour-participant Rebecca opened it to find a diamond engagement ring. The other visitors showered the happy couple with rainbow colored sprinkles.

★ Ben & Jerry's 1996 annual report included a box of crayons scented like the company's eight new Sorbet flavors and pages for stockholders to color.

★ When Ben & Jerry's named one of its ice creams "Cherry Garcia," the Grateful Dead's Jerry Garcia attempted to sue the company.

Tom Cruise and Nicole Kidman

In 1989, Australian actress Nicole Kidman landed a starring role in the movie thriller *Dead Calm* opposite Sam Neill and Billy Zane. Receiving critical acclaim for her performance, Nicole was also noticed by actor Tom Cruise, who had starred in the box-office hits *Risky Business, Top Gun,* and *Rainman.* While attending a film festival in Japan, Nicole received a telephone call from Tom, who asked her to audition in Los Angeles for his next film, *Days of Thunder.* Searching for a leading lady, Tom flew Nicole to Los Angeles.

"My first reaction to meeting Nic was pure lust," Tom reportedly said. He cast her in her first American film as a young Australian neurologist at the Daytona Beach Hospital who treats injured race-car driver Tom Cruise and falls in love with him. She stole Tom's heart both on and off screen. Nicole said it was love at first sight. "He basically swept me off my feet," she told *Vanity Fair* magazine. "I fell madly, passionately in love."

At the time Tom and Nicole met, he had just announced his separation from his wife of three years, actress Mimi Rogers. Tom and Nicole became inseparable during their five months together on the set of *Days of Thunder.* Upon completing the film, they moved in together.

After a whirlwind courtship, the couple wed on Christmas Eve, 1990, in a private, candle-lit ceremony in Telluride, Colorado.

★ After eleven years of marriage, Tom and Nicole divorced in August 2001, citing career conflicts.

★ Tom Cruise, born Thomas Cruise Mapother IV on July 3, 1962, in Syracuse, New York, is dyslexic.

★ Nicole Kidman, born on June 20, 1967, in Honolulu, Hawaii, to a clinical psychologist and a nursing instructor, was raised in Sydney, Australia.

★ Tom attended fifteen different schools by the time he was fourteen.

★ In her first stage role, Nicole played a bleating sheep in an elementary school Christmas pageant.

★ At Nicole's first school dance, no one asked her to dance. She was nicknamed "Storky" because of her height.

★ At age fourteen, Tom attended a Franciscan seminary to become a priest. He dropped out after one year.

★ Tom took up acting after losing his place on a high school wrestling team due to a knee injury.

★ Nicole dropped out of high school at age sixteen to pursue an acting career, landing a role in the Australian holiday favorite *Bush Christmas*.

★ When her mother was diagnosed with breast cancer, seventeen-year-old Nicole took a massage course so that she could provide physical therapy for her mother, who eventually beat the cancer.

★ Tom graduated from Glen Ridge High School in 1980.

★ Tom made his film debut with a small part in the 1981 movie *Endless Love*.

★ Working with actor Paul Newman on the 1986 movie *The Color of Money* helped awaken Tom's political consciousness. Subsequently, Tom chose to star in the 1989 anti-war film *Born on the Fourth of July* to counter his contribution to the 1986 jingoistic movie *Top Gun*.

★ Tom was married to actress Mimi Rogers from 1987 to 1990.In *Days of Thunder*, Nicole plays a neurosurgeon who, oddly, has no qualms about riding a motorcycle without a helmet.

★ In 1990, Tom renounced his devout Catholic beliefs, embraced the Church Of Scientology, and claimed that Scientology had cured him of dyslexia.

★ Tom and Nicole adopted two children, Isabella and Connor.

★ Tom and Nicole starred together in three movies: *Days of Thunder, Far and Away,* and *Eyes Wide Shut.*

★ Tired of denying tabloid attacks that their marriage was a cover-up for Tom's alleged homosexuality, Tom and Nicole successfully sued *The Star* for a story claiming that a sex therapist coached the couple through love scenes for Stanley Kubrick's 1999 sexual thriller *Eyes Wide Shut.*

★ In 2001, Tom filed a 100 million dollar defamation lawsuit against Michael Davis for claiming to have videotapes of himself having sex with the actor. That same year, he filed a 100 million dollar defamation lawsuit against porn star Kyle Bradford, who claimed in the French magazine *Actustar* that he had had a homosexual affair with the actor. Bradford later insisted that the magazine misquoted him. In 2003, Tom won a ten million dollar default judgment against porn star Chad Slater, who claimed he had had a homosexual affair with the actor.

Tony Curtis and Janet Leigh

In 1950, 25-year-old actor Tony Curtis, having been signed by Universal Studios and having made his film debut in *Criss Cross*, spotted 23-year-old actress Janet Leigh at a cocktail party at RKO Studios, where she was standing in a corner, talking with billionaire Howard Hughes. Hughes, then head of RKO, planned to feature Janet in the movie *Jet Pilot*, in the hopes that their professional relationship would blossom into a romantic one. Unintimidated by the wealthy and powerful Hughes, Tony walked over and introduced himself to Janet, prompting Hughes to back off.

A few months later, Tony Curtis became friendly with actress Judy Garland, who happened to be good friends with Janet Leigh. Judy, Tony, and Janet went to a party together and became part of a dynamic young Hollywood crowd that included Jerry Lewis. Tony and Janet grew closer and fell in love. Neither Universal nor RKO Studios wanted Tony and Janet to marry, fearing fans would abandon the two sex symbols. Despite this opposition, they got engaged on May 26, 1951, and married nine days later, with Jerry Lewis serving as best man. Ironically, the marriage heightened Tony and Janet's popularity. The media called them Hollywood's Perfect Young Couple. In fact, after the wedding, the studio developed a sexier image for Janet, dying her hair blonde and dressing her in tight outfits that hugged her svelte figure.

STRANGE ENCOUNTERS

★ Tony Curtis, born Bernard Schwartz on June 3, 1925, in the Bronx, New York, changed his last name to an anglicized version of Kertész, the name of one of his Hungarian ancestors.

★ Janet Leigh, born Jeanette Helen Morrison on July 6, 1927, in Merced, California, skipped several grades and finished high school at age fifteen.

★ As a teenager, Tony was a member of a notorious Bronx street gang.

★ Janet Leigh eloped at age fourteen, but the marriage was later annulled.

★ Although she appeared in more than fifty movies, Janet is best remembered for the forty-five minutes that she was on the screen in the 1960 Alfred Hitchcock movie *Psycho*.

★ Actress Norma Shearer noticed a photograph of Janet on the front desk at a Northern California ski resort where Janet's father worked, leading to a screen test for Janet at MGM and a starring role in the 1947 movie *The Romance of Rosy Ridge*.

★ Born to a Jewish tailor from Hungary, Tony speaks fluent Hungarian.

★ In *Psycho*, the famous shower scene ends with an extreme closeup of Janet Leigh's eye, her pupil tightly contracted. When people die, their pupils dilate.

★ Tony and Janet appeared together in six movies: *Houdini, The Black Shield of Falworth, The Vikings, The Perfect Furlough, Pepe*, and *Who Was That Lady?*

★ Tony and Janet divorced after ten years of marriage, leaving Janet with custody of their two daughters: Jamie Lee Curtis and Kelly Curtis.

★ Tony married five times, to Janet Leigh, Christine Kaufman, Leslie Allen, Lisa Deutsch, and Jill Vanderberg.

★ Janet married four times, to John Carlyle, Stanley Reames, Tony Curtis, and Robert Brandt.

★ Tony's fifth wife, Jill Vandenberg, is 45 years his junior.

Roger Daltrey and Pete Townshend

In 1962, after leaving Acton County Grammar School, eighteen-year-old Roger Daltrey formed a skiffle band called the Detours. He invited his former class-mate John Entwistle, an accomplished musician who studied piano and played French horn with the Middlesex Youth Orchestra, to join his group. When the Detours needed a new rhythm guitarist, John suggested they invite his friend Pete Townshend to join the band. Pete had played banjo and John had played trumpet in the Aristocrats, a Dixieland band formed by Pete in 1959 while they were students at Acton County Grammar School. When the Detours' lead singer, Colin Dawson, left the band in 1963, Roger took over as lead vocalist and Pete switched to lead guitar. The Detours soon renamed themselves the Who.

In 1964, at the insistence of manager Pete Meaden, the Who renamed themselves the High Numbers, took on a Mod image, and released the single "I'm the Face," which flopped. In 1965, the group added drummer Keith Moon, found new managers, and renamed themselves the Who again. They recorded the demo record, "I Can't Explain," and landed a record deal with Decca Records. The single received little attention until the band played the song on the television show *Ready, Steady, Go,* culminating with Pete smashing his guitar and Keith kicking over his drums. The havoc sent sales of the single soaring and established the Who as the ultimate violent, antiestablishment band.

STRANGE ENCOUNTERS

★ Roger Daltrey, born on March 1, 1945, in Hammersmith, London, earned a living as a sheet-metal worker.

★ Pete Townshend was born on May 19, 1945, in Chiswick, London. His mother sang with the Sidney Torch Orchestra, and his father played saxophone in a Royal Air Force dance band called the Squadronaires.

★ When Pete was a young boy, his parents separated and left him with his maternal grandmother, who was clinically insane.

★ When a club manager asked the group the name of their band, they responded, "the Detours." The manager replied, "The who?" The band replied, "Yeah, that's right. The Who."

★ In 1964, while performing at the Railway Hotel in Harrow, England, Pete, swinging his arm like a windmill, accidentally smacked his guitar against the low ceiling, snapping off the neck. When the audience failed to react, he smashed the rest of the guitar on the stage. Drummer Keith Moon followed suit by kicking over his drums, giving birth to a memorable new gimmick for the group.

★ In 1965, EMI rejected the Who's demo record because the group didn't write their own songs. Pete Townshend sat down and wrote "I Can't Explain," which was released eight weeks later by Decca as their first single.

★ Session musician Jimmy Page (later of the band Led Zeppelin) played guitar on "I Can't Explain."

★ In 1965, Roger Daltrey was quoted as saying, "When I'm thirty I'm going to kill myself, 'cos I don't ever want to get old."

★ On May 20, 1966, when John Entwistle and Keith Moon failed to show up at a scheduled Who performance at the Riki Tik club in Newbury, England, Pete and Roger performed with a substitute bassist and drummer. When John and Keith finally showed up, Pete hit Keith over the head with his guitar, giving the drummer a black eye.

★ The Who pioneered the rock opera with the albums *Tommy* and *Quadrophenia*.

★ Although the Who made their farewell concert tour in 1982, the group continued to play live and frequently went on tour over the next twenty years.

Matt Damon and Ben Affleck

In 1980, eight-year-old Ben Affleck lived with his family in Cambridge, Massachusetts, where his mother worked as a schoolteacher and his father worked as a janitor at Harvard University. Two blocks away, ten-year-old Matt Damon, whose parents had divorced when he was two, lived with his mother (a professor of child development) and his older brother in a communal home shared with five other families. Matt's mother and Ben's mother became friends and introduced the two boys.

As kids, Matt and Ben played Little League baseball together, enjoyed Dungeons and Dragons and video baseball, followed the comic book adventures of *The Superfriends* and *The X-Men*, and went to double-feature movies on Saturdays. They dressed up as superheroes, flying around the house with red towels around their necks. They enjoyed rap music, called each other "Matty D" and "Biz," and learned how to breakdance.

Ben introduced Matt to acting. In 1979, Jan Egleson, a friend of Ben's mother, hired seven-year-old Ben to appear in his independent feature film, *The Dark End of the Street*. The following year, his mother's best friend cast him as the lead in the PBS series, *The Voyage of the Mimi*. Ben soon had an agent in New York and worked during school vacations.

As students at Cambridge Rindge and Latin High School, Ben and Matt took acting classes together. When Matt was sixteen, Ben introduced him to his agent, and the two did extra work in several films shooting in the Boston area. "One of the reasons we're so tight is we always had a lot in common, a lot of similar interests and sensibilities," explained Matt.

After high school, Matt studied English at Harvard University. Ben attended the University of Vermont, dropped out after a few months, and moved to Los Angeles. Inspired by *Lawrence of Arabia*, he took up Middle Eastern studies at Occidental College in Los Angeles but soon dropped out to seek his fortune as an actor. In 1992, Matt dropped out of Harvard twelve credits short of his degree and joined Ben in Los Angeles to pursue acting. Soon fed up with life as a struggling actor, Matt asked Ben to help him finish a screenplay he had started writing at Harvard.

The duo sold the script for *Good Will Hunting* to Castle Rock, enduring years of rewrites—until director Kevin Smith sent the script to Harvey Weinstein, co-chairman of Miramax. Weinstein bought the script from Castle Rock and hired Gus Van Sant to direct Matt and Ben in the 1997 movie. The lifelong friends shared an Academy Award for Best Original Screenplay.

STRANGE ENCOUNTERS

★ Matthew Paige Damon was born on October 8, 1970, in Cambridge, Massachusetts, to a tax preparer and a college professor.

★ Born in Berkeley, California, on August 15, 1972, Benjamin Geza Affleck received his middle name in honor of a Hungarian friend of the family.

★ Both Matt's parents and Ben's parents are divorced.

★ When young Ben asked his mother for a dog, she tested him by making him walk an imaginary dog for a week. Ben lasted only five days and failed to get the dog.

★ Ben's first acting experience was in a Burger King commercial as a child.

★ Matt landed a small part in the 1988 film *Mystic Pizza*, starring newcomer Julia Roberts.

★ Both Matt and Ben worked as extras on the 1989 film *Field of Dreams*. During the shoot, Matt went down on the field of Boston's Fenway Park to take some blades of grass as a memento for his father.

★ Matt and Ben appeared together in seven movies: *School Ties, Glory Daze, Chasing Amy, Good Will Hunting, Dogma, Jay and Silent Bob Strike Back*, and *The Third Wheel*.

★ In 1993, Ben directed the short film *I Murdered My Lesbian Wife, Hung Her on a Meat Hook, and Now I've Got a Three-Picture Deal With Disney*.

★ Ben's father worked as a janitor at Harvard University, inspiring Matt and Ben to give the character Will Hunting a job as a janitor at M.I.T. in their movie *Good Will Hunting*.

★ In 1999, Ben was fined 135 dollars for driving in Massachusetts with a suspended license.

Ellen DeGeneres and Anne Heche

C omedienne Ellen DeGeneres, star of the hit television sitcom *Ellen*, appeared on the cover of the April 10, 1997, issue of *Time* magazine under the headline "Yep, I'm Gay," making television history by becoming the first openly gay lead on a sitcom. On April 30, ABC-TV aired a historic episode of *Ellen*, in which the main character revealed that she was gay. The show attracted 42 million viewers.

In May, Ellen meet actress Anne Heche at a party thrown by *Vanity Fair* magazine after the Academy Awards. Several weeks later, Ellen and Anne announced their romantic partnership on Oprah Winfrey's show, and soon after they were seen together arm-in-arm talking to President Bill Clinton at a White House dinner. Ellen and Anne's high-profile relationship quickly made them role models for gays and lesbians.

A year later, both Ellen and Anne became even more outspoken, accusing the Hollywood establishment of turning against them for being so vocal about their lesbian partnership. ABC, citing poor ratings, cancelled *Ellen*, and the studios seemed unwilling to cast Anne in any new movies. "What we've found," said Ellen, "is that this is a very hard town to be truthful in."

In 1999, Ellen and Anne announced their intention to marry the moment voters in Vermont passed legislation to legalize gay marriages.

STRANGE ENCOUNTERS

★ In August 2000, Ellen and Anne split up—without explaining why. "Unfortunately, we have decided to end our relationship," the couple said in a statement issued to the New York *Daily News*. "It is an amicable parting, and we greatly value the 3 1/2 years we have spent together. We hope everyone will respect our privacy through this difficult time."

★ On the same day that Ellen and Anne announced their separation, Anne parked her Toyota sport-utility vehicle along a highway in Fresno County, California, walked a mile, wandered into a home, and began making irrational statements. She was taken to a local hospital and examined by doctors for two hours.

★ Ellen DeGeneres, born on January 26, 1958, in New Orleans, Louisiana, worked as a paralegal before becoming a comedienne.

★ Anne Heche (pronounced "Haytch") was born on May 25, 1969, in Aurora, Ohio.

★ Anne's family moved eleven times before she was twelve. She attended Ocean City High School in Ocean City, New Jersey.

★ At age eighteen, Ellen confessed to her mother, Betty DeGeneres, that she was lesbian.

★ Anne had been in relationships only with men prior to meeting Ellen, including a two-year relationship with comedian Steve Martin.

★ Ellen's brother Vance DeGeneres starred as Mr. Hands in the *Mr. Bill* films seen on *Saturday Night Live*.

★ When Ellen came out as a lesbian on her show, ABC's affiliate in Birmingham, Alabama, refused to air the landmark episode. Some of the show's sponsors, including Chrysler, withdrew their advertisements.

★ Ellen was initially reluctant to do a love scene with Sharon Stone in *If These Walls Could Talk 2*, but Anne, who directed the segment, urged her to do it.

★ On September 1, 2001, Anne married cameraman Coleman Laffoon. Six months later, on March 2, 2002, Anne gave birth to a son, Homer Heche Laffoon.

★ In her autobiography *Call Me Crazy*, written in just six weeks, Anne claims to have an alter ego named Celestia. (Her middle name is Celeste.)

Joe DiMaggio and Marilyn Monroe

On March 13, 1952, a United Press newswire report revealed that Marilyn Monroe had posed nude in 1949 as "Miss Golden Dreams" for a calendar. Marilyn told reporter Aline Mosby, "Oh, the calendar's hanging in garages all over town. Why deny it? You can get one anyplace. Besides, I'm not ashamed of it. I've done nothing wrong. I was told I should deny I'd posed . . . but I'd rather be honest about it."

Two days later, determined to endear herself to the American public, Marilyn agreed to go on a blind date with recently retired baseball hero Joe DiMaggio, with the understanding that her friend, show business columnist Sidney Skolsky, would report the news in his column. DiMaggio, intrigued by a publicity photograph of Marilyn posing with baseball player Gus Zernial, had asked his friend David March, then Marilyn's press agent, to arrange the date. At 6:30 p.m. on Saturday, March 15, DiMaggio, March, and March's girlfriend sat in a booth in the Villa Nova restaurant on Hollywood's Sunset Boulevard waiting to meet Marilyn. She showed up two hours late. "There's a blue polka dot exactly in the middle of your tie knot," she said to DiMaggio, who wore a gray flannel suit with a blue polka-dot tie. "Did it take you long to fix it just that way?"

DiMaggio, known for his quiet demeanor, said very little that evening. March told stories about his adventures in Hollywood. Mickey Rooney, who happened to be dining there, joined the group, fawning over his baseball hero. Around ten o'clock, Marilyn went home.

The next day, DiMaggio telephoned Marilyn and invited her to join him for a more intimate dinner. Soon after, a blue Cadillac with the license plate JOE D was frequently seen parked outside Marilyn's apartment on Doheny Boulevard in Hollywood.

STRANGE ENCOUNTERS

★ Joe DiMaggio was born Giuseppe Paolo DiMaggio, Jr., on November 25, 1914, in Martinez, California.

★ Marilyn Monroe, born Norma Jean Mortenson on June 1, 1926, in Los Angeles, California, was a natural brunette who wore glasses. Her mother Gladys renamed her daughter with the last name Baker—her first husband's last name. Ultimately, Norma Jean used her mother's maiden name—Monroe. Marilyn was a direct descendant, on her mother's side, of President James Monroe.

★ Marilyn was raised by foster parents Wayne and Ida Bolender for the first seven years of her life.

★ At age nine, Marilyn was placed in an orphanage, where she remained for the next two years.

★ Marilyn claimed to be an orphan to hide the fact that her mother, diagnosed with paranoid schizophrenia, spent many years living in Agnews State Hospital in San Jose.

★ No one knows the identity of Marilyn's father. Her mother listed her second husband, Edward Mortenson, as Marilyn's father. However, Mortenson had deserted Gladys two years earlier.

★ In 1942, at age sixteen, Marilyn dropped out of Van Nuys High School and married 21-year-old aircraft plant worker James Dougherty. The marriage lasted four years.

★ Marilyn first used the name Marilyn Monroe in 1946, but she did not legally change her name until 1956.

★ Marilyn roomed with actress Shelley Winters when they were starting out in Hollywood.

★ In 1947, Marilyn was voted Miss California Artichoke Queen.

★ In 1953, Hugh Hefner shrewdly bought the rights to use Marilyn's nude calendar photograph for five hundred dollars and made her "Sweetheart of the Month" for the centerfold of the first issue of his new magazine, *Playboy*.

★ Marilyn affectionately called DiMaggio "Slugger."

★ When Marilyn's agent Charlie Feldman advised her to buy the screen rights to a novel and commission a screenwriter to tailor the script to her, DiMaggio chose *Horns of the Devil*.

★ DiMaggio helped Marilyn negotiate a new contract with Twentieth Century Fox by convincing her to refuse to make the movie *The Girl in Pink Tights* until she had a new deal.

★ On January 14, 1954, 27-year-old Marilyn married 39-year-old DiMaggio in a civil ceremony in San Francisco City Hall. He wore the same tie he had worn the night he met Marilyn.

★ Marilyn offered to convert to Catholicism for DiMaggio, but the Catholic Church refused to let her convert because she was divorced.When the couple married, the church automatically excommunicated DiMaggio, who was divorced from his first wife Dorothy Arnold, for bigamy. In 1962, Pope John XXIII's Ecumenical Council struck down this edict.

★ Marilyn and Joe spent their wedding night at the Clifton Motel in Paso Robles, in a room that cost $6.50 for the night.

★ DiMaggio objected when Marilyn refused to wear panties beneath her tight skirts when she went out in public, appeared in the first issue of *Playboy*, and posed for several hours on Lexington Avenue at 52nd Street before an estimated fifteen hundred fans to film the famous scene in which her skirt flies up from a gust of wind from a subway grate for the movie *The Seven Year Itch*. Two weeks after this publicity stunt (the actual sequence was re-shot in the studio), Marilyn announced her divorce from DiMaggio. The marriage had lasted only eight months.

★ Despite a reported affair with President Kennedy in 1962, Marilyn and Joe DiMaggio announced that they would remarry on August 8 that year.

★ On August 5, 1962, Marilyn was found dead by her housekeeper. The death was not reported for three hours, leading to innumerable theories as to what actually happened.

★ Joe DiMaggio arranged Marilyn Monroe's funeral, banning the Kennedys, Frank Sinatra, and Dean Martin from the guest list. When Sinatra showed up, guards prevented him from entering.

★ The song "Candle in the Wind" by Elton John and Bernie Taupin is a tribute to Marilyn Monroe. In 1997, Elton and Bernie rewrote the lyrics in memory of Princess Diana.

★ According to *The Book of Lists*, from the time of Marilyn's death in 1962 until his own death in 1999, DiMaggio had fresh red roses delivered to her grave three times a week.

Michael Douglas and Catherine Zeta-Jones

In August 1998, actor Michael Douglas, the 53-year-old star of such hit films as *Fatal Attraction, Wall Street,* and *The Game,* met actress Catherine Zeta Jones, twenty-five years his junior, at the Deauville Film Festival in France. After a screening of the movie *The Mask of Zorro,* starring Catherine as a seductress opposite Antonio Banderas, Michael, promoting the thriller *A Perfect Murder,* convinced Catherine to have dinner with him. He had recently divorced his wife Diandra Luker, with whom he had a nineteen-year-old son, after twenty years of marriage. Seventeen months later, on New Year's Eve 1999, Michael and Catherine got engaged in Aspen, Colorado. At the time, Catherine was two months pregnant with Michael's child.

On August 8, 2000, Catherine gave birth to a son named Dylan. Three months later, on November 18, 2000, Michael married Catherine at the Plaza Hotel in New York City (with his 22-year-old son Cameron serving as best man), followed by a lavish reception estimated to have cost more than 1.5 million dollars. To keep the paparazzi away from their wedding, Michael and Catherine sold the photography rights to just one magazine from each country. Although the couple tried to keep the location of the wedding secret from the press, a disgruntled florist leaked the information.

★ Michael Douglas, born on September 25, 1944, in New Brunswick, New Jersey, to actor Kirk Douglas and Diana Dill, graduated from the University of California at Santa Barbara.

★ Catherine Zeta-Jones was born on September 25, 1969, in Swansea, West Glamorgan, Wales, to a candy factory manager. Her parents named her after her grandmothers: Catherine Fair and Zeta Jones.

★ As an infant, Catherine suffered from a virus that hindered her breathing, prompting doctors to give her a tracheotomy. She retains the scar.

★ While starting out as an actor in New York City, Michael roomed with fellow actor Danny DeVito.

★ When Catherine was three years old, Michael starred as young, hot-headed Inspector Steve Kellyer opposite veteran actor Karl Malden on the television police drama *The Streets of San Francisco*.

★ Michael produced the 1975 movie version of Ken Kesey's novel *One Flew Over the Cuckoo's Nest*.

★ As a child, Catherine, who speaks Welsh fluently, sang and danced in the performing troupe of a Catholic church.

★ At age fifteen, Catherine, cast as the second understudy to the lead role in the British revival of the musical *42nd Street*, played the lead one night after both the star and first understudy called in sick. The producer, who happened to be in the audience that night, gave the lead to Catherine for the rest of the run.

★ In 1998, Michael was named a United Nations Messenger of Peace to focus worldwide attention on nuclear disarmament and human rights.

★ Michael and Catherine share the same birthday, September 25—exactly twenty-five years apart.

★ Michael and Catherine have starred together in one movie—*Traffic*—but they do not share any scenes. Catherine's character was rewritten as a pregnant woman because the actress was pregnant with Michael's child.

Dwight Eisenhower and Mamie Geneva Doud

O n Sunday, October 3, 1915, Lieutenant Dwight "Ike" Eisenhower, a recent graduate of West Point Military Academy, was serving as Officer of the Day at Fort Sam Houston, in San Antonio, Texas. In the late afternoon he stepped out of his quarters, strapping his gun belt around his waist. Across the street, on the lawn of a house occupied by a Major Harris and his wife, Lulu, a group of civilians dressed in their Sunday best sat in deck chairs. Ike's fellow junior officer, Leonard "Gee" Gerow, talking with Lulu, beckoned Ike to come over. Gee had told the gathered women that the heartbroken Ike had sworn off women. This description intrigued the ladies, especially Mamie Geneva Doud, the eighteen-year-old daughter of a wealthy meat packer. Mamie wore a flowered skirt, a large black hat, and—as Ike later recalled—"a saucy look." He invited her to take a walk with him to inspect the guard, promising to get her back in time for the date that would be picking her up at eight o'clock.

The walk turned out to be a three-mile hike. Mamie pretended that her brand-new, tightly-laced boots were not killing her feet. As promised, Ike returned her to their starting point so she could prepare for her date.

The next day, Ike visited her home in San Antonio, only to discover that Mamie, a recent debutante, had dates scheduled for weeks. While waiting for her hectic schedule to open up, Ike spent his off-duty hours in the Doud's home, befriending Mamie's parents and sisters and making his presence known whenever rival dates picked up or dropped off Mamie. Mamie seemed reluctant to date the persistent Ike, until her father told her, "Stop this flighty nonsense, or the Army boy will give up in disgust."

Ike courted Mamie by taking her to local Mexican restaurants and the movies, eventually capturing her heart. For Christmas, he gave her a heart-shaped silver jewelry box engraved with her initials. On Valentine's Day 1916, Ike and Mamie announced their engagement. Shortly afterward, Ike applied for a transfer to the aviation division, but Mamie said she'd refuse to marry him if he was chosen to become a pilot. When the transfer came through, Ike turned it down.

Ike applied to the Army for a twenty-one day leave to get married, but while waiting for the paperwork to travel through the bureaucracy for approval, the Doud family returned to their summer home in Denver, Colorado. When the Army, preparing to enter World War I, finally granted Ike an abbreviated ten-day leave, he insisted that Mamie marry him right away. At noon on July 1, 1916, Ike married Mamie in her parent's house in Denver, in a traditional Anglican wedding ceremony conducted by Reverend William Williamson, a visiting English Episcopalian minister.

S T R A N G E   E N C O U N T E R S

★ Mamie Geneva Doud, born in 1896 in Boone, Iowa, was raised in San Antonio, Texas, and spent summers in Denver, Colorado.

★ Dwight David Eisenhower, born David Dwight Eisenhower on October 14, 1890, in Denison, Texas, was raised in Abilene, Kansas, where his father worked as a mechanic in a creamery. His parents called him Dwight, and he reversed his first and middle names before he reached high school.

★ Ike's 1909 high school yearbook predicted that he would become a history professor at Yale University.

★ On August 5, 1915, just two months before meeting Mamie, Ike proposed marriage to Gladys Harding, a girlfriend in Abilene. After twelve days with no response, Ike wrote her a long love letter. Gladys,

a pianist, left Abilene on September 1 to go on a concert tour. She wrote to Ike, explaining that her career came first. She later returned to Abilene and gave up her career to marry a widower named Cecil Brooks.

★ On his wedding day, Ike was promoted to first lieutenant. He refused to sit down before the wedding ceremony to avoid creasing the trousers of his uniform.

★ During Ike and Mamie's two-day honeymoon at Eldorado Springs, a resort outside of Denver, Mamie's parents showed up uninvited.

★ After they married, Ike quickly discovered that his new bride could neither cook nor clean, forcing the couple to eat in restaurants.

★ While serving as a regimental supply officer in 1917, Ike was struck by lightning.

★ In 1943, Ike had to tell his driver and personal assistant Kay Summersby that her fiancé had been killed while inspecting a mine field. In her autobiography, *Past Forgetting*, Kay claims that she and Ike became romantically involved but never consummated their relationship. Some of Kay's closest friends disputed the claim that they were entangled.

★ Ike's parents, David and Ida Eisenhower, belonged to the Church of the Brethren in Christ and opposed war or any kind of violence. Ike became the supreme commander of the Allied armies in Europe during World War II.

★ Ike and Mamie had two sons: Doud Dwight Eisenhower (who died of scarlet fever at the age of three) and John Selton Doud Eisenhower (appointed United States Ambassador to Belgium by President Richard M. Nixon).

★ In 1937, Ike, working under General Douglas MacArthur to establish the Philippine Air Force and the Philippine Military Academy, obtained his pilot's license at the age of forty-seven.

★ In 1948, after retiring from the military, Ike served as president of Columbia University.

★ In 1948, both the Republican and Democratic parties attempted to draft Ike as their presidential nominee. Ike turned down both offers.

★ President Dwight D. Eisenhower played golf nearly every Sunday on a course near Gettysburg, Pennsylvania. Unbeknownst to Eisenhower, a 1794 state law made it illegal to play golf in Pennsylvania on Sunday. The law was not repealed until 1960.

★ The Eisenhowers had four grandchildren. In 1968, their only grandson, David, married Julie Nixon, the younger daughter of Ike's vice-president, Richard M. Nixon.

Queen Elizabeth II and Prince Philip

On July 22, 1939, English King George VI and his family sailed up the river Dar aboard the royal yacht *Victoria and Albert* and dropped anchor off the shore of Dartmouth Royal Naval College, where the king had been a cadet. He planned to revisit his old haunts with his cousin, Lord Louis Mountbatten and his family

While George and Mountbatten toured the campus, Mountbatten's two daughters Patricia and Pamela, played with the king's thirteen-year-old daughter, Princess Lilibet (and her nine-year-old sister Margaret) at the house of Admiral Sir Frederick Dalrymple-Hamilton, who ran the college.

While the girls played, Lord Mountbatten's nephew, eighteen-year-old Prince Philip o: Greece, a cadet at the college, stopped by to visit. According to Lilibet's governess, Marion Crawford, Philip and the girls played together with clockwork trains on the floor of the nursery. "We had ginger crackers and lemonade in which he joined," recalled Crawford, "and then he said, 'Let's go to the tennis courts and have some real fun jumping the nets.'"

At the tennis courts, Philip did not pay Lilibet any special attention, but she immediately fell in love with him. That evening, Philip and a group of his fellow cadets joined the royal family aboard their yacht for dinner, and the following day he kept the girls company. When the yacht departed that afternoon, the cadets hopped into boats and escorted the royal family down the river and out to sea. When his fellow cadets turned back, Prince Philip continued rowing after the yacht, as Lilibet watched admiringly through a pair of binoculars.

STRANGE ENCOUNTERS

★ Lilibet and Philip are both the great-great-grandchildren of Queen Victoria and Prince Albert, meaning they share the same great-great-grandparents (one of sixteen pairs).

★ Philip was born on June 10, 1921, on the Greek island of Corfu, to Prince Andrew of Greece and Princess Alice of Battenberg.

★ Lilibet, born on April 21, 1926, in London to the Duke and Duchess of York, was christened Elizabeth Alexandra Mary Windsor.

★ At two years old, Elizabeth pronounced her own name as "Lilliebeth." Her grandfather, King George V, affectionately called her Lilibet, and from then on, her family addressed her as Lilibet.

★ In 1922, when Turkish troops defeated the Greek army and imprisoned Philip's father, Prince Andrew of Greece, in Athens and threatened to execute him, the British cruiser *HMS Calypso*, by order of King George V, secretly rescued Philip and his family.

★ Educated in England, Philip served as a lieutenant in the British Navy with the Mediterranean Fleet and the British Pacific Fleet during World War II. During this time he frequently corresponded with his cousin Lilibet, and when the war ended, the couple began courting.

★ In 1947, Philip renounced his title and rights of succession to the throne of Greece, became a British citizen, and took Mountbatten for his last name.

★ The 21-year-old Lilibet married 26-year-old Philip Mountbatten on November 20, 1947, in Westminster Abbey. The day before the wedding, King George VI made Philip Duke of Edinburgh.

★ In 1948, when her father's health began to fail, Lilibet and Philip began assuming many of his royal obligations. Lilibet became queen upon the death of her father, King George VI, on February 6, 1952.

★ In 1957, Lilibet gave Philip the title of Prince of the United Kingdom.

★ Lilibet and Philip have four children: Charles, Anne, Andrew, and Edward.

F. Scott Fitzgerald and Zelda Sayre

On a hot Saturday night in July 1918, a month after her graduation from Sidney Lanier High School, eighteen-year-old Zelda Sayre attended a dance at the country club in Montgomery, Alabama. F. Scott Fitzgerald, a first lieutenant stationed at Camp Sheridan a few weeks earlier, also attended that dance. When Zelda performed the "Dance of the Hours," Scott, watching from the edge of the dance floor, asked a friend to introduce him to this vivacious young woman. Scott and Zelda were soon dancing together.

From that night on, Scott saw Zelda whenever he was free from military duty and telephoned her every day, twice if he could not see her. Zelda invited him to dinner to meet her family. Scott carved their initials into the door of the country club where they met. On September 7, Scott noted in his journal that he had fallen in love with Zelda. Zelda, however, refused to limit herself to just one man, encouraging other suitors—to fuel Scott's passion for her. Still, they spent many afternoons together, sitting in the porch swing outside the Sayers' house.

On October 26, the Army sent Scott to Camp Mills on Long Island to await shipment to France to fight in World War I. While he waited, the war ended, and Scott returned to Montgomery to await his discharge. Once again, he was seeing Zelda steadily. She soon confessed her love for him, and the two began planning their future together. Scott insisted upon setting himself up in New York City as a journalist before letting Zelda join him. On February 18, 1919, Scott moved to New York. He and Zelda wrote to each other every day. Toward the end of March, Scott sent his mother's engagement ring to Zelda.

During her long-distance engagement to Scott, Zelda accepted a fraternity pin from a golfer while attending a party at Georgia Tech in Atlanta, Georgia. Upon returning home to Montgomery, she decided to return the pin along with a sentimental note to the golfer, but accidentally put them in an envelope addressed to Scott in New York. Scott took the next train to Montgomery and proposed they marry immediately. Zelda refused, and Scott took his mother's engagement ring back to New York.

Devastated, Scott quit his job and proceeded to get drunk for the next three weeks (until Prohibition closed all the bars). On July 4, he took a train home to St. Paul to write his novel, *This Side of Paradise,* using material from his rejected first novel *The Romantic Egoist.* He finished the novel in August, and a month later he received a publishing contract from editor Maxwell Perkins at Scribner's. Convinced that publishing the book would help him win back Zelda, Scott wrote to Perkins, asking him to publish it immediately. "I have so many things dependent on its success," he wrote, "including, of course, a girl."

In October, having had no contact with Zelda since their breakup in June, Scott wrote to her about his success and asked if he could visit her. She said yes. While in Montgomery, they renewed their engagement and agreed to marry upon the publication of his novel. He returned to New York, leaving Zelda with a copy of his manuscript for *This Side of Paradise.* Scott signed with an agent, began selling his short stories to magazines, and made frequent visits to Montgomery. The Sayers announced their daughter's engagement on March 20, 1920. Six days later, Scribner's published *This Side of Paradise.* Zelda took a train to New York and married Scott on Saturday, April 3, in the rectory of St. Patrick's Cathedral.

S T R A N G E   E N C O U N T E R S

★ Zelda Sayre, born on July 24, 1900 at home in Montgomery, Alabama, was the youngest of six children.

★ F. Scott Fitzgerald, born Francis Scott Key Fitzgerald on September 24, 1896, in St. Paul, Minnesota, was named after the lawyer who composed the Star Spangled Banner.

★ Zelda was voted The Prettiest and The Most Attractive girl in her high school class.

★ Beneath Zelda's picture in her high school yearbook is the verse:

> "Why should all life be work,
> when we all can borrow.
> Let's only think of today,
> and not worry about tomorrow."

★ As an undergraduate at Princeton University, Scott contributed to the campus humor magazine, the *Princeton Tiger*, and the campus literary magazine, the *Nassau Lit*.

★ Scott dropped out of Princeton University in his senior year to join the army.

★ Scott wrote his first novel, *The Romantic Egotist*, in 1917 on weekends while stationed at Fort Leavenworth. Maxwell Perkins, an editor at Scribner's, rejected the book in August 1918.

★ During Scott's first dinner at the Sayre house, Zelda's father chased her around the dining room table with a carving knife.

★ In a section of *This Side of Paradise* called "The Débutante," Scott used portions of Zelda's letters and diary to create Rosalind, a character based on Zelda and his earlier girlfriend, Ginevra King.

★ Zelda celebrated the success of Scott's first novel, *This Side of Paradise,* by dancing on the dinner table at parties.

Jane Fonda and Ted Turner

In 1989, while broadcasting magnate Ted Turner was hunting and fishing at his Avalon estate in Tallahassee, Florida, with former President Jimmy Carter, he read that actress Jane Fonda had announced her plans to divorce her husband of sixteen years, political activist Tom Hayden. As founder of the Turner Broadcasting System, Cable News Network, and Turner Network Television, Ted was one of the richest men in the world. A year earlier, his second marriage had ended in divorce after twenty-four years and three children. Ted turned to Carter, confessed his admiration for Jane as both an actress and activist, and said, "I think I'm going to ask her for a date."

When Jane, in the midst of a divorce, received a telephone call from Ted, she told him she was not yet ready to date. Ted persisted, and she eventually agreed to go out with him. They shared much in common. Both had a parent who committed suicide. They had each been married twice. They were both committed to using their power and money to improve the world. Ted accompanied Jane to the 1989 Academy Awards. She accompanied him to a dinner at the White House with President George Bush and to a dinner at the Kremlin with Mikhail Gorbachev. They went horseback riding at Ted's ranch in Montana and consummated their relationship in one of the cabins.

★ Jane Seymour Fonda, born on December 12, 1937, in New York City to actor Henry Fonda and socialite Frances Seymour Brokaw, was kicked out of the Girl Scouts for telling dirty jokes.

★ Ted Turner, born Robert Edward Turner III, on November 19, 1938, in Cincinnati, Ohio, was raised in Savannah, Georgia, where his father bought a billboard-advertising company and renamed it Turner Advertising Company.

★ On April 14, 1950, Jane's mother, Frances Seymour Brokaw, living in a psychiatric clinic, committed suicide by cutting her own throat with a razor. Henry Fonda, who had been having an affair with 22-year-old Susan Blanchard, told his twelve-year-old daughter Jane and ten-year-old son Peter that their mother had died from a heart attack. A few weeks later, while reading a fan magazine article about her father, Jane learned the truth about her mother's death.

★ Jane suffered from bulimia from ages thirteen to thirty-seven. She claimed that as a model she lived on cigarettes, coffee, amphetamines, and strawberry yogurt.

★ Legend holds that while attending Vassar College, Jane refused to wear the elegant white gloves and pearls required to attend the daily Tea in the Rose Parlor. When confronted, she purportedly returned to the parlor wearing the gloves, pearls, and nothing else. While Jane did attend Vassar College, she never showed up for Tea in the buff.

★ Ted was expelled from Brown University for smuggling a young woman into his dorm room in violation of university rules.

★ Jane made her screen debut in the 1960 movie *Tall Story*, in which she makes out with actor Anthony Perkins while standing in a shower stall. Later that year Perkins, starring as Norman Bates in the Alfred Hitchcock movie *Psycho*, would become renowned for a more macabre shower scene.

★ In March 1963, Ted's father committed suicide, leaving his son in charge of the Turner Advertising Company.

★ Ted met his second wife, flight attendant Jane Smith, in 1964 at a campaign rally for Republican presidential candidate Barry Goldwater.

★ Jane turned down the lead roles in the movies *Bonnie and Clyde* and *Rosemary's Baby* to star in the 1968 sexual science fiction movie *Barbarella*, directed by her first husband Roger Vadim.

★ In 1970, Jane was arrested for allegedly kicking a police officer who found her in possession of a large quantity of pills. The police dropped all charges after identifying the pills as vitamins.

★ In 1970, Ted bought a television station, Atlanta-based independent Channel 17, then losing more than half a million dollars annually, and used the station to found the WTBS "Superstation" cable network.

★ In July 1972, Jane staged a controversial anti-Vietnam War demonstration by visiting the Viet Cong in Hanoi and recording speeches that Radio Hanoi broadcast to American troops, garnering her the nickname "Hanoi Jane." At a Hanoi press conference, Jane, joined by American prisoners of war, demanded that the United States withdraw from Vietnam and told reporters, "It is not a policy of the North Vietnamese to torture prisoners." During this time, prisoner of war John McCain, later elected Arizona Senator, had his arms broken for refusing to pose for photos with Fonda.

★ In 1977, Ted, having served as captain of the Brown University sailing team, won the America's Cup race aboard his yacht *Courageous*.

★ Jane starred together with her father, Henry Fonda, in only one movie: *On Golden Pond*.

★ In 1986, Ted purchased the MGM/UA Entertainment Company for 1.6 billion dollars, acquiring the rights to more than four thousand movies. His attempts to colorize many black-and-white films triggered fierce debate among film historians and critics.

★ In 1987, Jane, having launched a fitness revolution with her first workout videos and books, had her breasts enlarged through plastic surgery.

★ Since Ted was worth an estimated 1.6 billion dollars compared to Jane's sixty million dollars, the couple worked out a prenuptial agreement, giving her ten million dollars worth of Turner Broadcasting stock and no claim on his estate.

★ Jane married Ted on her fifty-fourth birthday, on December 12, 1991, on his eight-thousand-acre Avalon Plantation in Florida. Jane wore a gown from her 1981 movie *Rollover*, in which she plays a retired film star who inherits a multimillion dollar empire when her husband is mysteriously murdered. Within a year of marrying Ted, Jane retired from her movie career, but continued making fitness videos.

★ In 1991, *Time* magazine named Ted "Man of the Year" for his efforts to promote international relations by founding the Goodwill Games, an international sports competition between the United States and the Soviet Union.

★ In 1995, Ted sold Turner Broadcasting to Time Warner for 7.5 billion dollars and became the largest shareholder in the company.

★ In 1997, Ted pledged one billion dollars—the single largest donation in philanthropic history—to the United Nations for good-works programs.

★ In 2000, America Online acquired Time Warner and reduced Ted's control over Turner Broadcasting. He resigned three years later.

★ Ted has been married and divorced three times, to Judy Nye, Jane Smith, and Jane Fonda. He has five children: Laura and Robert (with Nye), and Rhett, Beauregard, and Jennie (with Smith).

★ Jane has been married and divorced three times, to Roger Vadim, Tom Hayden, and Ted Turner. She has two children: Vanessa (with Vadim) and Troy (with Hayden).

★ Jane is the daughter of actor Henry Fonda, sister of actor Peter Fonda, and aunt of actress Bridget Fonda.

★ Jane and Ted divorced on May 22, 2001, possibly due to religious differences. Shortly after parting ways, Jane become a born-again Christian; Ted has fiercely criticized religion.

★ Ted, the largest private landowner in the United States, owns roughly 1.75 million acres in New Mexico, Montana, South Dakota, and Nebraska.

Gerald Ford and Betty Bloomer

One night in the fall of 1947, Peg Newman, whose husband Frank was working with 34-year-old lawyer Gerald Rudolph Ford, Jr., to raise money for cancer research, called her 29-year-old friend Betty Ann Bloomer to invite her out for a beer with Frank and Jerry. Betty, in the process of a divorce from her husband of five years, did not date. When Betty said no, Jerry got on the phone and convinced her to join them for twenty minutes. While growing up in Grand Rapids, Michigan, Betty had heard about Jerry Ford (a football hero at South High School and the University of Michigan), but had never met him. During her marriage, she had seen Jerry at Saturday night dances at the Kent Country Club. "He picked me up at my apartment," recalled Betty, "we went down to a place on the corner of Division and Hall streets, and the next time I looked at my watch, an hour had passed."

Jerry and Betty began going out together occasionally. When Betty's divorce came through, she and Jerry continued seeing each other frequently. Neither of them intended to get serious. Jerry's former girlfriend, a New York model, had broken his heart and he feared further heartache. Betty's divorce had left her emotionally scarred as well. They agreed to see other people. Yet, Betty suspected that things were heating up when she overheard Jerry asking another one of her dates if his intentions were serious.

Betty helped Jerry and his friends build a one-room cabin on their property in Caberfae, Michigan. Jerry helped Betty buy ski equipment, taught her how to ski, and took her skiing every weekend. Betty went to great lengths to get off work early from her job as a fashion coordinator at Herpolsheimer's

Department Store. Jerry took Betty home to his family for Thanksgiving. When Jerry went skiing without her in Sun Valley for three weeks for the Christmas holiday, they corresponded daily. She sent him a homemade Christmas stocking that included a pipe lighter engraved with the words "To the light of my life."

In February, Jerry proposed, but told Betty they couldn't be married for a year because he intended to run for Congress. Jerry's mother, however, urged him to announce his engagement to help his candidacy. "I always accuse him of marrying me to give himself a respectable image," wrote Betty. After they married on October 15, 1948, she spent the next two weeks working at Herpolsheimer's Department Store during the day and licking envelopes at Jerry's campaign headquarters each night. He was elected to Congress on November 2.

STRANGE ENCOUNTERS

★ Gerald R. Ford, Jr., was born Leslie Lynch King, Jr., on July 14, 1913, in Omaha, Nebraska, to Leslie Lynch King and Dorothy Gardner. His parents divorced two years later, and his mother brought him back to her family in Grand Rapids, Michigan. Dorothy married Gerald R. Ford, the owner of the Ford Paint and Varnish Company, whom she met at a church social. Ford adopted her son, and the couple renamed him Gerald R. Ford, Jr.

★ Betty Ford, born Elizabeth Ann Bloomer on April 8, 1918 in Chicago, Illinois, was raised in Grand Rapids, Michigan. Her father worked as a traveling salesman for the Royal Rubber Company, selling conveyor belts to factories.

★ In 1936, Jerry worked as a ranger at Yellowstone National Park.

★ When Betty was sixteen her father died of carbon monoxide poisoning. He was working under the car in the garage with the engine running. Five years later, Betty's mother Hortense married widower Arthur Godwin, a banker in Grand Rapids.

★ Betty dropped out of Bennington College in Vermont after her sophomore year to study dance in New York City with famed dancer Martha Graham.

★ In 1940, Jerry, a partner in a New York modeling agency, appeared on the cover of *Cosmopolitan* magazine with his girlfriend, Phyllis Brown.

★ Jerry went steady for four years with a New York model he met while attending Yale Law School. She refused to marry him because he intended to practice law in his hometown of Grand Rapids, Michigan. While he served in the Navy in World War II, she married—and divorced—someone else.

★ At age twenty-four, Betty married furniture salesman Bill Warren, who had taken her to her first dance when she was twelve years old. The Presbyterian minister performed an Episcopal service.

★ During World War II, Betty worked in a frozen-food factory in Syracuse, New York.

★ When Betty went to New York City to see the new spring fashions for Herpolsheimer's Department Store, Jerry arranged for his close friend, magazine illustrator Brad Crandel, to invite Betty to his apartment for cocktails. Unbeknownst to Betty, Brad also invited Jerry's former girlfriend.

★ According to Betty, Jerry never told her that he loved her until after they were officially engaged.

★ "We were married on a Friday, because it was fall, and in the fall we couldn't miss a Saturday [University of Michigan] football game," recalled Betty. "I chose Friday, October 15, and all the ushers were furious because they were duck hunters and October 15 was the opening of the duck season."

★ As a divorcée, Betty married Jerry in a sapphire blue satin dress.

★ In November 1963, President Lyndon B. Johnson appointed Jerry to serve on the Warren Commission to investigate the assassination of President John F. Kennedy.

★ Jerry was the first Eagle Scout to become Vice President of the United States.

★ Jerry was the first person to serve as both Vice President and President of the United States without being elected to either office.

★ Comedian Flip Wilson called Betty Ford the "First Momma," a moniker she incorporated as her CB handle.

★ Two women attempted to assassinate Jerry in California in September 1975. On September 6, 1975, Lynette "Squeaky" Fromme attempted to kill the president to impress Charles Manson. On September 22, 1975, Sara Jane Moore made an assassination attempt because she was bored. She was declared mentally unstable.

★ Betty had a mastectomy for cancer less than two months after Gerald Ford became president.

★ In March 1976, at the request of President Gerald Ford, Congress appropriated 135 million dollars for a federal campaign to inoculate the entire United States population against a virus with swine flu characteristics that had first appeared a month earlier among soldiers at Fort Dix in New Jersey. Vaccinations began in the fall, resulting in twenty-three deaths and hundreds of lawsuits against the government for adverse reactions, including heart attacks and paralysis. The government ended the program in December 1976.

★ In 1976, during a debate with Democratic presidential nominee Jimmy Carter, President Gerald Ford incorrectly claimed, "Eastern Europe has never been under Soviet domination."

★ Betty, having battled substance abuse, founded the Betty Ford Clinic.

Michael J. Fox and Tracy Pollan

I n 1982, Michael J. Fox, having moved to Los Angeles to break into acting two years earlier, landed the role of Alex P. Keaton on the television sitcom *Family Ties*. His energetic portrayal of politically conservative, money-hungry, egocentric Alex won him two Emmy Awards and launched his movie career. He starred in the feature films *High School U.S.A.*, *Teen Wolf*, and *Poison Ivy*.

In the fall of 1985, during the fourth season of *Family Ties*, Alex Keaton left for Leland College, where he met his intellectual match in the brilliant Ellen Reed, played by actress Tracy Pollan. While Ellen became the love of Alex's life for one season, Michael and Tracy never dated during this time. Ellen broke up with Alex in an emotional scene at a train station, leaving the usually resilient Alex heartbroken and vulnerable. Alex eventually bounced back and began dating Lauren Miller, played by actress Courtney Cox, a psychology student who saw right through his cockiness but loved him anyway.

In 1987, Michael and Tracy met again when they both costarred in the movie *Bright Lights, Big City*, based on the best-selling novel by Jay McInerney. They married on July 16, 1988.

STRANGE ENCOUNTERS

★ Michael J. Fox, born Michael Andrew Fox on June 9, 1961, in Edmonton, Canada, was raised in Burnaby, a suburb of Vancouver.

★ Tracy was born on June 22, 1960, on Long Island, New York.

★ Michael dropped out of high school, made his professional acting debut in the situation comedy *Leo and Me* at age fifteen, and moved to Hollywood when he was eighteen. Michael has called his decision to quit high school a "stupid youthful mistake." In 1995, he obtained his high school equivalency degree.

★ Tracy's best friend is actress Jennifer Grey, who starred in the movie *Dirty Dancing*. They met while students at the Dalton School in New York City.

★ Michael went to school in Vancouver with rock musician Bryan Adams.

★ While trying to break into television acting, Michael survived on boxes of macaroni and cheese.

★ Michael originally decided against using his middle initial A so his name would not read "Michael, A Fox." Since another actor went by the name Michael Fox, Michael decided to use the middle initial J in homage to Michael J. Pollard, best known for his role in the 1968 movie *Bonnie and Clyde*.

★ *Family Ties* producer Gary David Goldberg originally asked Matthew Broderick to play the part of Alex P. Keaton. Broderick did not want a long-term TV obligation.

★ Tracy once dated actor Kevin Bacon.

★ Michael dated Nancy McKeon, best known for her role as Jo on the television sitcom *Facts of Life*. They costarred in the 1985 movie *Poison Ivy*.

★ Michael starred in the movies *Bright Lights, Big City*, *Casualties of War*, *Doc Hollywood*, and the three *Back to the Future* films.

★ In 1991, while filming *Doc Hollywood*, Michael noticed three of his fingers twitching uncontrollably. He saw a doctor and was diagnosed with Parkinson's Disease. He made his disease public knowledge in the December 7, 1998, issue of *People* magazine.

★ In 2000, Michael left the television sitcom *Spin City* because of his illness.

★ Michael's sister is actress Kelli Fox.

★ Michael and Tracy have four children: Sam, twins Aquinnah and Schuyler, and Esme.

Bill Gates and Paul Allen

I n 1967, Bill Gates' parents enrolled their gifted twelve-year-old son in Lakeside School, a private preparatory school in Seattle, Washington, known for its challenging academic environment.

In the spring of 1968, the Lakeside faculty, determined to acquaint their students with computers, organized a fund-raiser and used the money to buy enough computer time on a DEC PDP-10 owned by General Electric to last one year. A handful of eager, young students—including Bill Gates and Paul Allen—became engrossed by the computer. They worked in the computer room day and night, writing programs and reading all the computer literature they could get their hands on. The students used up a year's worth of computer time in just a few months.

In the fall of 1968, Lakeside struck a new deal for computer time with the newly launched, Seattle-based Computer Center Corporation, one of whose chief programmers had a child attending Lakeside. Before long, Bill and his classmates hacked into the computer system, caused several crashes, broke the security system, and altered the files that recorded the amount of computer time they were using. The Computer Center Corporation banned the overzealous students from using the system for several weeks.

In late 1968, Bill, Paul, and two other Lakeside students formed the Lakeside Programmers Group in the hopes of finding constructive and profitable outlets for their computer skills. The Computer Center Corporation, impressed by the ingenuity of the group's previous assault on the computer, hired the students to find bugs and expose weaknesses in the computer system in exchange for unlimited computer time. "It was when we got free time at C³ [Computer Center Corporation] that we really got into computers," recalled Bill. "I mean, then I became hardcore. It was day and night."

When Computer Center Corporation went out of business in 1970, the Lakeside Programmers Group arranged for computer time on a few computers at the University of Washington, where Paul's father worked. In 1971, Information Sciences, Inc., hired the group to program a payroll system, giving the group free computer time, a source of income, and royalties on any money made from the group's programs.

Bill and Paul started their own company, Traf-O-Data, producing a small computer to measure traffic flow. They grossed some twenty thousand dollars. During Bill's junior year, the Lakeside administration offered him a job computerizing the school's scheduling system. In his senior year, defense contractor TRW hired Bill and Paul to fix the bugs in its computer system. At TRW, Bill and Paul turned into serious programmers and began talking about forming their own software company.

In the fall of 1973, Bill began his pre-law studies at Harvard University, but soon located the school's computer center and lost himself in cyberspace. He remained in close contact with Paul, discussing ideas for future projects and a business partnership. That summer they both worked for Honeywell.

In December 1974, Paul traveled to Harvard to visit Bill. Along the way, he stopped to browse at a magazine stand and discovered that the cover of the latest issue of *Popular Electronics* featured a picture of the Altair 8080 under the headline "World's First Microcomputer Kit to Rival Commercial Models." He bought a copy and raced over to Bill's dorm room. Realizing the imminent explosion of the home computer market and the impending demand for software for the new machines, Bill telephoned MITS (Micro Instrumentation and Telemetry Systems), the maker of the Altair, and lied that he and Paul had developed a version of the computer programming language BASIC that could be used on the company's new microcomputer. When the MITS company expressed interest in seeing their version of BASIC, Bill immediately began developing the code for the program and Paul began devising a way to simulate the Altair with the school's PDP-10.

Two months later, without ever seeing an Altair or the chip that ran the computer, Paul flew to MITS to demonstrate the program. Paul entered the program into the Altair, it worked perfectly, and MITS brought the rights to Bill and Paul's BASIC. In his junior year, Bill Gates dropped out of Harvard and, together with Paul Allen, founded Microsoft, creating the software market.

★ Bill Gates was born William Henry Gates III on October 28, 1955, in Seattle, Washington.

★ Paul Allen was born on January 21, 1953, in Seattle, Washington.

★ In 1980, Bill and Paul developed MS-DOS, an operating system for IBM personal computers. The duo offered to sell the rights to IBM, but IBM declined, deciding instead to lease Microsoft's operating system. Microsoft then went on to license its operating system to computer companies building IBM clones, making MS-DOS the industry standard and turning Bill and Paul into millionaires.

★ In 1990, Bill and Paul developed Windows 3.0, a program that makes IBM computers operate like user-friendly Macintosh computers.

★ Bill is the world's richest self-made billionaire in history.

★ In 1994, Bill, 37, married Melinda French, 28, a Microsoft marketing manager he met at a company dinner six years earlier. The couple has three children.

★ In his 1995 book *The Road Ahead*, Bill predicted a future where you will be able to watch *Gone With the Wind* "with your own face and voice replacing Vivien Leigh's or Clark Gable's."

★ Bill and his wife, Melinda, have endowed a foundation with more than 24 billion dollars to support philanthropic initiatives in the areas of global health and learning.

★ Paul plays guitar in the rock band Grown Men.

Rudy Giuliani and Judith Nathan

In 1999, registered nurse Judith Nathan, a divorcée working for Bristol-Myers Squibb, was dining with a friend at a Manhattan restaurant when New York Mayor Rudy Giuliani invited them to join him at his table. The mayor and Judi had reportedly met before, at an event at their children's private school. At the time, Rudy was living in Gracie Mansion with his wife, Donna Hanover, and their two children, Andrew and Caroline. Judi was living in midtown Manhattan with her teenage daughter and her boyfriend, psychologist Manos Zacharioudakis, but their relationship had deteriorated to the point where they were living in separate rooms and leading separate lives.

A few weeks later, Rudy invited 47-year-old Judi to Gracie Mansion. In May, Judi began spending weekends at her condominium in Southampton, where she was joined throughout the summer by Rudy, complete with police escorts. In August, Judi began visiting Rudy at City Hall, claiming she was visiting his assistant of seventeen years, Denny Young. Young, in the midst of a divorce, would act as a chaperone for Judi. By September, she moved into her own apartment on 94th Street.

Over the next several months, Judi attended the dedication of City Hall Park and a Yankee victory party at Gracie Mansion, and frequently dined alone with Rudy in the private, curtained-off Romeo and Julieta Room at Cuker's restaurant. She showed up at Town Hall meetings, the State of the City speech, the Saint Patrick's Day Parade, and tagged along on the campaign trail through upstate New York as Rudy ran for Senate against First Lady Hillary Clinton.

On March 10, 2000, Judi sat next to Rudy at the Inner City, an annual political lampoon hosted by the press, raising speculation about the nature of their relationship. Soon after, Rudy's wife, Donna, filed for divorce and said she would continue to reside in Gracie Mansion with their two children and announced that she would costar with Kirstie Alley and Hazelle Goodman for two weeks in the off-Broadway hit *The Vagina Monologues*—a show written by one of Hillary Clinton's close friends and supporters.

A week later, Rudy was diagnosed with prostate cancer and withdrew from the Senate race. After the *New York Post* published a photograph of Rudy and Judi leaving a restaurant together, the mayor held a surprise press conference and went public with his relationship with Judi, whom he credited with helping him through his arduous cancer treatments. Judi began appearing with Rudy regularly.

On November 24, 2001, five months after his divorce was finalized, Rudy asked Judi to marry him, giving her an oval Ceylon sapphire set in platinum and surrounded by ten diamonds. They married on May 24, 2003.

STRANGE ENCOUNTERS

★ Rudy Giuliani, born Rudolph William Lewis Giuliani III on May 28, 1944, in Brooklyn, New York, served as mayor of New York City from 1994 to 2001.

★ Judith Nathan, born Judith Stish in Hazelton, Pennsylvania, sold surgical supplies in Charlotte, North Carolina.

★ Judi has a daughter, Whitney (adopted with first husband Bruce Nathan).

★ Rudy has been married three times, to Regina Peruggi (his second cousin), Donna Hanover, and Judith Nathan. The Catholic Church annulled Rudy's fourteen-year marriage to Regina because the couple failed to obtain a church dispensation required when second cousins marry.

★ In 1982, Rudy began introducing Donna as his fiancée while he was still married to Regina Peruggi, president of Marymount Manhattan College.

★ During his marriage to Donna, Rudy reputedly had a long-term affair with one of his staff members, Cristyne Lategano.

★ Rudy's second wife, Donna Hanover, an anchorwoman at New York's WPIX-TV and a correspondent on WNYW-TV's *Good Day New York*, played a news reporter in the movie *Ransom*, Ruth Carter Stapleton in the movie *The People vs. Larry Flynt;* and a variety of characters on various soap operas.

★ Judi, a registered Republican, did not vote in any of the three races in which Rudy ran for mayor.

★ In 2001, Queen Elizabeth II knighted Rudy, and *Time* magazine named him "Person of the Year" for his work in the wake of the terrorist attacks on New York City on September 11, 2001.

★ In the 2003 made-for-TV movie *Rudy*, James Woods starred as Rudy Giuliani.

Jackie Gleason and Art Carney

In 1950, Jackie Gleason, having starred in the final season of the television comedy series *Life of Riley*, was hired to replace Jerry Lester as the host of the television variety show *Cavalcade of Stars*, on the DuMont network. Jackie, determined to build a huge following, employed two comedy writers, Coleman Jacoby and Arnie Rosen.

In the first sketch written for Jackie, entitled "The Man of Compunction," Jacoby and Rosen created "that devil-may-care playboy," Reginald Van Gleason III. In the sketch, Reggie agrees to pose for an advertisement for a liquor company, and drinks shot after shot of whiskey while a photographer shoots picture after picture—until Reggie falls down drunk. For the photographer, Jacoby and Rosen suggested hiring a comedian unknown to Jackie—Art Carney.

32-year-old Art, a former stand-up comedian and impressionist, had played Newton the Waiter on *The Morey Amsterdam Show.* After Jackie and Art performed the sketch on the July 15, 1950, broadcast of *Cavalcade of Stars,* Jackie asked Art to return the following week and instructed his writers and producers to create material specifically for him.

In 1951, comedy writers Joe Bigelow and Harry Crane helped Jackie create a sketch called "The Honeymooners," featuring New York City bus driver Ralph Kramden and his nagging wife Alice, originally played by Pert Kelton. In the first Honeymooners sketch, performed on *Cavalcade of Stars* on October 5, 1951, Art appeared briefly as a befuddled policeman. In a later sketch he became sewer worker Ed Norton, the perfect foil for Ralph Kramden.

★ While Jackie never won an Emmy Award, Art won three for best supporting actor for his portrayal of Ed Norton in *The Honeymooners* (in 1952, 1954, and 1955).

★ Both Jackie and Art were Irish.

★ While trying to break into show business, Jackie worked as a stuntman in high-speed automobile exhibitions at a local carnival.

★ Art, a native of Mount Vernon, New York, worked in a jewelry store until his brother, who worked for the MCA agency, got him a booking with the Horace Heidt Orchestra as a singer/comedian.

★ Jackie's real name was Herbert John Gleason.

★ Drafted into the Army in 1944, Art served in the Normandy invasion, where he was wounded in action.

★ Jackie and Art could have been equal partners in a comedy team, but Jackie remained the boss and Art as second banana.

★ While Ralph Kramden and Ed Norton were bosom buddies, Jackie and Art spent very little time together offstage. When they were not working together, they rarely communicated.

★ Ralph Kramden's address on *The Honeymooners* —328 Chauncey Street—was Jackie's boyhood address in Brooklyn.

★ Art owned the battered hat he wore as Ed Norton. "I bought it in 1935 when I was in high school," he insisted.

★ In 1960, Art starred on Broadway as the original Felix Unger opposite Walter Matthau as Oscar Madison in *The Odd Couple*.

★ Art played the Archer on the television series *Batman* and won an Academy Award for his starring role in the 1974 movie *Harry and Tonto*.

★ Engraved on one of the risers to Jackie's grave in Miami, Florida, is Jackie's signature catchphrase, "And Away We Go."

Daryl Hall and John Oates

I n 1967, Daryl Hall, a student at Temple University, sang lead with his band, the Temptones, to compete in a battle-of-the-bands in the Adelphi Ballroom in Philadelphia, Pennsylvania. Another Temple University student, John Oates, competed in the contest, leading his soul band, the Masters. A gang fight broke out, and both Daryl and John fled from the scene in the same freight elevator. Admiring each other's talents and recognizing their shared musical interests, Daryl and John decided to team up to perform together in various rhythm-and-blues and doo-wop groups.

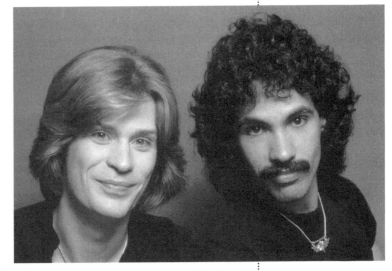

When John transferred to another college, Daryl formed the soft-rock band Gulliver, recording an album in 1969. After earning a degree in journalism, John rekindled his friendship with Daryl, who invited him to join Gulliver. Soon, Gulliver broke up. John traveled through Europe. Daryl continued pursuing a music career, singing back-up for the Stylistics, the Delfonics, and the Intruders. When John returned from his travels, he reunited with Daryl and the twosome began to perform around Philadelphia as Hall and Oates, writing their own acoustic songs together.

In 1972, Atlantic Records signed the duo and released their debut album, *Whole Oats*, which bombed. Undaunted, Daryl and John continued playing Philadelphia clubs, building a loyal following. They moved to New York's Greenwich Village and continued honing their craft, attracting a legion of committed fans. In 1974, Daryl and John released their second album, *Abandoned Luncheonette*. "She's Gone," a single from the album, reached #60 on the Top 100, and six months later became a #1 hit for the band Tavares. Encouraged by their success, Hall and Oates released another version of "She's Gone" in 1976, which became a Top Ten hit. Their next single, "Sara Smile," became their first gold record, establishing the duo in the pantheon of popular musicians.

STRANGE ENCOUNTERS

★ John Oates, born on April 7, 1949, in New York City, started playing guitar at age eight and played in a band in the sixth grade, covering Motown songs.

★ Daryl Hall, born Daryl Franklin Hohl, on October 11, 1949, took piano and voice lessons as a child.

★ Both Daryl and John, raised in Philadelphia suburbs, frequented African American neighborhoods, absorbing music influences and later joining rhythm-and-blues and doo-wop groups.

★ Care-Free chewing gum sponsored Hall and Oates' 1978 concert tour. The duo played free concerts at high schools that had sent in the most gum wrappers.

★ Serial killer David Berkowitz, known as the Son of Sam, claimed that Hall and Oates' hit song "Rich Girl" motivated his crimes. Shocked and appalled, Hall and Oates responded by recording the song "Diddy Doo Wop (I Hear the Voices)" on their 1980 album *Voices*.

★ *The 1982 World Book Encyclopedia* listed Hall and Oates under "Black Music," though they are both white.

★ At the 1985 Live Aid concert at JFK Stadium in Philadelphia, Hall and Oates backed Mick Jagger and Tina Turner's performance.

Jerry Hall and Mick Jagger

In the summer of 1976, Bryan Ferry, lead singer of the English glam-rock band Roxy Music, introduced his fiancée, 20-year-old model Jerry Hall, to his friend, 33-year-old Mick Jagger, backstage at a Rolling Stones concert in London. "He looked really small and slim and fragile and feminine," recalled Jerry. "He sort of scared me. . . . It was definitely a sexual feeling."

Despite his five-year marriage to Brazilian socialite Bianca Perez Morena de Macias, Mick, clearly attracted to Jerry, arranged a few more meetings with the American model. In May 1977, while Ferry was on a concert tour of the Far East, hairdresser Ara Gallant, who worked for photographer Richard Avedon, invited Jerry to a dinner party at a New York restaurant. On May 21, Jerry showed up to discover that the other guests included actor Warren Beatty, model Penelope Tree, and Mick Jagger, whom, she later learned, had engineered the meeting. After dinner, the group went club hopping, ending up at Studio 54, then the trendiest discotheque in New York City. "The next day, he called up and he was really calling up and calling up, from the studio, from here, from there, and always sending flowers," recalled Jerry in her autobiography, *Jerry Hall's Tall Tales.* "And I thought, 'God, this guy is really keen.'"

Jagger (still married to Bianca) and Jerry (still engaged to Ferry) began meeting clandestinely. When Ferry went to Switzerland to record a new album, Jerry secretly accompanied Mick to Morrocco for a vacation, which the press soon discovered and reported. Incensed, Ferry spread rumors that, prior to their engagement, Jerry had been romantically involved with the Shah of Iran.

In 1977, Jerry canceled her engagement to Ferry to be with Jagger, who was still married to Bianca. Finally, on May 11, 1978, Bianca filed for a divorce from Mick due to irreconcilable differences. Mick and Jerry lived together for twelve years and had two children together before finally marrying in a Hindu ceremony on the Indonesian island of Bali in 1990.

STRANGE ENCOUNTERS

★ Mick Jagger was born Michael Philip Jagger on July 26, 1943, in Dartford, England.

★ Jerry Hall, born on July 2, 1956, in Gonzalez, Texas, graduated from North Mesquite High School and left home at age seventeen to pursue a modeling career in Paris, France, where she was discovered by fashion photographer Helmut Newton.

★ The photograph on the cover of Brian Ferry's solo album *The Bride Stripped Bare* depicts Ferry standing in an empty movie theater, mooning a picture of Jerry Hall projected on the silver screen.

★ Jerry had a small part in the 1989 movie *Batman* as the Joker's girlfriend.

★ In 1992, Mick became a grandfather when his daughter Jade (with first wife Bianca) gave birth to a child named Assisi.

★ In 1999, Jerry filed for divorce from Mick on the grounds that he had impregnated Brazilian model Luciana Morad. Mick claimed that his 1990 Hindu wedding to Jerry on Bali did not constitute a legal marriage. Later that year, Jerry agreed to an annulment with an accompanying fifteen-million-dollar settlement and ownership of their eight-million-dollar London mansion.

★ Mick has seven children: Karis (from a relationship with actress Marsha Hunt), Jade (with first wife Bianca), Elizabeth, James, Georgia, and Gabriel (with second wife Jerry Hall), and Lucas (with Luciana Morad). He has also been romantically linked to models Vanessa Neumann, Jane Rajlich, and Carla Bruni.

★ In 2000, Jerry starred as Mrs. Robinson in the musical production of *The Graduate* on the London stage.

Bill Hanna and Joe Barbera

In 1929, while working for his father's engineering firm on the construction of the Pantages Theatre in Hollywood, California, Bill Hanna learned that a new animation company, run by Hugh Harman and Rudolf Ising, had been contracted to create cartoons for Warner Brothers. With no formal art training, Hanna applied for a job with Harman-Ising Studios. He quickly rose to head the ink-and-paint department. Before long, he was composing lyrics and music for Warner Brothers' "Looney Toons" and "Merrie Melodies."

When Harman-Ising moved to Metro-Goldwyn-Mayer to produce cartoons under the banner "Happy Harmonies," Hanna directed his first short, *To Spring*, released in June 1936. The next year, MGM ended its contract with Harman-Ising, established its own in-house cartoon division, and offered Hanna a job as a director of animation. The studio, scouting artists in New York, also hired animator Joe Barbera.

Barbera had begun his career as a professional cartoonist while working as an accountant for the Irving Trust Company. He took art classes at night, eventually selling his cartoons to *Collier's* magazine. He landed a job with Van Beuren Studios, and within six months he was working as a full-fledged animator and story writer. When Van Beuren Studios lost its distribution deal with RKO, Paul Terry, owner of the Terrytoons studio in New Rochelle, hired Barbera as an animator.

In 1937, MGM paired Hanna with Barbera to work on a cartoon about a cat and mouse duo named Tom and Jerry. Hanna wrote the script, Barbera created the drawings, and their first collaboration for MGM, *Puss Gets the Boot*, introduced a unique twist on the adversarial cat-and-mouse relationship. Over the next twenty years, Hanna and Barbera created more than one hundred *Tom and Jerry* cartoons, winning seven Academy Awards.

In 1957, when MGM studios threatened to shut down its animation department, Hanna and Barbera decided to strike out on their own.

"We were sitting in a room waiting for the place to fold," recalled Barbera, "and I said to Bill, 'Why don't we try a cartoon of our own?'"

"Joe's talents are a little different than what talents I have," said Hanna, "and between the two of us, we covered all the bases in production: creation, development, execution, animation, music, the whole thing. We thought it was a good idea to put them together."

The team decided to create cartoons directly for television. Rather than hiring teams of animators to spend months completing a dozen cartoon shorts for cinema release, Hanna and Barbera reduced the heavy production costs by reusing backgrounds and cels. Their first foray onto the small screen featured a clever cat and a dumb dog, *Ruff and Reddy*. By the end of the year, they had their own animation studio. Three years later, they created *The Flintstones*, the first prime-time animated show with half-hour storylines.

STRANGE ENCOUNTERS

★ William Denby Hanna, born on July 7, 1910, in Melrose, New Mexico, was raised in Los Angeles.

★ Joseph Roland Barbera, born on March 24, 1911, in New York City's Little Italy, was raised in Flatbush, Brooklyn.

★ As a youth, Barbera was an amateur boxer.

★ Barbera took a job with the New York cartoon studios of Max Fleischer, where he worked on *Betty Boop* and *Popeye*. He quit after only four days.

★ In the 1945 feature film *Anchors Aweigh*, the animated mouse Jerry danced with a live-action Gene Kelly!

★ Hanna and Barbera created *Huckleberry Hound; Yogi Bear; Quick Draw McGraw; The Flintstones; The Jetsons; Top Cat; Magilla Gorilla; Johnny Quest; Scooby-Doo, Where Are You?; Speed Buggy; Touche Turtle; Josie and the Pussycats;* and *The Smurfs*.

★ Tom and Jerry have been parodied in the pages of *National Lampoon* as Kit 'n' Kaboodle and on *The Simpsons* as Itchy & Scratchy.

★ *The Flintstones* was based on the television sitcom *The Honeymooners*, starring Jackie Gleason.

★ Legend holds that a television executive thought up the name Scooby Doo while sitting on a plane listening to a recording of "Strangers In The Night," in which Frank Sinatra sings, "Scooby dooby doo… "

★ Hanna-Barbera modeled the psychedelic Mystery Machine on *Scooby Doo* after the brightly painted bus driven by hippie author Ken Kesey and popularized in Tom Wolfe's book *The Electric Kool-Aid Acid Test*.

★ Besides acting as executive producers for the 1994 *Flintstones* movie starring John Goodman and Elizabeth Taylor, Hanna made a cameo appearance as an executive in the boardroom and Barbera played a random bystander.

Goldie Hawn and Kurt Russell

I n 1967, while playing a dancer in the Disney movie *The One and Only, Genuine, Original Family Band,* 22-year-old Goldie Hawn met seventeen-year-old Kurt Russell, a young actor playing one of the children in the film. "I remember he was five years younger than me and that he always seemed to be watching me when I was limbering up," recalled Goldie years later. Nothing happened between them.

Goldie went on to achieve fame as the giggly dumb blond on *Rowan and Martin's Laugh-In.* She starred in several hit films including *Cactus Flower, Butterflies Are Free, Sugarland Express, Foul Play, Seems Like Old Times,* and *Private Benjamin,* went through two failed marriages (the first with choreographer/actor Gus Trikonis, the second with comedian Bill Hudson, with whom she had two children —Oliver and Kate), and had an affair with French actor Yves Renier.

In 1983, Goldie began producing the movie *Swing Shift.* Kurt, having starred in the movies *Escape From New York, The Thing,* and the television biography *Elvis,* tried out for the part of Lucky, Goldie's love interest in the film. "When I

met Kurt again, he felt like family," recalled Goldie, who had seen Kurt a year earlier in *The Thing.* "I felt extremely comfortable with him, and I was instantly attracted."

Goldie interviewed Kurt for the part, then continued their discussion at a restaurant. When Goldie got up to leave, Kurt yelled, "Even if I don't get the part, I'd love to take you out sometime." Kurt's four-year marriage to Season Hubley, his costar from *Elvis,* had recently ended in divorce, giving Hubley custody of their son, Boston.

Kurt won the role of Lucky. "When we started filming," recalled Goldie, "I realized that my feelings for him went much deeper than friendship." One night, after a day spent filming *Swing Set* and an evening spent dancing at the Playboy Club, Goldie and Kurt wanted to be alone. Unfortunately, they had no place to go. Kurt, who lived in Aspen, Colorado, was staying in Los Angeles with his brother-in-law; Goldie and her kids were staying in her mother's condominium in Malibu while waiting for their home in Pacific Palisades to be renovated. Impassioned, Goldie and Kurt broke into the house under renovation. "So we were on the floor of the master bedroom," recalled Kurt, "and the next thing we knew, there were flashlights shining in our eyes. A local security company had come to the house to check to see if there had been a break-in." The couple promptly went to a nearby motel.

STRANGE ENCOUNTERS

★ Goldie Hawn was born on November 21, 1945, in Tacoma Park, Maryland.

★ Kurt Russell was born on March 17, 1951, in Springfield, Massachusetts.

★ Goldie's father, Edward Rutledge Hawn, was a descendant of Edward Rutledge, the youngest signer of the Declaration of Independence and the first governor of South Carolina.

★ Kurt's father Bing, a former baseball player, played Deputy Clem Foster on *Bonanza*.

★ Goldie dropped out of American University in Washington D.C. after her freshman year to work as a can-can dancer in a chorus line in the Texas Pavilion at the 1964 World's Fair in New York City.

★ Goldie worked as a go-go dancer at New York's notorious Dudes 'n' Dolls night club.

★ Kurt played professional baseball as second baseman for the California Angels until 1973, when a torn shoulder muscle forced him to retire.

★ Kurt appeared in an episode of *Gilligan's Island*, as a jungle boy who gets off the island in the basket of a helium balloon sewn together from the castaways' raincoats.

★ In 1984, Kurt went to Miami to star in the film *Mean Season*. Goldie remained in Los Angeles to film the first half of the movie *Protocol*. On weekends the enamored actors would fly to Dallas to be together.

★ Together, Goldie and Kurt have a son, Wyatt Hawn Russell, born in 1986.

★ Goldie and Kurt have appeared together in only three movies: *The One and Only, Genuine, Original Family Band; Swing Shift*; and *Overboard*.

★ Goldie's third husband, Bill Hudson, married actress Cindy Williams, who starred as Shirley Feeney on the classic sitcom *Laverne and Shirley.*

★ Goldie arranged a meeting with director Ridley Scott in 1991 in the hopes of starring in the film *Thelma & Louise,* but Scott turned her down, fearing that her star status would distract from the script.

★ In 1991, Goldie and Kurt, having lived together for seven years, gathered their four children together and asked them to vote on whether their parents should marry. The children voted no.

★ Goldie's daughter, Kate Hudson, appeared on the television series *Party of Five* and starred as Penny Lane in the 2000 movie *Almost Famous.*

Adolf Hitler and Eva Braun

In 1929, after graduating from convent school, seventeen-year-old Eva Braun got a job as an office assistant to well-known photographer Heinrich Hoffmann, who happened to be the personal photographer and close friend of Adolf Hitler. Shortly after Braun started her job, Hitler entered the shop and Hoffmann introduced him to Braun, who, lacking interest in politics, knew little about the leader of the Nazi party and author of *Mein Kampf.* At the time, Hitler was romantically involved with his 21-year-old niece, Geli Raubal, the daughter of his half-sister. Braun did, however, feel an immediate attraction to Hitler. At dinner that night, Braun asked her father about Hitler. She described him to her sister, Ilse, as "a gentleman of a certain age with a funny moustache and carrying a big felt hat."

Although her father expressed disdain for Hitler and his political ideas, Braun began reading about him and became more entranced. They met several more times at Hoffmann's photography studio, and after Braun slipped a love letter into Hitler's pocket, he started asking her out to restaurants and the theater. A few weeks after meeting, Hitler invited her to his mountain retreat at Berchtesgarden in the Alps.

Braun was soon developing film in Hoffmann's laboratory and helping him process pictures of Hitler.

In 1931, Giel Raubal was found shot to death in Hitler's apartment in Munich. According to the official report, she committed suicide. Braun soon became Hitler's mistress, living in his Munich apartment, despite objections from her father. In 1932, after Braun attempted suicide, Hitler bought her a villa in a Munich suburb and provided her with a Mercedes-Benz and a chauffeur. In 1935, after she made a second suicide attempt, the Führer bought her a villa near his own home.

In 1936, the reserved and politically indifferent Braun moved into Hitler's mountain villa, Berghof, in Obersalzberg near Berchtesgarden, where she played the role of hostess and led a completely isolated life. Hitler spent one week each month at Berghof, leaving Braun free to use the house as she pleased.

For the next sixteen years, Braun lived in luxury as Hitler's Third Reich put millions of people to death. Braun spent most of her time exercising, musing, reading cheap novelettes, watching romantic movies, and concentrating on her appearance. She loved going up to Hilter's Kehlsteinhaus (Eagles' Nest), built atop a 6,013-foot-tall mountain peak not far from Berghof. After Hitler survived an assassination attempt in July 1944, Braun summed up her deep feelings for him in an emotional love letter. "From our first meeting," she wrote, "I swore to follow you anywhere—even unto death—I live only for your love."

STRANGE ENCOUNTERS

★ Adolf Hitler was born on April 20, 1889, in Braunnau, Austria, a small border town just across the Inn River from Germany.

★ Eva Braun was born on February 6, 1912, in Munich, Germany.

★ Hitler failed the entrance examination to the Academy of Fine Arts in Vienna, Austria—twice.

★ While living in Vienna, Hitler earned money by shoveling snow, carrying suitcases at the railroad station, working as a day laborer on construction sites, and making posters for shop owners.

★ In 1924, Hitler was imprisoned for five years for attempting to overthrow the Bavarian government. From his jail cell, he began writing *Mein Kampf*, stating his plan to conquer much of Europe, his belief in a German master race, and his desire to install a dictatorship and rid Germany of all Jews.

★ In 1935, German Chancellor Adolf Hitler posed for a photograph with a blond boy on his lap as the model of a pure Aryan child. The postcard made of it sold hundreds of thousands of copies throughout Germany. The Nazis later discovered that the "ideal Aryan child" was actually the Jewish grandson of Rabbi Wedell of Düsseldorf.

★ Hitler labeled atomic research "Jewish physics" and refused to support it. His anti-Semitic policies prompted Jewish physicists Albert Einstein, Edward Teller, and Lise Meitner to emigrate to the United States—where they helped develop the atomic bomb.

★ In 1939, Hitler gave Braun one of the first Volkswagens ever produced.

★ Hitler and Braun rarely appeared in public together and few Germans even knew of her existence.

★ Braun affectionately called Hitler "Wulf."

★ Hitler's closest associates remained unaware of the true nature of his relationship with Braun. Hitler never displayed his affection for Braun in public and seemed uncomfortable in her presence.

★ In his first will of May 2, 1938, Hitler bequeathed Braun the equivalent of nine hundred dollars a year for life.

★ On the night of June 5, 1944, Hitler took sleeping pills and gave orders that he not be woken. At dawn on June 6, 1944, the Allied Forces launched their D-Day invasion of Normandy Beach with parachute landings. German General von Rundstedt immediately ordered two Panzer divisions to defend the region. However, German headquarters in Berlin ordered that von Rundstedt halt until he received direct authorization from Adolf Hitler. When Hitler finally woke up, the Allies had won the invasion.

★ On the morning of April 29, 1945, as Allied forces closed in on Berlin, a local magistrate married Adolph Hitler to Eva Braun in the bomb shelter beneath the Reich Chancellery. The next day, at around 3:30 p.m., Hitler and Braun bit into thin glass vials of cyanide. Hitler also shot himself in the head with a 7.65 mm Walther pistol.

★ Aides carried Hitler and Braun's dead bodies into the garden of the adjacent Reich Chancellery, doused them with gasoline, and set them on fire.

★ Adolf Hitler promised that his Third Reich would last one thousand years. It lasted twelve years.

★ In May 1945, Soviet troops, having found the charred bodies of Hitler and Braun, took the bodies with them as they moved west, ultimately burying the remains behind Smersh's East German headquarters in Magdeburg, where they remained for twenty-five years, under a yard later owned by a waste-disposal company. In 1970, the Soviets excavated and destroyed the remains.

★ Eva Braun's family survived World War II. Her mother, Franziska, lived in an old farmhouse in Ruhpolding, Bavaria, and died in 1976 at age ninety-six.

Abbie Hoffman and Jerry Rubin

In 1966, when called before the House Un-American Activities Committee (HUAC), Jerry Rubin, a political activist who had organized one of the first teach-ins against the war in Vietnam, showed up wearing the uniform of a 1776 American Revolutionary. In New York City, political activist Abbie Hoffman, impressed by Jerry's costumed appearance before HUAC, began following his activities. Abbie admired Jerry's antics, such as when he lay down in front of troop trains in Oakland, California, and ran for mayor of Berkeley, capturing twenty-two percent of the vote.

In 1967, Dave Dellinger, editor of the left-wing magazine *Liberation,* invited Jerry to New York to work as a project director on the National Mobilization Committee to End the War in Vietnam. Dellinger, similarly impressed with Jerry's organizational skills and political activities, wanted to utilize Jerry's ingenuity to help organize a peace march in Washington, D.C. When Jerry heard that a political activist named Abbie Hoffman had been burning money in public, he wanted to meet this kindred spirit. "Just as Che needed Fidel and Costello needed Abbott, Jerry Rubin and I were destined to join forces," recalled Abbie in his autobiography. At the time, Abbie was about to stage a theatrical protest inside the New York Stock Exchange.

On August 24, 1967, Abbie and a group of friends, including newcomer Jerry Rubin, dressed as hippies, went to the visitor's gallery on the third floor of the New York Stock Exchange and threw dollar bills down onto the trading floor. The stockbrokers on the floor looked up to see the floating bills, cheered, and then scrambled for the dollars. The event disrupted the day's trading briefly and garnered national media attention.

Abbie and Jerry then put their minds together to devise a dramatic protest for the impending peace march in Washington, D.C. Jerry suggested that they march from the Lincoln Memorial to the Pentagon, rather than to the Capitol Building as was originally planned. Abbie, inspired by the writings of French theater director Antonin Artaud, suggested they encircle the Pentagon, chant exorcism incantations, and levitate the building three hundred feet into the air. According to *Time* magazine, Abbie received permission from the Pentagon administrator "to raise the building a maximum of ten feet." On October 21, 1967, tens of thousands of protestors showed up for the event, including novelist Norman Mailer, poet Robert Lowell, and author Dr. Benjamin Spock, galvanizing the debate against the war in Vietnam.

STRANGE ENCOUNTERS

★ Abbie Hoffman, born Abbott Hoffman on November 30, 1936, in Worcester, Massachusetts, graduated from Brandeis University, where he was on the wrestling team.

★ Jerry Rubin, born on July 14, 1938, in Cincinnati, Ohio, worked as a sports reporter.

★ In his autobiography, Abbie described the stock exchange incident as "the TV-age version of driving the money changers from the Temple."

★ In 1968, Abbie and Jerry founded the Youth International Party, hoping to turn apolitical hippies into revolutionary "yippies."

★ To protest the Vietnam War outside the 1968 Democratic National Convention in Chicago, Abbie and Jerry announced the presidential candidacy of a hog named Pigasus. The police confiscated the pig, prompting the yippies to chant, "Free the pig!" Abbie and Jerry also announced that they were considering putting LSD in the water supply, prompting Mayor Richard Daley to send thousands of National Guard troops to surround the city's reservoirs. Abbie and Jerry were arrested, along with their cohorts.

★ During the Chicago Eight Trial in 1969, Abbie and Jerry appeared in court wearing judicial robes to mock the authority of Judge Julius Hoffman. When the judge ordered Abbie and Jerry to remove their robes, Jerry took his robe off to reveal that he was wearing a police officer's uniform.

★ In April 1970, Abbie appeared on *The Merv Griffin Show* wearing a shirt with an American flag motif. CBS censors masked the shirt with a blue square, bringing him even greater media attention. More than 88,000 viewers called CBS to protest the censorship, protests took place in front of CBS offices in three cities, and Merv Griffin publicly apologized. Prior to Hoffman's appearance, Ricky Nelson, Raquel Welch, Roy Rogers, and Ryan O'Neal had worn similar shirts on television.

★ Arrested for possession of cocaine in 1973, Abbie jumped bail and went underground. Under the alias Barry Freed, Abbie organized a grass-roots campaign to save the St. Lawrence River and received a commendation from New York Governor Hugh Carey.

★ Jerry repudiated activism, became a stockbroker, and organized Jerry Rubin's Business Networking Salon in New York.

★ In 1980, Abbie published his autobiography, *Soon to Be a Major Motion Picture,* resurfaced on the television show *20/20,* surrendered to authorities, and was sentenced to less than a year in prison.

★ In 1985, Abbie and Jerry toured the nation to conduct Yippie-versus-Yuppie debates.

★ Unable to cope with Manic Depression, a medical condition he kept secret, Abbie committed suicide in 1989.

★ While jaywalking in Los Angeles on November 28, 1994, Jerry was hit by a car and killed.

Sherlock Holmes and Dr. John H. Watson

In 1882, after being discharged from the British Army, Dr. John Watson returned to London to recuperate from a bullet wound to the shoulder received during the battle of Maiwand, and a subsequent bout with enteric fever. With financial assistance from the British government, he took up residence in a private hotel in the Strand, but soon decided to seek less expensive accommodations. While at the Criterion Bar, Watson ran into "young Stamford," a colleague with whom he had once worked at St. Bartholomew Hospital. When Watson told Stamford that he was looking for reasonably priced lodgings, Stamford mentioned that an acquaintance working in the hospital's chemical laboratory had that very morning bemoaned his inability to find a roommate to share an available apartment. Young Stamford reluctantly agreed to introduce Watson to his acquaintance, Sherlock Holmes, whose studies he described as "desultory and eccentric."

Stamford brought Watson to the hospital laboratory to find Holmes absorbed in his work. "I've found it!" exclaimed Holmes, running toward Stamford and Watson with a test tube in his hand. "I have found a re-agent which is precipitated by hemoglobin, and by nothing else."

"Dr. Watson, Mr. Sherlock Holmes," said Stamford, introducing the two men.

"How are you?" said Holmes, shaking Watson's hand firmly. "You have been in Afghanistan, I perceive."

"How on earth did you know that?" queried Watson.

"Never mind," replied Holmes. He chuckled to himself and proceeded, with great excitement, to demonstrate his new bloodstain test, explain its usefulness, and list several criminal cases where his test could have been used to convict the defendant.

Stamford explained that Watson was interested in sharing an apartment. Holmes, delighted by the idea, agreed to meet the following day at noon to show him the suite he had found at 221b Baker Street, where Watson would become Holmes' biographer and closest friend.

STRANGE ENCOUNTERS

★ Sir Arthur Conan Doyle began writing stories while practicing medicine and waiting for patients to arrive. His first novel, *A Study in Scarlet*, published in 1887, introduced Sherlock Holmes.

★ Sherlock Holmes, born on January 6 in an undisclosed year in an unnamed city in England, was educated at either Lincoln or Balliol College.

★ Exhibiting extraordinary powers of observation and deductive reasoning, Holmes attended St. Bartholomew's College in London. He dropped out after two years, but continued pursuing his keen interest in Criminology.

★ Dr. John Watson received his doctorate in medicine from the University of London in 1878 and served in the Royal Army as assistant surgeon during the second Afghan war.

★ Sir Arthur Conan Doyle based Sherlock Holmes on eminent Edinburgh surgeon Dr. Joseph Bell, under whose tutelage Doyle had studied medicine.

★ Sherlock Holmes is the world's best-known fictional detective.

★ In *A Study in Scarlet*, Doyle tells us that during the second Afghan War Watson received a bullet wound in his shoulder. In his 1890 novel, *The Sign of Four*, Doyle puts the wound in Watson's leg.

★ Doyle killed off Sherlock Holmes in a story published in 1893, but public demand forced the author to resurrect the beloved detective in his next story.

★ Holmes appeared in fifty-six short stories and four novels: *A Study in Scarlet*, *The Sign of Four*, *The Hound of the Baskervilles*, and *The Valley of Fear*.

★ Holmes never speaks the words, "Elementary, my dear Watson" in any of Doyle's novels or stories. In the short story "The Crooked Man," first published in 1893, Holmes does reply "Elementary" to Watson. In the movies, actor Basil Rathbone does say "Elementary, my dear Watson." Nigel Bruce starred as Dr. Watson.

★ Holmes did not smoke the Calabash pipe frequently associated with him—until American actor William Gillette portrayed the great detective onstage. Gillette needed a pipe that would stay in his mouth when he spoke his lines.

★ Holmes narrated only two of his stories: "The Blanched Soldier" and "The Lion's Mane."

★ In 1926, Doyle departed from detective stories and wrote *The History of Spiritualism*.

★ Contrary to popular belief, Sir Arthur Conan Doyle was not knighted to honor his stories about Sherlock Holmes. He was knighted for the pamphlets and articles he wrote in defense of the British concentration camps during the Boer War.

Chet Huntley and David Brinkley

In the summer of 1956, NBC producer Reuven Frank teamed former UPI reporter David Brinkley with former Los Angeles television news reporter Chet Huntley to anchor the network's television coverage of the Democratic and Republican national conventions. Chet had delivered the news on CBS radio in Los Angeles for twelve years, followed by four years on television at ABC in Los Angeles. In 1955, NBC brought him to New York as a newscaster, with the promise of a major news program. David joined NBC in 1943 as a radio news writer in Washington, D.C., where he eventually became an on-air correspondent for John Cameron Swayze's *Camel News Caravan*, NBC's early television news effort.

The duo successfully attracted the largest share of the convention television audience, prompting NBC to formalize the Huntley-Brinkley partnership with the debut of *The Huntley-Brinkley Report*, a nightly national newscast first broadcast in October 1956. Unlike typical news programs of the day, which featured an announcer who read the news between filmed reports similar to movie theater newsreels, the innovative *Huntley-Brinkley Report* originated the technique of cutting between Chet in New York (reporting international news) and David in Washington, D.C. (reporting national stories). Chet and David delivered the news in terse, declarative sentences and added biting analysis. Every newscast ended with the same comforting signature: From New

York, Chet said, "Good night, David." From Washington, David replied, "Good night, Chet."

In 1963, NBC expanded the highly rated and critically acclaimed nightly newscast from fifteen minutes to thirty minutes. With an estimated twenty million viewers watching *The Huntley-Brinkley Report* every night, a 1965 survey revealed that more American adults recognized Chet and David than such famous stars as Cary Grant, James Stewart, and the Beatles.

STRANGE ENCOUNTERS

★ Chet, born Chester Robert Huntley on December 10, 1911, in Cardwell, Montana, was raised in Bozeman, Montana.

★ David, born on July 10, 1920, in Wilmington, North Carolina, attended the University of North Carolina at Chapel Hill, Emory University, and Vanderbilt University.

★ During his senior year at the University of Washington in Seattle, Chet worked at local radio station KPCB.

★ Chet frequently voiced his personal opinions on the air, and a critic once accused him of editorializing with his eyebrows.

★ In his only apparent disagreement with David, Chet crossed an American Federation of Television and Radio Artists' picket line in 1967, insisting that news anchors did not belong in the same union with actors, singers, and dancers.

★ When Chet retired on August 1, 1970, and said "Good night, David," for the last time, David changed his signature signoff to "Goodbye, Chet."

★ Chet was married twice, to Ingrid Rolin and Tipton Stringer.

★ David was married twice, to Ann Fischer and Susan Benfer, and had four children: Alan, Joel, and John (with Fischer), and Alexis (with Benfer).

★ Chet retired to his native Montana, became a spokesman for American Airlines, and developed the Big Sky resort. He died of lung cancer on March 20, 1974, in Bozeman.

★ After Chet retired, David hosted *NBC Nightly News* and *NBC Magazine with David Brinkley*. In 1981, ABC hired him to host the Sunday program *This Week With David Brinkley*, where he discussed the week's news events with other Washington insiders. He died after suffering complications from a fall on June 11, 2003.

King Hussein and Queen Noor

In January 1977, Lisa Halaby, a graduate of Princeton University, helped design new airport facilities in Amman, Jordan, for Alia, the Royal Jordanian Airline. At the dedication ceremony, Lisa's Syrian-American father, Najeeb Halaby, then chairman of the board for Pan-American Airlines, introduced his 25-year-old daughter to 42-year-old King Hussein, who had served as king of Jordan since age sixteen. At the time, the king was married to his third wife, Queen Alia Toukan.

Later that year, Queen Alia was killed in a tragic helicopter crash, sending King Hussein into a state of despair.

In the spring of 1978, King Hussein rekindled his acquaintance with Lisa and her father over dinner at his Zahran Palace. Lisa brightened the king's spirits, and he began taking her out secretly at night for rides through the hills of Amman on the back of his BMW motorcycle. After six weeks, the couple was engaged. Shortly before their wedding, Lisa, a non-practicing Protestant, converted to Islam and adopted the Arabic name "Noor Al-Hussein" or "Light of Hussein"—a name chosen by the king to allude to her blond hair and the joy she brought back into his life. After providing a dowry of a reported 3.3 million dollars, Lisa married Hussein on June 15, 1978, in a small, private ceremony in Amman.

★ King Hussein was born Hussein bin Talal on November 14, 1935, in Amman, the capital city of the newly formed country Transjordan, then a British emirate ruled by his grandfather, Emir Abdullah bin Al-Hussein.

★ Queen Noor, born Lisa Najeeb Halaby on August 23, 1951, in Washington, D.C., was a cheerleader while an undergraduate at Princeton University.

★ In 1946, when Hussein was ten years old, Great Britain granted independence to Transjordan, which became the Hashemite Kingdom of Jordan, with Hussein's grandfather Abdullah bin Al-Hussein as its first king.

★ In 1951, King Abdullah took his fifteen-year-old grandson, Hussein, to pray at the Al-Aqsa Mosque in Jerusalem. On the temple steps, a Palestinian shot the king to death and fired a bullet at Hussein, which bounced off a medal he was wearing over his heart.

★ After King Abdullah's death, Hussein's father Talal, who suffered from schizophrenia, became king of Jordan. Within a year, he was declared unfit to rule and was sent to a mental institution.

★ On August 11, 1952, sixteen-year-old Hussein, attending private boarding school in England, became king of Jordan. A regency oversaw the country's affairs until May 1953, when King Hussein would reach the age of eighteen according to the Islamic calendar and could assume his full constitutional powers. In the meantime, the young king attended Sandhurst military school in Great Britain, where drill sergeants called him "Mr. King Hussein, sir."

★ King Hussein's first wife, Dina bint Abedelhamid, was his distant cousin. After one year of marriage and the birth of a daughter, Princess Alia, Hussein divorced Dina.

★ In 1961, Hussein married his second wife, Antoinette "Toni" Gardner, the daughter of a British army officer. Toni converted to Islam and took the name Princess Muna. They had four children: Prince Abdullah, Prince Feisal, Princess Zein, and Princess Aisha.

★ In 1972, after divorcing his second wife, Hussein married Alia Toukan. They had three children: Princess Haya, Prince Ali, and an adopted daughter, Abeer Muhaisin. In 1977, Queen Alia died in a helicopter crash.

★ King Hussein and Lisa Halaby had four children: Prince Hamzah, Prince Hashim, Princess Iman, and Princess Raiyah.

★ The press compared Queen Noor to Princess Grace, another blond American woman who married foreign royalty. Noor, however, pointed out that Grace had moved to the peaceful European resort of Monaco, while she had moved to a distressed nation in the troubled Middle East.

★ During his reign, Hussein escaped several assassination attempts, including a 1957 coup attempt by Jordanian army officers, a 1958 attempt by Syrian jets to intercept his plane and force it down, and a 1960 attempt by Jordanian palace officials working for Syria to poison his food and put acid in his nose drops.

Michael Jackson and Lisa Marie Presley

In 1975, rock 'n' roll legend Elvis Presley, performing in Lake Tahoe, Nevada, arranged for his seven-year-old daughter Lisa Marie to go backstage to meet the lead singer of the Jackson 5, seventeen-year-old Michael Jackson.

Nineteen years later, in 1994, Lisa Marie, heir to Elvis's 100-million-dollar estate, divorced her husband, Danny Keough, after six years of marriage, and won custody of their two children. Lisa Marie had met Danny while living in the Scientology Celebrity Center in Hollywood. She had embraced Scientology to help combat her problems with drug abuse.

On May 18, 1994, twenty days after Lisa Marie divorced Keough, Judge Hugo Francisco Alvarez Perez married 37-year-old Michael and 27-year-old Lisa Marie in a secret ceremony in Santo Domingo in the Dominican Republic. For nearly two months, Michael and Lisa Marie denied that they had married. Gossip columnists speculated that the marriage was merely a masquerade to boost Michael's public image. A few months earlier, Michael had paid several million dollars to settle out of court with a thirteen-year-old boy who claimed the singer had sexually molested him.

In June 1995, Michael and Lisa Marie appeared together on *Primetime Live* on ABC-TV and declared that they were deeply in love and trying to conceive a child together. When asked if their marriage was a publicity stunt designed to legitimize Michael, Lisa Marie replied, "How can you fake this twenty-four hours a day—sleeping with somebody, waking up with somebody? I'm not going to marry somebody for any reason other than the fact that I fall in love with them." Lisa Marie legally changed her name to Lisa Marie Presley-Jackson. She and her children traveled around the world with Michael.

In December 1995, after Michael's massively promoted *HIStory* album flopped and the singer canceled a New York concert scheduled to air on HBO, the couple separated after just twenty months of marriage, and Lisa Marie filed for divorce in January 1996, citing irreconcilable differences.

STRANGE ENCOUNTERS

★ Michael Jackson, born Michael Joseph Jackson on August 29, 1958 in Gary, Indiana, has been nicknamed the "King of Pop," "Wacko Jacko," and "The Gloved One."

★ Lisa Marie Presley was born on February 1, 1968, in Memphis, Tennessee, to rock legend Elvis Presley and Priscilla Presley.

★ Michael's parents, former guitarist Joseph Jackson and his wife Katherine Scruse, pushed their children Jackie, Tito, Jermaine, Michael, and Marlon into showbiz as the Jackson 5. Buoyed by his captivating singing and dancing talents, Michael quickly rose to the forefront as the dominant voice of the group. The Jackson 5 performed as an opening act for the O-Jays and James Brown, until singer Gladys Knight brought the group to the attention of record producer Berry Gordy, launching their chartbusting career as Motown recording artists.

★ As a child, Lisa Marie received one-hundred dollar bills from the Tooth Fairy.

★ Elvis named his private jet *Lisa Marie* and bought furs and jewels for Lisa Marie as a toddler.

★ After leaving Elvis, Priscilla moved four-year-old Lisa Marie from Graceland to Los Angeles, to live with karate champion Mike Stone.

★ For Lisa Marie's tenth birthday in 1978, her mother Priscilla arranged for her to have lunch with heartthrob John Travolta, who eventually introduced them to Scientology.

★ In 1977, after Elvis Presley died, leaving his one hundred-million-dollar estate to his eleven-year-old daughter, his ex-wife Priscilla took control of Lisa's trust fund. With no income and upkeep of the Graceland mansion quickly devouring the reserves, Priscilla opened Graceland to the public to generate funds.

★ Michael's 1984 solo album *Thriller* became the best-selling album of all time, with more than 46 million copies sold worldwide. The second best-selling album of all time is Michael's *Dangerous,* followed by his album *Bad.*

★ Michael holds the record for most Grammy Awards won in a single year—eight for his 1984 solo album *Thriller.*

★ With the release of *Thriller*, Michael became the first recording artist in music history to achieve seven Top Ten hits from one record.

★ Michael's 2,700-acre Neverland Valley Ranch near Santa Ynez, California, contains an amusement park (co-designed by child actor Macaulay Culkin), a private theater and dance stage, and a private zoo filled with exotic animals. His constant home companion was once a chimpanzee named Bubbles. Michael's house on the property contains a fully functional roller coaster.

★ Michael, a vegetarian and former Jehovah's Witness, suffers from vitiligo, a degenerative skin disease.

★ Michael has reputedly had four nose jobs, two nose adjustments, and a cleft put into his chin. Some experts claim that Michael's face has been disfigured by excessive plastic surgery.

★ Michael has been married and divorced twice, to Lisa Marie Presley and Debbie Rowe. He has three children: Prince and Paris (with Rowe), and Prince II (whose mother remains anonymous).

★ Lisa Marie has been married and divorced three times, to Danny Keough, Michael Jackson, and Nicolas Cage. She has two children: Danielle and Benjamin (with Keough).

★ At Liz Taylor's 1991 wedding to Larry Fortensky, Michael gave the bride away.

★ In 2002, Michael dangled his third child, infant Prince Michael II, over a balcony on the fourth floor of a hotel in Berlin, Germany, for his gathered fans to see.

★ In 2003, Lisa Marie released her debut album, *To Whom It May Concern*, featuring the single "Lights Out."

Mick Jagger and Keith Richards

In 1950, seven-year-old Mick Jagger met fellow seven-year-old Keith Richards at Westworth Country Primary School in Dartford, England. The two boys lived two blocks from each other. "We weren't great friends," recalled Mick, "but we knew each other." In 1954, when the two eleven-year-old boys went to different secondary schools, they lost touch. Mick was placed with brighter, more promising students at Dartford Grammar School. Keith was placed at Dartford Technical College, a vocational school.

Seven years later on a cold morning in 1961, Mick met his old schoolmate Keith on the platform of the Dartford train station. At the time, Mick attended the London School of Economics on a scholarship. Keith, a student at Sidcup Art College, recognized Mick and noticed that he was carrying record albums by Little Walter, Muddy Waters, and Chuck Berry. Realizing they shared an interest in rock 'n' roll and the blues, Keith invited Mick to his house for tea. "He started playing me these records," recalled Keith, "and I really turned on to it."

Mick, who had been singing with a band called the Blues Boys invited Keith, who played guitar, to join the group. In 1962, Mick and Keith joined Blue Incorporated, a band that included guitarist Brian Jones and drummer Charlie Watts. At the end of the year, several members of the group—Mick, Keith, Brian, Charlie, and bassist Bill Wyman—broke away to form a new band, the Rolling Stones, playing their first gig together on February 24, 1963, at the Crawdaddy nightclub in London.

STRANGE ENCOUNTERS

★ Keith Richards, born on December 18, 1943, in Dartford, England, sang in a trio as part of the Dartford Technical College choir and performed the "Hallelujah Chorus" at the coronation of Queen Elizabeth II on June 2, 1953, in Westminster Abbey. He was later expelled from Dartford Technical College.

★ Michael Philip Jagger, born on July 26, 1943, in Dartford, England, worked as a temporary postman and as a porter at Bexley Mental Hospital.

★ Mick's mother, Eva Jagger, worked as an Avon lady.

★ Beatles John Lennon and Paul McCartney wrote the song "I Wanna Be Your Man" specifically for the Rolling Stones. It became the Stones first Top Ten Hit and inspired Mick and Keith to write their own music.

★ Mick sat in on the orchestral session for the Beatles' song "A Day In The Life."

★ Director Stanley Kubrick originally conceived the 1971 movie *A Clockwork Orange* as a vehicle for the Rolling Stones, with Mick playing the role of Alex.

★ Mick and Keith refer to themselves as the Glimmer Twins.

★ Mick starred in the 1970 movie *Performance* as a retired rock star, singing his first solo song, "Memo from Turner."

★ The Rolling Stones' best-selling album, *Sticky Fingers*, released in 1971, includes the hit songs "Brown Sugar," "Wild Horses," and "Dead Flowers."

★ In an interview in the 1970s, Mick said, "I'd rather be dead than singing 'Satisfaction' when I'm forty-five." Since turning forty-five in 1988, Mick has sung "Satisfaction" on several Rolling Stones tours.

★ Mick sang backup vocals on Carly Simon's hit song "You're So Vain."

★ Keith had three children with former partner Anita Pallenberg: Marlon, Angela, and Tara (deceased).

★ Keith married model Patti Hansen on his fortieth birthday. The couple has two daughters: Theodora and Alexandra.

★ Mick sang on the Jacksons' hit song, "State of Shock."

★ Mick has recorded four solo albums: *She's the Boss, Wandering Spirit, Primitive Cool,* and *Goddess in the Doorway.*

★ Mick made his first solo appearance at the 1985 Live Aid benefit concert in Philadelphia.

★ Keith has recorded three solo albums: *Live at the Hollywood Palladium, Main Offender,* and *Talk Is Cheap.*

★ In 2002, Queen Elizabeth knighted Mick Jagger.

★ Mick and Keith performed together at the 2002 Concert for New York, a benefit for the victims of the September 11, 2001, terrorist attack on the World Trade Center.

Penn Jillette and Teller

On April 10, 1974, aspiring magician Weir Chrisimer introduced nineteen-year-old Penn Jillette, a friend who had worked as a juggler on the New Jersey boardwalk and attended Ringling Bros. Barnum & Bailey Clown College, to another friend, 26-year-old Teller, a graduate of Amherst College who taught high school Latin in Lawrenceville, New Jersey.

Penn, Teller, and Weir teamed up to create a magic act called the Othmar Schoeck Memorial Society for the Preservation of Unusual and Disgusting Music. They soon renamed their act the Asparagus Valley Cultural Society. Their unconventional show combined magic and comedy, featuring Teller's East Indian Needle Mystery, shadows, fire-eating, juggling, suspension, and unusual music—Penn played bass, Teller played keyboard and slide-whistle, and Weir played accordion.

In 1981, Weir dropped out of the group, prompting a name change to Penn & Teller. Four years later, having performed at scores of small clubs, theaters, and Renaissance Fairs, Penn and Teller brought their stage show to an off-Broadway theater, landing the duo on *Late Night with David Letterman* and *Saturday Night Live*. In 1987, the national attention catapulted Penn and Teller's stage show to Broadway.

STRANGE ENCOUNTERS

★ Teller, born Raymond Joseph Teller on February 14, 1948, in Philadelphia, Pennsylvania, legally changed his name to Teller. He possesses one of the few United States passports issued with a single name.

★ Penn Fraser Jillette, born on March 5, 1955, in Greenfield, Massachusetts, wears red nail polish on one fingernail in honor of his mother. When he began performing, she advised him to get a manicure because people would be looking at his hands. Penn responded by having his nails painted red.

★ Among their many television appearances, Penn and Teller have guest-starred on *Hollywood Squares, The Drew Carey Show, Friends, Dharma & Greg, Babylon 5, Home Improvement, The Simpsons,* and *Just Shoot Me.*

★ The license plate on Penn's bright pink-sport-utility vehicle reads "6SIX6."

★ Penn and Teller have starred in the television specials *Penn & Teller Go Public, Penn & Teller's Sin City Spectacular, Penn & Teller's Home Invasion, Penn and Teller's Invisible Thread, Don't Try This At Home, The Unpleasant World of Penn & Teller, Penn & Teller's Phobophilia,* and in the movie *Penn & Teller Get Killed.*

★ Teller's driver's license reads "NFN Teller." "NFN" is an abbreviation for "No First Name."

★ Penn and Teller have written three books together: *Cruel Tricks for Dear Friends, How To Play With Your Food,* and *How To Play In Traffic.*

★ Penn and Teller serve as Visiting Scholars at MIT, and have lectured at the Smithsonian Institution and Oxford University.

★ Although Teller's trademark is that he never speaks, he has spoken on several television shows.

Steve Jobs and Steve Wozniak

In 1968, thirteen-year-old Steve Jobs met eighteen-year-old Steve Wozniak while the two were working for Hewlett-Packard in Palo Alto, California. In his spare time, Wozniak, a recent dropout from the University of California at Berkeley, built blue boxes, illegal pocket-sized devices that attach to telephones, enabling the user to make free long-distance calls. Jobs helped Wozniak sell the blue boxes, beginning a partnership that would lead to the invention of the world's first mass-marketed personal computer.

Six years later, Jobs dropped out of Reed College in Oregon after one semester and took a job as a video game designer at Atari. He rekindled his friendship with Wozniak, also working at Atari, and began attending meetings of Wozniak's Homebrew Computer Club in Palo Alto. Jobs persuaded "Woz," still working at Hewlett-Packard, to help him build a personal computer.

By 1976, Jobs and Wozniak developed a prototype for the Apple I, the first single-board computer with a built-in video interface and on-board ROM, which enabled the machine to load programs from an external source. Jobs sold his Volkswagen van and Wozniak sold his programmable calculator to raise 1,300 dollars to start their company, Apple Computer Corp., in Jobs' parents' garage in Los Altos. Within a few weeks, Jobs sold fifty Apple I computers at 666 dollars each. Wozniak immediately quit his job at Hewlett-Packard. A year later, Jobs and Wozniak developed the Apple II, which attached to a color video monitor. Jobs challenged computer programmers to create applications for the Apple II, resulting in a library of more than sixteen thousand software programs.

In 1980, Apple went public, making Jobs and Wozniak multimillionaires.

STRANGE ENCOUNTERS

★ Steven Paul Jobs, born in 1955 in Los Altos, was adopted that year by Paul and Clara Jobs of Mountain View, California.

★ Steve Wozniak, born on August 11, 1950, grew up in Sunnyvale, California. He received his HAM radio license when he was in the sixth grade.

★ The Apple name alludes to the happy summer Jobs spent picking apples in Oregon. The company logo depicts an apple with a bite taken out of it to symbolize the computer term *byte*—a sequence of binary digits processed as a unit by a computer.

★ The original Apple II computer hooked up to a cassette recorder to record data.

★ Six years after its founding, Apple was listed in the Fortune 500.

★ In 1981, Wozniak, injured in a plane crash, left Apple, got married, and returned to college at Berkeley under the name Rocky Clark (a combination of his dog's name and his wife's maiden name) to complete his degree in electrical engineering and computer science.

★ In 1984, Wozniak attended the Democratic National Convention as a delegate for Gary Hart for President.

★ In 1985, when Apple President John Sculley laid off twelve hundred employees, Jobs resigned as CEO and sold over twenty million dollars-worth of his Apple stock. Wozniak, who had returned to the company in 1983, also resigned.

★ After leaving Apple, Wozniak did volunteer work in Silicon Valley schools, teaching local Hispanic children.

★ Jobs purchased a majority stake in Pixar, a San Rafael computer animation studio spun off from LucasFilm. In 1995, Pixar produced the hit film *Toy Story*.

★ In 1995, Jobs returned to Apple to serve as the company's interim CEO, a position he held until 1999, when he was made the permanent CEO.

★ Wozniak has been married three times, to Alice Robertson, Candice Clark, and Suzanne Mulkern. He has three children (with Clark).

Elton John and Bernie Taupin

In 1967, American-based Liberty Records opened a branch office in London and put eighteen-year-old Ray Williams in charge of recruiting new talent. Ray ran a quarter-page advertisement in the June 17 issue of the *New Musical Express* inviting new talent to audition for him. Twenty-year-old keyboardist Reggie Dwight, whose band Bluesology played backup for blues singer Long John Baldry, responded with a handwritten letter (penned with help from his mother) and secured an appointment for an audition.

In Ray's office, Reggie played piano and mournfully sang several songs, starting with the country-western song "He'll Have to Go," by Jim Reeves, and ending with "Mammy," by Al Jolson. Impressed by Reggie's unconventional style, Ray brought Reggie to Regent Sound to cut a demo record. At the recording session, Reggie insisted that his strength lay in composing music, not in writing lyrics. Ray suddenly remembered another letter he had received in response to his advertisement. Seventeen-year-old Bernie Taupin, a native of Owmby-by-Spital in Lincolnshire, confessing an inability to compose music, had sent him a sheaf of typed song lyrics. Ray gave the lyrics to Reggie, asked him to set them to music, and promised to arrange for him to meet Bernie Taupin.

When Ray's bosses, unimpressed by Reggie's demo, refused to put the piano player under contract, Ray got Reggie a job with music publisher Dick James. A week later, having received a letter of invitation from Ray Williams, Bernie Taupin traveled to London. Ray explained that he had no immediate use for Bernie's lyrics but wanted him to meet a piano player named Reggie Dwight at Dick James Music. The next day, Bernie showed up at the in-house music studio and, after, the two young men walked over to the Lancaster Grill on Tottenham Court Road for a cup of coffee. "We were complete opposites," recalled Bernie, "town mouse and country mouse." Despite their different upbringings, they both shared an encyclopedic knowledge of music trivia, a love for the music of Bob Dylan and the Beatles, and an insatiable passion for writing music. They decided to team up.

Reggie set Bernie's poem "Scarecrow" to music and recorded the demo track at Dick James Music. A week later, they had created more than a dozen songs.

STRANGE ENCOUNTERS

★ Elton John was born Reginald Kenneth Dwight on March 25, 1947, in Pinner, England.

★ Bernie Taupin, born on May 22, 1950, in Sleaford, England, dropped out of school at age fifteen, and worked on a chicken farm.

★ At age eleven, Elton, a musical prodigy, entered the prestigious Royal Academy of Music, but dropped out three weeks before graduation to pursue a rock career.

★ The same advertisement that attracted Reggie and Bernie helped Ray Williams discover the Bonzo Dog Doo-Dah Band and Jeff Lynne (who later joined Electric Light Orchestra).

★ Elton and Bernie's first song together, "Scarecrow," never appeared as a single or on any album.

★ In December 1967, Reggie left Bluesology and renamed himself Elton John, after Bluesology's tenor-sax player Elton Dean and singer Long John Baldry.

★ Bernie and Elton worked separately. Bernie wrote the lyrics alone at home in Owmby-by-Spital, then sent them by mail or hand-delivered them to Elton, who went off on his own and set them to music.

★ Elton legally changed his name to Elton Hercules John.

★ In 1979, Elton John became the first Western rock star to perform in Israel and the USSR.

★ Elton has been married once, to Renate Blauel. The couple divorced after three years of marriage. Elton eventually admitted that he is bisexual and has had a longterm relationship with Daniel Furnish.

★ Elton and Bernie re-worded their song "Candle in the Wind," originally written about Marilyn Monroe, in tribute to Princess Diana. Elton sang the new version at Diana's funeral. The song became the best-selling single of all time.

★ In 1998, Queen Elizabeth knighted Elton in honor of his contribution to music and his fundraising efforts for AIDS charities. Elton donates all profits from his singles to AIDS charities. The Elton John AIDS Foundation is one of the world's largest nonprofit AIDS organizations.

Lyndon Johnson and Lady Bird Taylor

On September 12, 1934, at a hearing of the Texas Railroad Commission in Austin, Texas, 26-year-old Lyndon Baines Johnson, working as secretary to Congressman Richard Kleberg, met 21-year-old Claudia Alta "Lady Bird" Taylor, the daughter of a wealthy family from Karnack, Texas. At the time, Lady Bird was working toward a journalism degree at the University of Texas.

Within two hours of meeting her, Lyndon invited Lady Bird to meet him at 8 a.m. the next morning for breakfast, followed by a drive through the countryside. During the drive, Lyndon told her all about himself—his dreams, his ambitions, "even about all the members of his family," recalled Lady Bird, "and how much insurance he carried." When Lyndon said he would like her to meet his mother, Lady Bird expressed interest. Lyndon immediately turned the car around and drove her to Johnson City, where his mother lived. Determined to win Lady Bird's heart, Lyndon brought her to Congressman Kleberg's impressive ranch in Corpus Christi, then drove her home to Karnack, Texas, so that he could meet her father, Thomas Taylor.

The next day Lyndon returned to Washington. "Lyndon came into my life and in one week's time he had become so much a part of me that when he left, I felt his absence terribly," recalled Lady Bird. "It was embarrassing to admit that so much could happen in a short time. Here was this man I barely knew talking about marriage and I was seriously considering the idea." From Washington, Lyndon stayed in close contact with Lady Bird, writing or telephoning daily. Seven weeks later, he returned to Texas, went straight to the Taylors' home in Karnack, and proposed to Lady Bird. She accepted. "Sometimes," she later said, "Lyndon simply takes your heart away."

The next week, on November 17, 1934, Lyndon married Lady Bird at Saint Mark's Episcopal Church in San Antonio, Texas. The newlywed couple, having known each other for less than three weeks, drove to Mexico for their honeymoon.

STRANGE ENCOUNTERS

★ Lyndon Baines Johnson was born on August 27, 1908, in a farmhouse near Stonewall, Texas, to two schoolteachers. He could read at the age of four and graduated from Johnson City High School at age fifteen.

★ Lyndon's grandfather, Samuel Ealy Johnson, Sr., founded Johnson City, Texas.

★ Claudia Alta Taylor was born on December 22, 1912, in Karnack, Texas. Her father, Thomas Jefferson Taylor, owned a general store and declared himself a "dealer in everything." When Lady Bird was five years old, her mother, Minnie Patillo Taylor, died in childbirth with her fourth child, who also died.

★ In 1913, a nurse gave two-year-old Claudia Alta Taylor the nickname "Lady Bird," insisting that the little girl was "as pretty as a lady bird."

★ In 1924, Lyndon drove to California in a 1918 Model T Ford with four friends (without telling his parents), and supported himself by working as an elevator operator, grape picker, dishwasher, law clerk, and auto mechanic.

★ Lyndon worked his way through Southwest Texas State Teachers College as a janitor and as secretary to the college president. Running out of money, he dropped out for a year and worked as a school teacher in Cotulla, Texas, saving enough money to complete his college education.

★ Lady Bird received a Bachelor of Arts degree from the University of Texas in 1933 and a journalism degree in 1934.

★ Lyndon and Lady Bird had two daughters: Lynda Bird and Luci Baines.

★ In 1953, 44-year-old Lyndon was elected Senate Democratic leader, making him the youngest person ever elected to lead either party in the Senate.

★ Elected Vice President of the United States on the ticket with John F. Kennedy in 1960, Lyndon became president upon Kennedy's assassination in 1963, and was re-elected in 1964.

★ Lyndon was the first Southerner to become President since Andrew Johnson.

★ During his presidency, Lyndon Baines Johnson's entire First Family had the initials LBJ, even his dogs, Little Beagle Johnson and Little Beagle Junior.

★ According to historian Doris Kearns Goodwin, Lyndon's passion for the grapefruit-flavored soda Fresca prompted him to have a soda fountain installed in the Oval Office that he could operate by pushing a button on his desk chair.

★ In 1966, Lyndon Johnson appointed the first black Cabinet member when he made Robert C. Weaver the secretary of the Department of Housing and Urban Development.

★ In 1967, Lyndon Johnson appointed the first black to the United States Supreme Court: Thurgood Marshall.

★ Lyndon Johnson died at his beloved LBJ Ranch on January 22, 1973.

Angelina Jolie and Billy Bob Thornton

In the spring of 1998, 22-year-old actress Angelina Jolie met 42-year-old actor/writer/director Billy Bob Thornton on the set of the movie *Pushing Tin*. At the time, Billy Bob, winner of an Academy Award for Best Adapted Screenplay for the 1996 movie *Sling Blade*, was living with actress Laura Dern. Angelina, separated from British actor Jonny Lee Miller, was dating actor Timothy Hutton. In *Pushing Tin*, Angelina and Billy Bob starred as an eccentric married couple. "They were extremely convincing as a couple in front of the camera," said producer Art Linson. "But I thought it was just real good acting and nothing more."

"He's always been my favorite director, the actor I love to watch, the writer I love to read, or hear his words said," claimed Angelina. "And I met him, and he was just such a good person: one of the funniest people on the planet, and really—just a great, great person. He doesn't judge anybody. He's the kind of person that I would like to be like, you know? So for all those reasons he's somebody I wanted as a friend. And, you know, he's the sexiest fucking creature that ever lived."

Two years later, the pair went public with their romantic relationship, just before the Academy Awards ceremony in March 2000. When Angelina won the Oscar for Best Supporting Actress for her role in *Girl, Interrupted*, she celebrated with Billy Bob at the Sunset Marquis hotel in Los Angeles. Soon afterward, Angelina sported a tattoo that read "Billy Bob" on her upper arm. "I'm madly in love with this man," she told *Talk* magazine, " and will be 'til the day I die."

On May 5, 2000, the couple eloped to Las Vegas and married in the Little Church of the West Wedding Chapel. Angelina wore a blue sleeveless sweater and jeans. Billy Bob wore jeans and his trademark baseball cap. The couple filed for divorce two years later, on July 18, 2002.

★ Billy Bob Thornton was born August 4, 1955, in Hot Springs, Arkansas, to an educator and a psychic.

★ In high school, Billy Bob played drums in a band called Stone Cold Fever.

★ Angelina Jolie was born Angelina Jolie Voight on June 4, 1975, in Los Angeles, California, to Academy Award-winning actor Jon Voight and actress Marcheline Bertrand.

★ As a child, Angelina dreamed of becoming a funeral director.

★ Billy Bob played drums and sang in the band Tres Hombres, which once opened for Hank Williams, Jr.

★ At age eleven, Angelina began studying acting at the Lee Strasberg Theater Institute, six years after making her film debut in *Lookin' to Get Out*, which starred her father.

★ Angelina graduated from Beverly Hills High School at age sixteen.

★ Billy Bob's mother, a psychic, predicted he would work with Burt Reynolds. He eventually did, appearing in three episodes of the sitcom *Evening Shade*.

★ In 1995, Angelina married actor Jonny Lee Miller, her costar in the 1995 movie *Hackers*. She wore black and had Jonny's name written across the back of her shirt in blood. They separated within a year and filed for divorce in 1999.

★ Angelina's numerous tattoos include the letter "H" on the inside of her left wrist (in honor of her brother, James Haven), a Tennessee Williams' quote ("A prayer for the wild at heart, kept in cages") on her left forearm, a dragon and two American Indian symbols on her lower back, a dragon on her upper left bicep, a large black cross on her lower left abdomen, the Latin phrase "Quod Me Nutrit Me Destruit" ("What nourishes me destroys me") across her abdomen, the Japanese symbol for death on her left shoulder blade, a blue rectangle on her lower back, and "Billy Bob" on her upper left bicep.

★ Billy Bob has many tattoos, including at least three on each arm.

★ Billy Bob has been married and divorced five times. His wives included Melissa Lee Gatlin, Toni Lawrence, Cynda Williams, Pietra Dawn Cherniak, and Angelina Jolie. He has four children: daughter Amanda (with Gatlin), sons William and Harry (both with Cherniak), and adopted son Maddock (a Cambodian baby adopted with Jolie).

★ In 1997, Billy Bob's fourth wife, Pietra, received a restraining order to keep Billy Bob away from her and their children.

★ Angelina and Billy Bob starred together in only one movie: *Pushing Tin*.

★ Billy Bob told *USA Today* that he suffers from an intense phobia of antique furniture.

Helen Keller and Anne Sullivan

Anne Sullivan, born in April 1866, in Feeding Hills, Massachusetts, to Irish immigrants, contracted trachoma, a disease of the eyes, around the age of five. Left untreated, Anne gradually lost most of her vision. When her mother died, her father sent Anne and her brother Jimmy to live with a series of relatives, who eventually sent the children to the state "poorhouse" in Tewksbury, Massachusetts, where nine-year-old Anne roomed with mental patients and prostitutes. Jimmy died from tuberculosis at Tewksbury, leaving Anne with no caring family.

When an investigating committee from the Board of Charities visited Tewksbury to inspect the institution, Anne threw herself at the mercy of the committee leader and pleaded to be sent to a school for the blind. Soon afterward, fourteen-year-old Anne, illiterate and half-blind, was sent to Perkins Institute for the Blind in Boston. Surgery partially restored her eyesight, and she graduated at the age of twenty as class valedictorian. When the school director learned of a deaf, blind six-year-old girl named Helen Keller in Alabama who needed a teacher, he offered the position to Anne.

In March 1887, Anne arrived in Tuscumbia to live with the Keller family as governess. Anne dedicated her life to Helen, who, in return, gave Anne a sense of family.

At nineteen months old, Helen Keller, born on June 27, 1880, in Tuscumbia, had come down with scarlet fever, which left her deaf and blind. Her parents, Arthur and Kate Keller, seeking help for their daughter, visited inventor Alexander Graham Bell in Washington, D.C. Bell, an activist in deaf education, recommended that they contact the Perkins School for the Blind in Boston and request a teacher for Helen.

Anne became Helen's live-in teacher, developing her own philosophy of teaching as she worked with Helen. Since Helen had already learned to communicate using some sixty gestures she had invented, Anne tried to teach her the names for things through finger-spelling into Helen's hand. Helen quickly learned the finger-spell patterns but considered them a game, unable to relate them to names for objects. The communication breakthrough came when, walking by the well house, Anne placed Helen's hand under the water coming from the pump and finger-spelled W-A-T-E-R. Suddenly Helen realized that the cool liquid had a name—as did all objects.

Four months later, Helen had a vocabulary numbering hundreds of words, was forming simple sentences, and knew the shapes of letters of the alphabet. By the end of the summer, she could write using block letters, began writing letters to her relatives, and learned the Braille alphabet.

In the spring of 1888, Anne brought seven-year-old Helen to the Perkins School in Boston, where Helen, a quick study with an exceptional memory for details, became known as the "miracle" child.

With funds raised by family friend Mark Twain, Helen attended Radcliffe College. Although college officials did not believe Helen could compete with the other students, she passed her entrance exams and attended regular classes with Anne Sullivan sitting by her side to spell the lectures into her hand. Helen graduated *cum laude* in 1904. At Helen's request, Anne stood beside her when she received her diploma.

STRANGE ENCOUNTERS

★ At age eight, Helen learned about other languages and began peppering her writing with Latin, French, and German phrases.

★ At age nine, Helen began to learn to speak. Her first speech teacher, Sarah Fuller, let Helen feel the shape of her mouth and the position of her tongue inside her mouth as she spoke.

★ Helen learned to read lips with her fingers.

★ During her college years, Helen wrote her autobiography, *The Story of my Life*. Harvard English instructor John Albert Macy, hired to help edit the book, married Anne on May 2, 1905.

★ Helen starred in the 1919 silent movie *Deliverance*, which told the story of her life.

★ In 1919, Helen began appearing with Anne in vaudeville shows. In their twenty-minute act, Anne demonstrated how she taught Helen language.

★ During World War II, Helen worked with soldiers who had been blinded in battle.

★ Anne died in October 1935 at age sixty-seven. Helen died in her sleep on June 1, 1968, at age eighty-seven.

★ Patty Duke and Anne Bancroft starred as Helen Keller and Anne Sullivan in the Broadway play and the 1962 movie *The Miracle Worker*.

★ Melissa Gilbert and Patty Duke Austin starred as Helen Keller and Anne Sullivan in the 1979 made-for-TV movie *The Miracle Worker*.

Grace Kelly and Prince Rainier

I n the summer of 1954, actress Grace Kelly, shooting a scene on the French Riviera for the Alfred Hitchcock movie *To Catch A Thief,* drove actor Cary Grant along the Moyen Corniche to lose a tailing police car, and pulled off the road for a picnic lunch. Looking out at the Mediterranean Sea, she noticed beautiful gardens.

"Whose gardens are those?" she later asked screenwriter John Michael Hayes. He told her they belonged to Prince Rainier III, the ruler of the principality of Monaco. Grace would not meet the prince until the next year.

In March 1955, back in New York City, Grace received a telephone call from Rupert Allan, an editor at *Look* magazine who had written three cover stories on her. He told Grace that the French government wanted her to attend the Cannes Film Festival in May. To entice her to attend, the Festival would screen her movie *The Country Girl*, and *Paris Match* had arranged a photo shoot for her with Prince Rainier.

The Prince and Grace met for forty-five minutes at his thirteenth-century pink palace. Rainier desperately needed a wife who would give him an heir to the throne. Otherwise, upon his death, Monaco would be returned to France and its citizens would be forced to pay taxes to the French government. Charmed by the Prince, Grace corresponded with him for the next eight months. Finally, he visited her family in Philadelphia for Christmas and proposed to Grace.

Grace married Prince Rainier III of Monaco on April 19, 1956, in a civil ceremony, as required by law, followed by a Roman Catholic mass in the Cathedral of St. Nicholas. Princess Grace then retired from her movie career.

★ Grace Patricia Kelly was born on November 12, 1929, in Philadelphia, Pennsylvania, to a former world champion oarsman and a former cover girl.

★ Prince Rainier was born Rainier Louis Henri Maxence Bertrand de Grimaldi in 1923.

★ After her high school graduation in 1947, Grace moved to New York City, where she worked as a model, attended the American Academy of Dramatic Arts, and made her debut on Broadway in 1949.

★ Grace starred as Gary Cooper's wife in the 1952 movie *High Noon* and won an Academy Award for her portrayal of an adulteress in the 1953 movie *Mogambo*, but her role in the 1954 Alfred Hitchcock movie *Rear Window* launched her to stardom.

★ Grace dated Clark Gable and William Holden.

★ When Grace left Hollywood, the roles she was slated to play in the movies *Designing Women* and *The Cobweb* were filled by Lauren Bacall.

★ Although marrying a movie star would inevitably increase tourism to Monaco, Prince Rainier demanded that the Kelly family provide a substantial dowry for Grace. The Kelly family diverted two million dollars from Grace's inheritance to avoid cheating her brother and two sisters.

★ Kelly's wedding gown, the most expensive garment ever made by MGM designer Helen Rose, required twenty-five yards of silk taffeta and one-hundred yards of silk net. MGM purchased 125-year-old rose point lace from a museum and Rose had thousands of tiny pearls sewn on the veil.

★ Grace Kelly hoped to return to acting in Alfred Hitchcock's 1964 movie *Marnie*, but the citizens of Monaco objected to the idea of their princess playing a thief and romancing Sean Connery.

★ Grace and Prince Rainier had three children: Princess Caroline, Prince Albert, and Princess Stephanie.

★ Grace assisted in preproduction of the 1983 made-for-TV movie *The Grace Kelly Story*, starring Cheryl Ladd, best known for her role as Kris Munroe on *Charlie's Angels.*

★ On September 14, 1982, Grace died in an automobile accident on a cliff road along the French Riviera—at a spot said to be the same place where the picnic scene for *To Catch a Thief* was filmed in 1954. She was 52 years old.

★ The inscription at her burial site in the Cathedral of St. Nicholas in Monte Carlo refers to Grace as *uxor principis* (Latin for "prince's wife").

★ Prince Rainier banned Grace Kelly's movies from being shown in Monaco.

★ In 1993, the United States and Monaco simultaneously issued a commemorative postage stamp honoring Grace Kelly. Since United States law prohibits postage stamps that depict foreign heads of state, the American stamp names her Grace Kelly, while the Monaco stamp names her Princess Grace.

John F. Kennedy and Jacqueline Bouvier

In 1949, Charlie Bartlett, a Washington correspondent for the *Chattanooga Times*, met nineteen-year-old Jacqueline Lee ("Jackie") Bouvier, the daughter of wealthy Wall Street broker, John V. Bouvier III, at a party at Merriwood, the mansion home of her mother and stepfather in McLean, Virginia. The two became platonic friends and frequent companions. Charlie, a devout Catholic, decided to match up Jackie with his friend, 32-year-old Jack Kennedy. He and Kennedy, both U.S. Navy veterans, had met around Christmas 1945 at El Patio, a nightclub in Palm Beach where the Kennedys had a home. Bartlett's family had a house in nearby Hobe Sound.

In the summer of 1949, Jackie accompanied Charlie to his brother David's wedding to Gladys Peggy Pulitzer at Puddle Duck Farm in Syosset, on the north shore of Long Island, New York. Charlie did not tell Jackie that his friend Jack Kennedy would also be at the wedding. Charlie never got the opportunity to introduce Jack to Jackie, who was well aware of Jack's reputation as a war hero, playboy, and rising politician. "Although they may have said hello to each other," recalled Charlie, "they missed the chance to meet."

Three years later, in the spring of 1951, Charlie's mentor, Arthur Krock, a friend of Jack Kennedy's father Joe, asked Charlie and his wife Martha to arrange a dinner party to introduce Jackie, now a senior at George Washington University, and Jack, now a Massachusetts Congressman. Martha, eager to divert Jackie's affections away from her husband, gladly arranged the dinner party and invited several friends to hide her real intent. Jack sat next to Jackie on the sofa and talked with the woman twelve years his junior. After dinner, all the guests played a variation of charades. Martha intentionally placed Jack and Jackie on opposing teams so they could better witness each other's sharp wit.

After the game, Jackie said she had to leave early. Charlie escorted Jackie outside to her convertible, followed by the Bartlett's fox terrier. When Jackie opened her car door, Jack appeared by Charlie's side and invited her to join him for a drink. Just then the Bartlett's dog jumped into the car and starting barking. Another man sat up in the backseat. Jackie's date, having spotted her parked car, had been hiding in the backseat, waiting for her. Jackie turned to Jack and said, "Some other time." He walked away, disheartened.

STRANGE ENCOUNTERS

★ John Fitzgerald Kennedy, born on May 29, 1917, in Brookline, Massachusetts, ran for president of his freshman class at Harvard, but lost the election.

★ Jackie Bouvier was born six weeks late on July 2, 1929, in Southampton, New York.

★ Jackie's parents, John Vernou ("Black Jack") Bouvier III and Janet Norton Lee, divorced when Jackie was ten years old due to Black Jack's womanizing. Two years later, her mother married Hugh Dudley Auchincloss, Jr., an heir to the Standard Oil fortune.

★ Kennedy, a graduate of Choate Academy in Wallingford, Connecticut, was voted "most likely to succeed" by his classmates.

★ Jackie majored in French Literature at Georgetown University, attended Vassar College and the Sorbonne in Paris, and worked briefly at *Vogue* magazine.

★ Jack dropped out of Stanford University Business School after six months.

★ In the spring of 1952, Jackie wrote a television script featuring the ghost of First Lady Dolly Madison haunting the Octagon House (the residence used to house the Madisons after the White House fire of 1812).

★ In 1952, Jackie worked as the "Inquiring Fotografer" at the *Washington Times Herald*.

★ In 1952, Jack telephoned Jackie to invite her out for drinks, having had no contact with her since their first meeting nine months before. Jackie had gotten engaged two weeks earlier to Wall Street stockbroker John Husted.

★ Jackie and Jack were married on September 12, 1953, at St. Mary's Church in Newport, with Jack's brother Robert Kennedy serving as the best man.

★ Jack's father, Joseph P. Kennedy, who made his fortune as a bootlegger during Prohibition, served as the first chairman of the Securities and Exchange Commission and as United States ambassador to Great Britain.

★ Jack was the first President born in the twentieth century and the first President of the Roman Catholic faith.

★ Jack and Jackie had three children: John F., Jr., (Nicknamed "John John" by the media), Caroline, and Patrick (who was born prematurely on August 7, 1963, and died two days later).

★ At age forty-three, Jack became the youngest man ever elected President of the United States and, at age forty-six, the youngest President to die in office.

★ On November 22, 1963, Jackie was sitting next to Jack when he was assassinated in Dallas.

★ The Warren Commission concluded that Lee Harvey Oswald fired three shots at the president's motorcade from the sixth-floor window of the Texas Book Depository, and that the first shot struck President John F. Kennedy in the base of his neck, exited from his throat (six inches higher than the entrance wound), hit Texas Governor John Connally in the back, shattered his fifth rib, emerged from his chest, passed through his right wrist, shattering bones, landed in Connally's left thigh, and was finally found in nearly pristine condition on a stretcher in Parkland Hospital. The Warren Commission also concluded that the third shot hit President Kennedy in the back of the head and thrust him backwards, violating the laws of physics.

John F. Kennedy, Jr., and Carolyn Bessette

After graduating from Boston University with a degree in elementary education, 22-year-old Carolyn Bessette took a marketing job with That's Entertainment, part of a Boston nightclub consortium. The manager of a local Calvin Klein boutique spotted her walking down Boston's trendy Newbury Street and hired her to be a personal shopper for celebrity clients.

When she actually met Klein, the fashion designer transferred her to his New York headquarters to work in publicity. Her poise, beauty, and grace personified the Calvin Klein look and image, making her the perfect press person for his design house.

Some gossip columnists claim that Carolyn met John F. Kennedy, Jr., then considered America's most eligible bachelor, while helping him shop for suits at Calvin Klein. Others claim they met while jogging in New York's Central Park. At the time, according to tabloid reports, John was living with actress Daryl Hannah. He broke up with the actress shortly after the death of his mother in May 1994.

John married Carolyn on Saturday, September 21, 1996, in a small, private ceremony in the First African Baptist Church on Cumberland Island, Georgia, keeping the wedding a complete secret from the press.

★ John was born on November 25, 1960, three weeks after his father was elected president.

★ Carolyn Bessette, born on January 7, 1966, in White Plains, New York, moved to Greenwich, Connecticut, when her parents divorced in 1974.

★ John attended New York City's Collegiate School for Boys, graduated from Phillips Academy in Andover, was rejected by Harvard University, and attended Brown University, graduating in 1983.

★ Carolyn was voted "The Ultimate Beautiful Person" by her classmates at St. Mary's High School.

★ While majoring in elementary education at Boston University, Carolyn posed for the cover of the calendar *The Women of BU*.

★ John graduated from New York University Law School and failed the bar exam twice, prompting the tabloids to nickname him "the hunk who flunked."

★ In 1988, *People* dubbed John the "Sexiest Man Alive."

★ John introduced his uncle, Senator Edward M. Kennedy, at the 1988 Democratic Convention, worked as a prosecutor for the Manhattan District Attorney (frequently bicycling to work), and in 1995, launched *George*, a glossy political magazine subtitled "Not Just Politics as Usual."

★ Carolyn dated *Baywatch* star Michael Bergin and Tampa Bay Lightning Assistant Coach John Cullen.

★ In 1996, paparazzi photographed John and Carolyn arguing in Central Park. He reportedly pulled a ring off her finger.

★ On July 16, 1999, John and Carolyn died when the single-engine plane John was piloting crashed into the Atlantic Ocean off Martha's Vineyard, Massachusetts. The couple was traveling to a Kennedy family wedding with Carolyn's sister, Lauren Bessette, who was also killed in the crash.

Stan Laurel and Oliver Hardy

In 1917, Stan Laurel, a vaudeville comedian who had worked as Charlie Chaplin's understudy, starred in the silent two-reel short *Lucky Dog*. Oliver Hardy, credited as Babe Hardy, played a bit part. They became friends, but did not cross paths again for several years. Stan appeared in numerous comedy shorts (as a clownish misfit clad in oversized clothes) and began writing and directing. In 1925, Stan and Ollie met again at the Hal Roach studios, where Stan directed Ollie in the cast of such silent comedy shorts as *Yes, Yes, Nanette* and *Wandering Papas*. Persuaded to return to acting, Stan appeared in the 1926 two-reel comedy *Forty-Five Minutes From Hollywood* with Oliver. Director Leo McCarey (best remembered for the movies *The Bells of St. Mary's* and *Going My Way*) persuaded Stan and Ollie to team up as full-fledged partners, which they did a year later in the 1927 movie *Duck Soup*, beginning a partnership that lasted thirty years. Stan played the befuddled featherbrain whose stupidity exasperated the overweight Ollie, who would twiddle his tie, stare incredulously into the camera, and proclaim, "This is another fine mess you've gotten us into." Stan would blink his eyes, remove his hat, scratch his head, and burst into tears. The duo became one of the most popular comedy teams in motion picture history.

★ Stan Laurel was born Arthur Stanley Jefferson on June 16, 1890, in Ulverston, England.

★ Oliver Norvell Hardy, Jr., was born on January 18, 1892, in Harlem, Georgia.

★ Ollie dropped out of the University of Georgia and opened a small movie theater.

★ In 1916, Stan impersonated Charlie Chaplin in a successful vaudeville act with the Keystone Trio.

★ Before being teamed with Ollie, Stan Laurel appeared in seventy-six movies.

★ The 1919 movie *Lucky Dog* was not released until 1922.

★ Stan's only son died nine days after birth in 1930.

★ Stan and Ollie made 117 films together.

★ Under the pen name Patrick LaBrutto, Stan wrote a short story parodying Sherlock Holmes called "The Little Problem of the Grosvener Square Furniture Van." Stan and Ollie adapted the story as the basis for their 1932 movie *The Music Box*, the only Laurel and Hardy film to win an Academy Award.

★ Stan was married six times. His wives included Mae Laurel, Virginia Ruth Rogers (twice), Lois Neilson, Vera Ivanova Shuvalova, and Ida Kitaeva.

★ Ollie was married twice, to Myrtle Lee Reeve and Virginia Lucille Jones.

★ After Ollie died in 1957, Stan became inconsolable and vowed never to perform again.

Jerry Leiber and Mike Stoller

In 1950, seventeen-year-old Mike Stoller, a student at Los Angeles Community College, played piano in a pick-up dance combo with a drummer who went to Fairfax High School. The drummer, impressed by Mike's playing, wrote down Mike's phone number and soon afterwards gave it to a schoolmate, Jerry Leiber.

Jerry, who attended Fairfax High School and worked after school at a record shop, called Mike on the phone to propose a meeting in hopes of finding someone to write music for his lyrics. The two teenagers, both originally from the East Coast, began collaborating that summer, writing songs that reflected their mutual love for Boogie Woogie and the Blues. By the end of the year, Jimmy Witherspoon recorded Jerry and Mike's song "Real Ugly Woman." The following year, Charles Brown recorded their first rhythm-and-blues hit, "Hard Times." In 1952, Texas bluesman Little Willie Littlefield recorded their song "Kansas City" (later covered by Wilbert Harrison, the Beatles, and hundreds of others). That same year, Willie Mae "Big Mama" Thornton recorded their blockbuster hit "Hound Dog," an event that would eventually change rock 'n' roll forever. In 1956, Elvis Presley covered the Big Mama recording, creating a #1 hit and launching his meteoric rise to superstardom.

In 1957, Jerry and Mike relocated to New York City and went from writing and producing rhythm-and-blues songs like "Smokey Joe's Cafe" (recorded by the Robins) to rock 'n' roll songs like "Yakety Yak," "Charlie Brown," and "Along Came Jones" (all recorded by the Coasters).

The two songwriters arranged their songs, selected the backing musicians, and supervised every aspect of the recording sessions. Jerry and Mike defined rock 'n' roll with such songs as "Searchin'," "Love Potion No.9," "Jailhouse Rock," "Yakety Yak," "On Broadway," "Stand By Me," "Kansas City," "Charlie Brown," "Young Blood," "Ruby Baby," "Along Came Jones," and "Poison Ivy." They also wrote the Peggy Lee classic "Is That All There Is?" The duo wrote many songs for Elvis Presley's movies, such as "Loving You," "Jailhouse Rock," "Treat Me Nice," "Baby, I Don't Care," "King Creole," "Trouble," "Girls, Girls, Girls," and "Bossa Nova Baby."

STRANGE ENCOUNTERS

★ Mike Stoller was bom on March 13, 1933, in Belle Harbor, New York.

★ Jerry Leiber was born on April 25, 1933, in Baltimore, Maryland.

★ Jerry and Mike's composition "Hound Dog," recorded by Elvis Presley in 1956, stayed #1 on the pop charts for eleven weeks, setting a world record that remains unbroken.

★ In 1956, after receiving a royalty check for five thousand dollars, Mike took his wife to Europe for three months and returned aboard the Italian ocean liner *Andrea Doria*. On that voyage, the *S.S. Stockholm* crashed into the *Andrea Doria*, killing more than fifty people and sinking the ship. Mike and his wife escaped in a lifeboat with a broken rudder and were rescued by a freighter.

★ Although Elvis Presley recorded Jerry and Mike's song "Love Me" in an entirely different way than the songwriters intended, they loved Elvis's interpretation of the song.

★ Jerry and Mike's songs have been sung by such recording artists as Elvis Presley, the Beatles, the Rolling Stones, the Beach Boys, the Coasters, the Drifters, John Lennon, Otis Redding, Jimi Hendrix, Frank Sinatra, Peggy Lee, and Edith Piaf.

★ Jerry and Mike showcased their hit songs in the Broadway musical *Smokey Joe's Cafe: The Songs of Leiber and Stoller.*

Jack Lemmon and Walter Matthau

One afternoon in the late 1940s, Broadway actor Jack Lemmon walked into Sardi's in New York City and spotted Walter Matthau, who was just beginning to make a name for himself as a character actor on Broadway, leaning against the wall in the corner. "I introduced myself, and he was very nice, but he looked kind of distant and pained," recalled Jack. "Every now and then he'd shift his weight and say, 'Ouch.' I said, 'What's the problem?' He said, 'Ah, hell, I'm going with a girl named Carol Marcus and she's a friend of Gloria Vanderbilt's. Last weekend we went to a big cocktail-do at Gloria's house at the beach. There were so many people, there was no place to sit. So there was a huge glass table by the fireplace, and I sat down and the whole goddamn thing cracked in half. It damn near cut my balls off. I don't know whether there was an aorta there or what, but blood was flying. I said, 'Get an ambulance!' People started running and hollering and screaming. And Gloria came over and looked down and said, 'What have you done to my table?!'" I don't remember what the hell he said after that—I cracked up."

Jack, having won an Academy Award for his role as Ensign Pulver in *Mr. Roberts,* was cast to costar with Walter, who had achieved stardom for his portrayal of Oscar Madison in the Broadway production of *The Odd Couple,* in their first movie together, *The Fortune Cookie.*

★ Walter Matthau, born Walter Matthow on October 1, 1920, in New York City to a pair of Russian-Jewish immigrants, grew up poor on the Lower East Side and started out selling soft drinks and playing bit parts at a Yiddish theater at age eleven.

★ Jack Lemmon was born Jack Uhler Lemmon III on February 8, 1925, in a hospital elevator in Newton, Massachusetts, to the president of a doughnut company.

★ Jack, whose middle initial was U., was frequently taunted as a child by kids calling him "Jack, u lemon."

★ After graduating from Seward Park High School, Walter worked as a gym instructor for the Works Progress Administration and as a boxing coach for policemen.

★ After graduating from Phillips Academy in Andover, Massachusetts, Jack attended Harvard University, where he was elected president of the Hasty Pudding Club.

★ During World War II, Jack served in the Naval Reserve as communications officer aboard the U.S.S. *Lake Champlain*.

★ During World War II, Walter served as a sergeant in the Army Air Corps and as a radio cryptographer in a heavy bomber unit in Europe.

★ While trying to break into acting, Jack played piano in a New York City beer hall.

★ Walter changed the spelling of his last name from Matthow to Matthau to make it sound more exotic.

★ Walter broke into acting as the understudy for the actor who played the 83-year-old Archbishop in the Broadway production of *Anne Of The Thousand Days*, starring Rex Harrison.

★ While filming the 1966 movie *The Fortune Cookie*, Walter's heavy smoking (and perhaps stress from his chronic gambling) caused him to suffer a serious heart attack.

★ Before any take Jack would say, "It's magic time."

★ Walter frequently embellished his life story. He once claimed that his father was an Orthodox priest in Czarist Russia who was removed after declaring that the Pope was infallible. He once said his wife's full name was Carol Wellington-Smythe Marcus, to make her sound more aristocratic.

★ When Walter signed up for Social Security in 1937, he listed his middle name as "Foghorn."

★ Jack admitted to a serious drinking problem at one time, which is one reason he considered his Academy Award-winning role as Harry Stoner in the 1973 movie *Save the Tiger* as one of the most gratifying performances of his career.

★ Walter claimed that his real name was Walter Matuschanskayasky as a joke to retaliate for being deceived into appearing in the 1974 movie *Earthquake* with a much larger part than he expected.

★ Jack was married twice. His wives included Cynthia Stone (with whom he had one son, Christopher, who appeared with him in *Airport '77*) and Felicia Farr (with whom he had one daughter, Courtney).

★ Walter was married twice, to Grace Geraldine Johnson (with whom he had two children, Jennie and David) and Carol Marcus (with whom he had a son, Charles).

★ A habitual gambler, Walter once estimated his lifetime gambling losses at five million dollars.

★ In 1993, after filming *Grumpy Old Men* in freezing weather in Minnesota, Walter was hospitalized for double pneumonia.

★ Jack and Walter appeared together in nine films: *The Fortune Cookie, The Odd Couple, The Front Page, The Gentleman Tramp, Buddy Buddy, JFK, Chaplin, Grumpy Old Men, The Grass Harp, Grumpier Old Men, Out to Sea,* and *The Odd Couple 2.* Jack directed Walter in the movie *Kotch.*

★ Walter died on July 1, 2000. Jack died 361 days later on June 27, 2001.

John Lennon and Paul McCartney

At 4:17 p.m. on Saturday, July 6, 1957, the Quarry Men Skiffle Group began playing at the St. Peter's Parish Church Garden Fête in the Liverpool suburb of Woolton. Sixteen-year-old John Lennon led the band, composed of guitarist Eric Griffiths, tea chest bassist Len Garry, drummer Colin Hanton, washboard player Pete Shotton, and banjo player Rod Davis.

About ten minutes into the Quarry Men's first set, fifteen-year-old Paul McCartney, clad in a white jacket and tight black pants, rode up to the church field on his bicycle. He parked the bike against a fence and found his Liverpool Institute classmate Ivan Vaughn near the middle of the field. Ivan, a neighbor of John's who sometimes played tea chest bass with the Quarry Men, had invited Paul, who loved rock 'n' roll, to the fête to meet John and his band. The two made their way toward the left side of the stage. John, wearing a checkered shirt, sang the Del Vikings' song "Come Go with Me."

"He didn't know the words," recalled Paul, "but it didn't matter because none of us knew the words either. There's a refrain which goes, 'Come little darlin', come and go with me, I love you darling.' John was singing, 'Down, down, down to the penitentiary.'"

When the Quarry Men finished their first set, Paul and Ivan roamed around the fête, then returned around 6 p.m. to listen to the second. Afterward, the Quarry

Men carried their instruments across the street to set up inside St. Peter's Church, where they would be playing for a dance that evening. Ivan brought Paul inside and introduced him to John and the other Quarry Men. John and Paul barely acknowledged each other—until left-handed Paul picked up John's right-handed guitar, held it upside down, and played "Twenty Flight Rock" by Eddie Cochran.

"I was very impressed by Paul playing 'Twenty Flight Rock,'" recalled John. "He could obviously play the guitar. I half thought to myself, 'He's as good as me.' I'd been kingpin up to then."

Paul went into "Be-Bop-a-Lula" by Gene Vincent, played a medley of Little Richard songs, and taught John how to play "Twenty Flight Rock" and tune his guitar.

"I turned round to him right then on first meeting and said, 'Do you want to join the group?'" recalled John. "And he said 'yes' the next day as I recall it."

S T R A N G E   E N C O U N T E R S

★ James Paul McCartney was born on June 18, 1942—the same day and year as his friend Ivan Vaughn.

★ John Winston Lennon was born on October 9, 1940, in Liverpool, England.

★ Also attending the St. Peter's Parish Church Garden Fête to hear the Quarry Men were John's mother Julia and his Aunt Mimi, who had no idea that her nephew was in a band.

★ John was frequently placed on detention at Quarry Bank Grammar School and received numerous canings for "insolence," "throwing blackboard duster out of window," "cutting class and going AWOL," and "gambling on school field."

★ John named his band the Quarry Men after the high school he and the other band members attended—Quarry Bank.

★ Paul's father, a musician, encouraged his son to play music. John's Aunt Mimi relegated her nephew's guitar playing to the porch.

★ The first instrument John learned to play was the harmonica.

★ At age fourteen, Paul wrote his first song, "I've Lost My Little Girl."

★ As teenagers, both Paul and John lost their mothers. Mary McCartney died of breast cancer on October 31, 1956, when Paul was fourteen. Julia Lennon was hit by a car and killed on July 15, 1958, when John was seventeen.

★ One night in 1957 at a cellar club called the Morgue, in the Liverpool suburb of Old Roan, Paul introduced John to fourteen-year-old George Harrison, a friend he had made years earlier on the daily bus to Liverpool Institute.

★ John Lennon and Stuart Sutcliffe named the band "The Beatles," changing the second letter *e* to *a*, to give the word a double meaning—inspired by the way the name of Buddy Holly's band, the Crickets, played off cricket the game and cricket the insect. After achieving worldwide fame, the Beatles met the Crickets who had no idea cricket was a game in England. George Harrison speculated that Sutcliffe, who admired Marlon Brando, took the name from a scene in the 1954 movie *The Wild One*, in which Lee Marvin, referring to a group of motorcycle chicks, says, "The Beetles have missed you." John claimed he changed the second letter *e* to an *a*, "because 'beetles' didn't mean two things on its own. When you said it, people thought of crawly things; and when you read it, it was beat music."

★ The Beatles were rejected in 1962 by Decca Records executive Dick Rowe, who signed Brian Poole & The Tremeloes instead, following back-to-back auditions by the groups. The Beatles' Decca audition tape was subsequently turned down by Pey, Philips, Columbia, and HMV.

★ The cover of Paul's solo album *Ram*, released in May 1971, features a photograph of Paul holding a ram by the horns. John's album *Imagine*, released in October 1971, includes a bonus photograph of John holding a hog by the ears.

★ Two songs on Paul's *Ram* album, "Too Many People" and "Dear Boy," seem directed to John, who responded on *Imagine* with "How Do You Sleep?"

John Lennon and Yoko Ono

In 1966, Beatle John Lennon, a former student at Liverpool College of Art, frequently visited private viewings at art galleries in London's West End. In November, John learned that avant-garde artist Yoko Ono would be holding a showing of her work, entitled "Unfinished Paintings and Objects," at the Indica, an art gallery run by John Dunbar, formerly married to singer Marianne Faithful. "I got the word that this amazing woman was putting on a show next week and there was going to be something about people in bags, in black bags, and it was going to be a bit of a happening and all that," recalled John. "So I went down to a preview of the show. I got there the night before it opened. I went in—she didn't know who I was or anything—I was wandering around, there was a couple of artsy type students there in the gallery, and I was looking at it and I was astounded. There was an apple on sale there for 200 quid, I thought it was fantastic—I got the humor in her work immediately."

John was particularly intrigued by a ladder leading to a painting hung on the ceiling. "It looked like a black canvas with a chain with a spy glass hanging on the end of it," said John. He ascended the ladder and looked through the spyglass to discover the word "yes" in minuscule letters.

"It's a great relief when you get up the ladder," said John, "and

you look through the spyglass and it doesn't say 'no' or 'fuck you' or something [negative], it said 'yes.'"

John Dunbar sent Yoko over to introduce herself to the wealthy Beatle. Dressed in all black, Yoko quietly handed John a card printed with the single word "Breathe." John responded by panting.

At the time, John was married to Cynthia Powell. Yoko was married to her second husband, Tony Cox. Amused by Yoko's absurd artistic sensibilities, John financed several of her exhibitions and kept a copy of her book, *Grapefruit*, next to his bed to flip through as a source of inspiration. He found himself intellectually stimulated by Yoko's unconventional ideas. "As she was talking to me, I'd get high, and the discussion would get to such a level, I'd be getting higher and higher. Then she'd leave, and I'd go back to this sort of suburbia. Then I'd meet her again, and my head would go open, like I was on an acid trip."

In 1967, while studying Transcendental Meditation with the Maharishi Mahesh Yogi in India (with a group that included his wife Cynthia, the other Beatles, folk singer Donovan, actress Mia Farrow, and Beach Boy Mike Love), John corresponded with Yoko. In May, after returning from India, John sent his wife Cynthia on vacation to Greece. While she was away, John invited Yoko to his mansion in Weybridge. He showed her his home studio, played her his experimental tapes of sound collages, and the two decided to make a tape together. "It was midnight when we started *Two Virgins*," recalled John. "It was dawn when we finished, and then we made love. It was very beautiful." A few days later, Cynthia returned home to find John and Yoko sitting together in her kitchen.

S T R A N G E   E N C O U N T E R S

★ Yoko Ono, born February 18, 1933, in Tokyo, Japan, was raised in Scarsdale, New York, and attended Sarah Lawrence College.

★ John Winston Lennon, born on October 9, 1940, in Liverpool, England, had an obsession with the number nine. He wrote the songs "One After 909," "Revolution #9," and "#9 Dream."

★ In English, the Japanese name Yoko translates to "Ocean Child."

★ Before meeting John, Yoko knew the name of only one Beatle: Ringo (whose name in Japanese means "apple").

★ John and Yoko became so inseparable that she accompanied him to nearly all of the Beatles' recording sessions.

★ Yoko can be heard singing in the chorus of the song "The Continuing Story of Bungalow Bill" on the Beatles' 1968 *White Album*.

★ When John and Cynthia separated, Paul McCartney wrote "Hey Jude" for their son Julian Lennon. After he broke up with actress Jane Asher, Paul jokingly proposed to Cynthia.

★ Inspired by his love for Yoko, John wrote the songs "Everybody's Got Something to Hide Except for Me and My Monkey," "I Want You (She's So Heavy)," "Don't Let Me Down," "Oh My Love," "Oh Yoko!" "Bless You," and "Woman."

★ After divorcing their respective spouses, John and Yoko were secretly married on March 20, 1969, at the British consulate on the Rock of Gibraltar. They flew to Paris to announce their marriage to the international press and then invited the press to join their seven day "bed-in" in the Amsterdam Hilton to promote world peace. John and Yoko sat in bed for seven consecutive days in a suite decorated with posters that proclaimed "Bed Peace" and "Hair Peace."

★ The Beatles' song "The Ballad Of John And Yoko" chronicles their wedding and honeymoon. The song, credited to Lennon/McCartney, was actually written single-handedly by John, and performed by John and Paul. Neither George nor Ringo were in England at the time.

★ In 1969, on the roof of Apple Records headquarters in London, before the Commissioner of Oaths, John Winston Lennon legally changed his name to John Ono Lennon.

★ In 1973, John and Yoko separated at her insistence. Yoko remained in New York in the Dakota apartment building. John moved to Los Angeles, began drinking heavily, and, in 1974, was escorted from the Troubadour Club by the bouncers, after heckling the Smothers Brothers, wearing a tampon on his forehead.

★ In 1974, John promised Elton John that if his version of "Lucy in the Sky with Diamonds" made it to #1 on the charts, he would perform onstage with Elton. It did. On November 28, 1974, John joined Elton onstage at Madison Square Garden to play the songs "Whatever Gets You Thru the Night," "Lucy in the Sky with Diamonds," and "I Saw Her Standing There." Unbeknownst to John, Elton had invited Yoko, who came backstage. They began dating again.

★ The Nixon administration, prompted by South Carolina Republican Senator Strom Thurmond, attempted to deport John from the United States. Lennon sued the United States government and won the case.

★ John's second son Sean was born on his thirty-fifth birthday.

★ John received a green card on July 4, 1976—the American bicentennial.

★ John used a number of pseudonyms in his musical work, including Dr. Winston O'Boogie, Dwarf McDougal, Rev. Fred Ghurkin, Musketeer Gripweed, Mel Torment, Dr. Dream, Honorary John St. John Johnson, Kaptain Kundalini, and Dad.

★ John Lennon had two sons: Julian (with his first wife Cynthia Powell) and Sean (with his second wife Yoko Ono).

★ Yoko Ono has been married three times, to Toshi Ichiyanagi, Anthony Cox, and John Lennon. She has two children: Kyoko Chan Cox and Sean Taro Ono Lennon.

★ Photographer Annie Liebowitz photographed John on the day he was assassinated for the cover of *Rolling Stone* magazine.

★ Mark David Chapman, a crazed fan, assassinated John on December 8, 1980, outside the Dakota. When apprehended, Chapman was flipping through the novel *The Catcher in the Rye* by J.D. Salinger.

★ John died at 11 p.m. on December 8, 1980, in New York City. In keeping with John's obsession with the number nine, in England on Greenwich Mean Time, his death occurred at 4 a.m. on December 9th.

★ Yoko used her photograph of John's blood-stained spectacles from his fatal shooting on the cover of her album *Season of Glass*.

★ Actor Mark Lindsay Chapman, cast to play the part of John Lennon in a made-for-TV movie biography, lost the part because he shared the same name as Lennon's killer.

Jay Leno and Mavis Nicholson

In January 1976, while performing at the Comedy Store in Los Angeles, comedian Jay Leno spotted a beautiful woman in the audience who, he claims, "even laughed in the right places." Determined to meet this young enchantress, he

waited by the women's restroom in the hopes that she would eventually need to use the facilities. When she finally crossed his path, he introduced himself and asked her out on a date. The young lady, Mavis Nicholson, accepted. A native of Los Angeles and the daughter of character actor Nick Nicholson, Mavis worked as a sitcom writer.

According to Jay, they consummated their relationship in the backseat of his 1955 Buick Roadmaster—the first car he bought in Los Angeles, a car he slept in while trying to break into show business, a car he still owns to this day. Jay and Mavis moved in together, and when Jay went on the road to perform at comedy clubs across the country, Mavis accompanied him.

After living together for four years, Jay, who had medical insurance, realized that Mavis did not. Jay, whose father sold insurance, suggested that they get married so that Mavis would be covered. Mavis agreed, and the couple got married on November 20, 1980—Jay's parents' wedding anniversary.

★ Jay Leno, born James Douglas Muir Leno on April 28, 1950, in New Rochelle, New York, to an Italian father and Scottish mother, was raised in Andover, Massachusetts.

★ In elementary school, Jay flushed tennis balls down the toilet as a prank and hid a dog in his locker.

★ On Jay's fifth-grade report card, the teacher wrote: "If Jay spent as much time studying as he does trying to be a comedian, he'd be a big star."

★ As a teenager, Jay, who suffered from dyslexia, applied for a job at Woolworth's but failed the employment test.

★ At age fourteen, Jay bought and restored his first automobile—a 1934 Ford V-8 truck. Today he owns more than thirty classic cars and some forty motorcycles.

★ In his senior year in high school, Jay worked at McDonald's. At the suggestion of the store manager, the wisecracking employee entered the company's Northeast talent show. When he won, he began to seriously consider a career in stand-up comedy. "Until then," he told *Time* magazine, "I just always thought I'd be a funny salesman."

★ A 1972 graduate of Emerson College in Boston, Jay made his first appearance on *The Tonight Show* on March 2, 1977.

★ As an aspiring actor, Jay appeared on an episode of *Good Times* as a patient in a VD clinic.

★ In the 1978 movie *American Hot Wax,* Jay played a character named Mookie.

★ Jay and Mavis do not have any children.

★ As chairperson of the Feminist Majority Foundation's Campaign to Stop Gender Apartheid in Afghanistan, Mavis helped combat the strict Islamic fundamentalist Taliban regime that required women to wear burkahs and prohibited women from attending school, driving cars, or holding jobs.

Jerry Lewis and Dean Martin

In September 1944, Catskills comedian Jerry Lewis and his friend, Sonny King, bumped into Dean Martin, then the host of his own radio show on WMCA, on the corner of 49th Street and Broadway in New York City. Sonny introduced Jerry to Dean.

After that, Dean and Jerry frequently crossed paths at various clubs. In March 1946, the Havana Club booked Jerry and Dean as separate acts to appear on the same bill. The comedian and the singer visited each others' acts, often joking out loud during the other's performance.

In July 1946, Jerry's agent booked him into the 500 Club in Atlantic City, New Jersey, where Dean was again booked on the same bill. Dean would go on first and sing, then Jerry would follow with his comedy routine. "We started horsing around with each other's acts," recalled Dean. "That's how the team Martin and Lewis started. We'd do anything that came to our minds, anything at all."

Dean and Jerry would perform their own routines, then join each other as a twosome at the end of their shows. When Dean sang, Jerry interrupted with zany clowning. They traded insults, ad-libbed, and acted like manic madmen. The audience loved it. "We lasted six weeks at the Club 500," recalled Dean. "It was wonderful."

In January 1947, Dean and Jerry launched their careers as a full-fledged team. They were soon playing to packed nightclubs and theaters across the country, and quickly became the most popular comedy team in the nation—breaking records in nightclubs and on radio and television.

★ Jerry was born Joseph Levitch on March 16, 1926, in Newark, New Jersey. Jerry took the last name Lewis from his father's stage name.

★ Dean was born Dino Paul Crocetti on June 7, 1917, in Steubenville, Ohio, to Italian immigrants Gaetano and Angella Crocetti. He spoke only Italian until age five.

★ Jerry claims he was thrown out of high school for punching out his principal, who insulted him with an anti-Semitic remark.

★ Dean worked as a steel mill laborer, gas station attendant, card shark, and prize-fighter under the name Kid Crochet. Recalled Dean: "I won all but eleven of twelve fights."

★ Jerry and Dean starred together in seventeen movies: *My Friend Irma, My Friend Irma Goes West, At War with the Army, Sailor Beware, That's My Boy, Jumping Jacks, Road to Bali, The Caddy, Scared Stiff, The Stooge, Living It Up, 3 Ring Circus, Money from Home, Artists and Models, You're Never Too Young, Hollywood or Bust,* and *Pardners.*

★ Jerry and Dean split up their act in 1956.

★ Dean was a member of the "Rat Pack," which included Frank Sinatra, Sammy Davis, Jr., Peter Lawford, and Joey Bishop. All five men appeared in the movies *Ocean's Eleven, Sergeants Three,* and *Robin and the Seven Hoods.*

★ Most of the alcohol Dean drank during his stage performances was actually apple juice.

★ Dean's 1964 hit song, "Everybody Loves Somebody," beat the Beatles to become the #1 hit in America for one week.

★ Jerry's eldest son, Gary Lewis, and his rock group, The Playboys, recorded the hit song, "This Diamond Ring."

★ Jerry wrote the screenplays for eight of his movies.

★ Jerry wrote, produced, and acted in the 1972 film *The Day the Clown Cried,* which was never released. The film purports to tell the tale of a clown at Auschwitz during World War II.

★ For nine years, Dean hosted *Dean Martin Celebrity Roasts* in which a panel comprised of the biggest names in show business would shower the guest of honor with insults.

★ Dean has two stars on the Hollywood Walk of Fame: one for his work in motion pictures, the second for his work in television.

★ Jerry has seven children: Gary, Ronald, Scott, Christopher, Anthony, and Joseph (with his first wife, Patti Palmer), and Danielle (adopted with his second wife SanDee Pitrick).

★ Dean had seven children: Craig, Claudia, Gail, and Dina (with first wife Betty McDonald); Dino, Ricci, and Gina (with second wife Jeanne Biegger); and adopted daughter Sasha (with third wife Catherine Mae Hawn). His son Craig married Lou Costello's daughter; his son Dino was killed in an Air

National Guard fighter plane crash; and his daughter Gina was married to the late Carl Wilson of the Beach Boys.

★ When Jerry taught a film class at the University of California, his students included directors Steven Spielberg and George Lucas.

★ Known as a clothes horse, Jerry allegedly gives away suits rather than having them cleaned and refuses to wear a pair of socks more than once.

★ Jerry, presented with the French Legion of Honor in 1984, was nominated for the Nobel Peace Prize in 1977 for his fundraising work for muscular dystrophy.

★ Dean died on Christmas Day 1995, the same day that his mother had died twenty-nine years earlier.

★ In 1995, Jerry became the highest-paid performer in Broadway history for his role as the Devil in *Damn Yankees*.

Meriwether Lewis and William Clark

Meriwether Lewis, born on August 18, 1774, at Locust Hill in Albemarle County, Virginia, in view of Thomas Jefferson's Monticello home, was the son of a plantation owner. When Lewis was five years old, his father, a close friend of Jefferson's, died in the Revolutionary War. Jefferson, who had no son of his own, took Lewis under his wing as his protégé, tutoring him in biology, astronomy, taxidermy, and navigation.

In 1794, twenty-year-old Lewis, bored with plantation life, turned the management of the Locust Hill plantation over to his mother and volunteered for the frontier militia, serving under 24-year-old William Clark. Clark had joined the frontier militia five years earlier. A native of Virginia's Caroline County, Clark had risen in rank to a captain in the Regular Army, commanding an elite company of riflemen-sharpshooters.

For six months, Lewis served under Clark. He discovered that the strong and adventurous Clark, who shared his love for the outdoors, had sailed the Ohio and Mississippi Rivers, worked as a surveyor, and built forts in the wilderness. Clark also knew how to fight Indians and negotiate with them. Lewis and Clark grew to trust each other implicitly. Clark resigned from the Army in 1796. Lewis rose in rank to become an Army captain.

In 1801, President-elect Jefferson summoned Lewis to the President's House to serve as his secretary. Jefferson envisioned expanding the United States of America, whose Western border was then the Mississippi River, across the continent to create an "Empire of Liberty." He also hoped to find an all-water passage that connected the Atlantic Ocean with the Pacific Ocean. Irked by Great Britain's plans to develop a land passage across the American West to the Pacific, Jefferson appointed Lewis to lead an American expedition to explore the land west of the Mississippi River. Through the summer of 1802 at Monticello, Jefferson taught Lewis astronomy, botany, ethnology, and zoology. In the fall, Lewis read the few accounts of the exploration of the Pacific coasts, studied maps, and drew up a budget for the expedition to propose to Congress. In the spring of 1803, Jefferson sent his protégé to Philadelphia to be schooled by a group of the President's friends.

In 1803, after securing funds from Congress to purchase the Louisiana Territory from France for fifteen million dollars, Jefferson convinced Congress to appropriate the money for the expedition west for the sole purpose of promoting commerce with the Indians who traded furs and pelts along the Missouri River. Jefferson, however, also intended to use the expedition to further scientific exploration, invade foreign territory, locate an all-water route to the Pacific, claim the Northwest for the United States, and pinpoint the whereabouts of native Indians living on the land. Lewis, requiring a second, equally qualified officer for his expedition, selected his former army captain William Clark, whom Lewis had not seen for eight years.

President Thomas Jefferson put Lewis in charge of the expedition and, at Lewis's suggestion, chose Clark to be second in command. Lewis and Clark agreed privately to be equal co-leaders.

STRANGE ENCOUNTERS

★ Meriwether Lewis was born on August 18, 1774, in Albemarle County, Virginia.

★ William Clark was born on August 1, 1770, on a plantation in Caroline County, Virginia, less than ninety miles from Lewis's home.

★ In 1792, eighteen-year-old Lewis volunteered to lead an expedition up the Missouri River and down the Columbia River. He was rejected. The man chosen never got past Kentucky.

★ President Thomas Jefferson believed that the unexplored western part of the North American continent contained a mountain made of pure salt, a lost tribe of Israel, the Welsh Indians, and an all-water route to the Pacific Ocean.

★ The budget Lewis presented to Congress for his twelve-man expedition west came to 2,500 dollars and included 696 dollars for "Indian presents."

★ The Lewis and Clark Expedition, the first exploration by the United States government of the northwestern wilderness, began in 1804 and lasted two years.

★ Lewis and Clark started up the Missouri River from St. Louis on May 14, 1804, and traveled almost 7,700 miles to the Pacific Coast.

★ The Lewis and Clark Expedition included a Shoshone Indian woman named Sacagawea, whose image was minted on the United States one-dollar coin beginning in 2000.

★ While crossing the Rocky Mountains, several horses used by the Lewis and Clark Expedition lost their footing and fell to their deaths. With fewer animals to hunt for food in the Rockies, the explorers killed and ate some of their horses.

★ On the return trip, Lewis followed the Marias River while Clark followed the Yellowstone River.

★ The Lewis and Clark Expedition returned to St. Louis on September 23, 1806, to be greeted by throngs of cheering people who had given them up for lost.

★ In 1807, Lewis became governor of the Louisiana Territory.

★ In 1809, Lewis, traveling from St. Louis to Washington, D.C., stopped for the night at an inn in central Tennessee. The next morning, he was found shot dead. No one knows to this day whether he was murdered or committed suicide.

The Lone Ranger and Tonto

Sometime in the nineteenth century, young Captain John Reid led a posse of five Texas Rangers to search for a gang of desperadoes known as the Butch Cavendish "Hole in the Wall" Gang. Unfortunately, the outlaws lured the Rangers into an ambush in a canyon at Bryant's Gap, shot them during a fierce gun bat-

tle, and left them for dead, killing five of the Rangers. Reid survived, and, while seriously wounded, crawled to safety near a water hole. A lone Mohawk Indian named Tonto discovered the massacred Rangers and found Reid, still alive. Having once been helped by the "lone" Ranger, Tonto returned the favor by carrying Reid to a cave and nursing him back to health.

When Reid told Tonto what had happened and vowed to avenge the deaths of his comrades (including his slain brother Dan), the Indian pledged to stay by his side. "You kemo sabe," said Tonto. "It mean 'trusty scout.'" Reid tore a piece of black fabric from the vest of his dead brother Dan to fashion a mask to hide his identity. He posed as an outlaw to get near the gang. The Lone Ranger and Tonto cornered Butch Cavendish and his notorious gang in a dramatic battle. Those who survived were hanged or imprisoned.

In memory of the massacre at Bryant's Gap, the Lone Ranger buried his past at the graves of the five dead Rangers, continued to wear his mask, and set out with Tonto to avenge wrongs and defend justice throughout the Old West (yelling "Heigh-ho Silver, away!" before sallying forth). Although he appeared to have no visible means of support and never accepted payment for help, the masked man survived on the income generated by the silver mine that he and his brother Dan had previously discovered. He occasionally returned to the mine, managed in his absence by an honest old man, to collect his share of the proceeds and replenish his supply of silver bullets.

Together, the Lone Ranger and his faithful Indian companion Tonto, riding their trusted horses Silver and Scout, helped maintain law and order throughout the Wild West.

STRANGE ENCOUNTERS

★ *The Lone Ranger,* created by George W. Trendel, began as a local radio show on WXYZ in Detroit in 1933 and was soon nationally broadcast through the newly formed Mutual Radio Network. Trendle created the inexpensive drama because WXYZ could not afford network programs. He gave the Lone Ranger a white horse with silver shoes and named the stallion Silver. Writer Fran Striker, recalling that Robin Hood had silver-tipped arrows, gave the Lone Ranger silver bullets.

★ Striker introduced Tonto in the tenth show because, as a radio character, the Lone Ranger needed to talk to someone to help explain the plot to listeners.

★ George Stenius starred on radio as the first Lone Ranger. Brace Beemer, one of the show's early announcers, eventually became radio's best-known Lone Ranger.

★ *The Lone Ranger* radio show opening was: "The Lone Ranger! 'Heigh-ho Silver!' A fiery horse with the speed of light, a cloud of dust and a hearty 'Heigh-ho Silver!' The Lone Ranger. 'Heigh-ho Silver,

away!' With his faithful Indian companion Tonto, the daring and resourceful masked rider of the plains led the fight for law and order in the early west. Return with us now to those thrilling days of yesteryear. The Lone Ranger rides again!"

★ The theme song to *The Long Ranger* is "The William Tell Overture," composed by Gioacchino Rossini in 1829.

★ The Lone Ranger never smoked, used profanity, or drank liquor.

★ Actor Lee Powell and Chief Thundercloud starred as the Lone Ranger and Tonto in the fifteen episodes of the 1938 movie serial *The Lone Ranger.*

★ The television series *The Lone Ranger* premiered on September 15, 1949, and told the story of how the character came to be.

★ Actor Clayton Moore and Jay Silverheels portrayed the Lone Ranger and Tonto on the television series, *The Lone Ranger,* which ran on ABC until 1950. To get the part, Clayton Moore had to train his voice to match that of the radio Lone Ranger. From 1952 until 1954, when Moore was off the show temporarily, actor John Hart portrayed the masked man.

★ Clayton Moore and Jay Silverheels reprised their role in the 1956 movie *The Lone Ranger* and the 1958 movie *The Lone Ranger and the Lost City of Gold*.

★ "Kemo Sabe" is Potawatomi Indian for "faithful friend."

★ The Lone Ranger Creed included such moral lessons as, "To have a friend, a man must be one"; "Everyone has within himself the power to make this a better world"; "God put the firewood there but that every man must gather and light it himself"; "A man should make the most of what equipment he has"; and "All things change but truth, and that truth alone, lives on forever."

★ After *The Lone Ranger* went off the air, Clayton Moore continued to make commercials and personal appearances dressed as the character. In 1975, Wrather Corporation, owner of the television series and the rights to the character, got a court order to stop Clayton from appearing in public as the Lone Ranger. The company released a new Lone Ranger movie with a new star, but after the film bombed, the company gave Clayton permission to again appear as the Lone Ranger.

★ The Lone Ranger never killed anyone. The bad guys usually killed themselves or each other.

★ The Lone Ranger spoke with perfect grammar.

★ Clayton Moore is the only person to have a star on the Hollywood Walk of Fame with his name and the name of the character he portrayed. It reads: Clayton Moore, The Lone Ranger.

★ George W. Trendle and Fran Striker, creators of *The Lone Ranger*, also created the television show *The Green Hornet*. Britt Reid, who fought crime disguised as the Green Hornet, was originally introduced to radio audiences as the Lone Ranger's nephew.

Martin Luther King and Coretta Scott

In 1951, while attending Boston University's School of Theology, 22-year-old Martin Luther King, Jr., having yet to encounter any girls that captured his heart, asked Mary Powell, a friend from Atlanta who was enrolled at the New England Conservatory of Music, if she could set him up with one of her girlfriends.

Mary gave him the telephone number of her friend Coretta Scott, a singer. Martin called 24-year-old Coretta, introduced himself, and said he would like to meet and talk with her. He suggested they have lunch the next day. She said yes. The next day, Martin picked her up in his green Chevrolet.

"She talked about things other than music," recalled Martin in his autobiography. "I never will forget, the first discussion we had was about the question of racial and economic justice and the question of peace. She had been actively engaged in movements dealing with these problems. After an hour, my mind was made up. I said, 'So you can do something else besides sing? You've got a good mind also. You have everything I ever wanted in a woman. We ought to get married.'"

"Coretta often made comparison between me and her father," recalled Martin. "Even in the early days of our courtship, she used to say, 'You remind me so much of my father.' I don't suppose any compliment could be more inflating to the male ego."

On June 18, 1953, Martin Luther King, Sr., performed the marriage between his son and Coretta in Marion, Alabama, on the Scott family's lawn.

★ Martin's name was Michael Luther King, Jr., until he was six years old. His father, a Baptist minister, changed both their names legally to Martin in honor of German religious leader Martin Luther.

★ Martin Luther King, Jr., born Michael Luther King on January 15, 1929, at home at 501 Auburn Avenue in Atlanta, Georgia, graduated from Booker T. Washington High School in 1944 at age fifteen, received his Bachelor of Arts degree in sociology from Morehouse College in 1948 at age nineteen, and received his Bachelor of Divinity degree from Crozer Theological Seminary in 1951 at age twenty-two.

★ Coretta Scott, born on April 27, 1927, in Heiberger, Alabama, graduated from Antioch College in Ohio. With the aid of a scholarship, she worked her way through the New England Conservatory in Boston, eager to pursue a career as a mezzo-soprano concert singer.

★ At age fourteen, Martin was forced to surrender his bus seat to a white passenger and stand for ninety miles.

★ Ordained as a Baptist minister in 1947 at age eighteen, Martin became pastor of the Dexter Avenue Baptist Church in Montgomery, Alabama, in 1954.

★ Martin became the leader of the American civil rights movement, gave his famous "I Have a Dream" speech on the steps of the Lincoln Memorial to more than 200,000 people in 1963, and was awarded the Nobel Peace Prize in 1964 for leading the black struggle for equality through nonviolent means.

★ Martin based his idea of "nonviolent resistance" on the teachings of Christianity, the ideas expressed by Henry David Thoreau in his book *Civil Disobedience*, and the methods of Mohandas Gandhi, who used nonviolence to free India from British rule.

★ "I am convinced that if I had not had a wife with the fortitude, strength, and calmness of Corrie," recalled Martin, "I could not have withstood the ordeals and tensions surrounding the movement."

★ Martin was assassinated at the age of thirty-nine on April 4, 1968 at the Lorraine Hotel in Memphis, Tennessee. Escaped convict James Earl Ray pleaded guilty to the crime in March 1969. However, in 1978, a special committee of the United States House of Representatives reported the "likelihood" that King was assassinated "as a result of a conspiracy."

★ Martin's tombstone reads: "Free at last, free at last, thank God Almighty, I'm free at last!"

★ In 1974, Martin Luther King's mother, Alberta King, was shot and killed during services at Ebenezer Baptist Church. In 1979, Marcus W. Chenault, a black university student, was convicted of her murder.

★ In 1983, Congress approved a federal holiday honoring Martin Luther King, Jr., to be celebrated on the third Monday in January, beginning in 1986.

Robert MacNeil and Jim Lehrer

In 1973, PBS news correspondents Robert MacNeil and Jim Lehrer teamed up to cover the Senate Watergate Hearings for PBS. Bob, a native of Canada, had worked for Reuters News Agency, NBC-TV, and the BBC. Jim, a former columnist and city editor of *The Dallas Times Herald*, had worked as a news correspondent for KERA-TV in Dallas before joining the Washington PBS affiliate, WETA-TV.

Following Bob and Jim's Emmy Award-winning coverage of the hearings, Jim became the sole anchor for PBS coverage of the House Judiciary Committee's impeachment inquiry of President Richard M. Nixon.

In 1975, Channel Thirteen, the PBS affiliate in New York, gave Bob his own half-hour nightly news analysis program called *The Robert MacNeil Report*, with Jim as the Washington correspondent—fashioned after *The Huntley-Brinkley Report*. The show, renamed *The MacNeil/Lehrer Report* the following year, dealt in depth with a single topic each night and received critical praise for its objectivity. In 1983, PBS expanded the innovative show into *The MacNeil/Lehrer NewsHour*, the first hour-long evening news program in the United States.

STRANGE ENCOUNTERS

★ Robert MacNeil, born Robert Breckenridge Ware MacNeil on January 19, 1931, in Montreal, Canada, was raised in Halifax, Nova Scotia.

★ Jim Lehrer, born James Charles Lehrer on May 19, 1934, in Wichita, Kansas, aspired to play for the Brooklyn Dodgers, but, realizing his limited athletic ability, turned to sports writing.

★ In 1954, as a senior at Carleton University, Bob worked for CBC-TV in Ottawa, Canada, where he hosted twenty-six episodes of a children's program, *Let's Go To a Museum.*

★ On November 22, 1963, while covering President John F. Kennedy's motorcade through Dallas, Texas, Bob heard three shots. He stopped the press bus, jumped out, raced toward the Texas Book Depository, and asked a man leaving the building where he could find the nearest telephone. The man pointed to another man inside the building and said, "Better ask him." Bob later learned that he had spoken to Lee Harvey Oswald, the man accused of assassinating Kennedy.

★ Jim's first novel, *Viva Max!,* about a band of Mexican soldiers who reclaim the Alamo as a tourist attraction, was published in 1966 and made into a movie starring Peter Ustinov and Jonathan Winters.

★ In 1968, Bob made a documentary for PBS about the 1968 Democratic national convention entitled *The Whole World Is Watching.*

★ Bob resigned from PBS in 1971 to protest against the Nixon administration's attempt to transform the network into an internal Voice of America.

★ In the presidential election campaigns of 1988, 1992, 1996, and 2000, Jim moderated nine of the nationally televised candidate debates.

★ Jim has written thirteen novels, two memoirs, and three plays. Bob has written two novels, several nonfiction books, and two memoirs.

★ After Bob retired in 1995, Jim continued hosting the news program, renamed *The NewsHour with Jim Lehrer.*

Madonna and Guy Ritchie

In the summer of 1998, pop singer Madonna met movie director Guy Ritchie at a luncheon thrown by Trudie Styler, the wife of rock star Sting, at the couple's fifty-two acre country estate in Wiltshire, England. Trudie had invested in Guy's forthcoming movie *Lock, Stock and Two Smoking Barrels*. Guy attended the party specifically to meet Madonna. At the time, Madonna lived with aspiring British actor Andy Bird, ten years her junior, with whom she had exchanged vows in a Kabbalah ceremony. Guy was involved in a long-term relationship with model and television presenter Robin Green, whose stepfather, banker Gilbert de Botton, had also invested in *Lock, Stock and Two Smoking Barrels*. Despite their romantic commitments to others, Madonna and Guy threw caution to the wind and had a brief love affair.

In January 1999, Madonna and Guy broke up with their respective lovers and started dating publicly. On March 19, while Madonna was in Los Angeles preparing for the Academy Awards, her former beau Andy Bird happened to meet Guy in the Met Bar in London. They talked peacefully until Andy's comments about Madonna apparently provoked Guy to punch him in the nose.

In April 2000, Madonna announced that she was pregnant with Guy's child. On August 11, two weeks before her scheduled delivery date, Madonna, diagnosed with placenta previa, began to hemorrhage. Doctors delivered the baby by emergency Caesarian section. Five days later, on her forty-second birthday, Madonna went home with her newborn baby Rocco to discover a small paper bag on the table in her bedroom. Inside she found a box containing a diamond engagement ring and a proposal note from Guy. On December 22, 2000, the couple got married—and baptized Rocco—at Skibo Castle in Scotland, with actress Gwyneth Paltrow as the maid of honor.

STRANGE ENCOUNTERS

★ Born Madonna Louise Veronica Ciccone on August 16, 1958, in Bay City, Michigan, Madonna was a cheerleader at Rochester Adams High School.

★ Guy Ritchie, born on September 10, 1968 in Hatfield, England, was raised in a seventeenth-century manor house in the English countryside near Shrewsbury, despite his claims that he grew up in poverty.

★ Madonna won a scholarship to study modern dance and drama at the University of Michigan, but dropped out in her sophomore year.

★ While trying to break into the music business in New York City, Madonna worked at a doughnut shop in Times Square.

★ On Madonna's nineteenth birthday, Elvis Presley died.

★ Guy suffers from dyslexia and dropped out of school at age fifteen, after being expelled from Strandbridge Earls School.

★ Guy worked in Greece digging sewers.

★ In 1985, Madonna started fashion trends with her unique style. She used rosaries and crosses as jewelry, black rubber typewriter bands as bracelets, and wore layers of lingerie over her clothes.

★ Madonna married actor Sean Penn on August 16, 1985. The celebrity couple was divorced four years later.

★ Guy was fired from his job as a furniture mover after he tied an antique table to the roof of his van and inadvertently drove through a low tunnel.

★ Madonna and Sean Penn starred together in the 1986 movie *Shanghai Surprise*, produced by former Beatle George Harrison. The film bombed.

★ In 1989, Pepsi hired Madonna to promote the soft drink in her video for her new album *Like a Prayer*. When the video featured images of burning crosses, murder, and racism, Pepsi broke the contract. The resulting controversy catapulted the single to #1 on the charts.

★ MTV banned three Madonna videos for lewdness: "Justify My Love," "Erotica," and "What It Feels Like For A Girl."

★ The Puerto Rican House of Representatives unanimously condemned Madonna for pulling a Puerto Rican flag between her legs during a 1993 concert.

★ In 1994, Madonna appeared on *The Late Show with David Letterman*, used the word *fuck* thirteen times, and handed a pair of her underwear to David and urged him to smell them.

★ In 1996, Madonna gave birth to a daughter named Lourdes, fathered by her fitness trainer, Carlos Leon. Madonna named the baby in tribute to her mother, who died before fulfilling her dream of visiting Lourdes, France (where the Virgin Mary reportedly appeared in 1858).

Nelson Mandela and Winnie Madikizela

In June 1957, Winnie Nomzama Madikizela, a 22-year-old social worker at Baragwanath Hospital, spotted 38-year-old lawyer and political activist Nelson Mandela walking up the steps to a court building in Johannesburg, South Africa, to conduct a case. At the time, Nelson, an organizational leader of the African National Congress and a fierce opponent of the country's apartheid system,

was on trial, along with 156 others, on charges of treason. Shortly afterwards, Winnie's friend Adelaide Tsukudi, a nurse at Baragwanath Hospital, introduced her to Nelson at a delicatessen. Infatuated with Winnie, Nelson invited her to join him for lunch the next day, ostensibly to discuss her possible participation in fund-raising efforts for the Treason Trial Defense Fund.

The following day, Nelson's friend Joe Matthews picked up Winnie and brought her to Azad's Indian restaurant, marking the beginning of her courtship with Nelson. "I was both courting her and politicizing her," recalled Nelson, in his autobiography *Long Walk to Freedom*. While Nelson never formally proposed, in June 1958, a year after they first met, he married Winnie, sixteen years his junior, at the ancestral home of her family, followed by a celebration at the Bizana town hall.

STRANGE ENCOUNTERS

★ Nelson Rolihlahla Mandela was born the eldest son of a Tembu tribal chieftain on July 18, 1918, in Umtata, South Africa. In 1940, he was expelled from University College at Fort Hare for organizing a student strike. He obtained his law degree from

Witwatersrand University and, in 1952, established the first black law practice in South Africa.

★ Winnie was born on September 26, 1934, in Bizana, South Africa, where her father worked as a school headmaster.

★ Winnie's grandfather, Chief Mazingi, had twenty-nine wives.

★ Nelson had two children with his first wife, Evelyn: Makgatho and Makaziwe.

★ After being arrested for treason in 1956, Nelson returned home from prison on bail to find himself abandoned by his first wife, who had taken his two children and all their possessions.

★ Winnie was the first black social worker hired by Baragwanath Hospital in Johannesburg, South Africa.

★ In his speech at Nelson and Winnie's wedding celebration, Winnie's father acknowledged that Nelson was married to the struggle against apartheid and advised his daughter, "If your man is a wizard, you must become a witch." In his letters to Winnie from prison, Nelson affectionately called her a witch.

★ In August 1962, Nelson was arrested again and sentenced to five years in jail for inciting a strike and traveling without proper documents. In 1964, the South African government brought additional charges against Nelson and increased his sentence to life in prison for sabotage, treason, and conspiring to overthrow the government. In prison, Nelson became an international symbol of the black struggle against white minority rule in South Africa.

★ Imprisoned on Robben Island, Nelson quarried limestone and harvested seaweed. In 1982, the government moved Nelson to Pollsmoor Prison outside Cape Town, where he spent much of the next six years in solitary confinement. His wife Winnie was allowed a thirty-minute visit with Nelson once a week.

★ In 1984, the South African government offered to free Nelson from prison on the condition that he settle in the officially designated black "homeland" of Transkei. He refused the offer and reaffirmed his allegiance to the African National Congress.

★ In 1987, Winnie began surrounding herself by a gang of boys called the Mandela United Football Club, who lived in the back of her house in Soweto and acted as vigilantes to protect her.

★ On February 11, 1990, South African president F. W. De Klerk released Nelson from prison unconditionally. Nelson, named head of the ANC after his release, began to negotiate the political future of a post-apartheid South Africa. He became the first president of a black-majority-ruled South Africa and a winner of the Nobel Peace Prize.

★ As president of South Africa, Nelson appointed Winnie to his cabinet. When evidence of Winnie's complicity in civil violence surfaced, Nelson divorced her and forced her resignation from the government.

★ In 1998, Nelson attended his eightieth birthday party with his new wife, Graça Machel, whom he had married that very day.

Karl Marx and Friedrich Engels

Karl Heinrich Marx, born in Trier, Prussia, in 1818, joined a group of radical leftist students and professors while attending the University of Berlin to oppose the Prussian government. In 1841, after obtaining a Doctorate in Philosophy from the university in Jena, Marx, unable to get a teaching position because of his opposition to the Prussian government, became a freelance journalist, creating and contributing to several radical journals. He married in 1843 and the newlywed couple moved to Paris. The following year in Paris, he met Friedrich Engels, a young German radical, who became his best friend.

Friedrich Engels, born in 1820 to a textile manufacturer in Barmen, Prussia, was a German social scientist, journalist, and professional revolutionary. In 1844, Engels, wanted by the Prussian police for his revolutionary activities, fled to Paris.

Marx and Engels collaborated on several articles and books. In 1845, Marx moved to Brussels, Belgium, and three years later moved to Cologne, Germany, where he edited the *Neue Rheinische Zeitung*, making him famous throughout Germany as an advocate of radical democratic reform. When the German revolution of 1848 failed, Marx fled to London, where he spent the rest of his life in exile. Engels had also returned to Germany for the revolution of 1848, and when the revolution collapsed, he too fled to England, where he got a job managing one of his father's factories and remained in close contact with Marx.

STRANGE ENCOUNTERS

★ Marx refused to get a steady job to earn a living, preferring a hand-to-mouth existence as a freelance writer and professional revolutionary. Engels occasionally sent Marx money to support his wife and six children.

★ Marx occasionally wrote freelance articles for newspapers, including the *New York Tribune* as a political reporter.

★ Marx suffered long periods of depression, and while greatly admired, he had few friends. His opinionated and arrogant demeanor alienated many.

★ Together, Marx and Engels wrote the books *The German Ideology, The Communist Manifesto* (originally published as a pamphlet) and several political columns.

★ Engels wrote the entire first draft of *The Communist Manifesto,* and wrote several articles published under Marx's name.

★ Engels introduced Marx to the study of economics. In return, Marx shared his knowledge of military and political affairs with Engels.

★ Engels wrote the books *The Condition of the Working Class in England* and *Herr Eugen Dühring's Revolution in Science,* which became a textbook for generations of socialists and communists.

★ Marx wrote his major work *Das Kapital* over a period of some thirty years. The first volume was published in 1867, and after Marx's death in 1883, Engels edited the second and third volumes.

★ While Marx's philosophy is often called *dialectical materialism,* a term taken from the writings of German philosopher Georg Wilhelm Friedrich Hegel, Marx never used this phrase. Engels did.

★ Marx saw all history as the struggle between the ruling and working classes. He advocated taking the means of production away from private ownership and placing it into the hands of the public to create social and economic equality.

★ Engels outlived Marx by twelve years.

★ Some scholars believe that Engels' philosophic writings after the death of Marx demonstrate a misunderstanding of Marx's ideas.

William Masters and Virginia Johnson

In 1955, gynecologist William Howell Masters, a teacher at Washington University Medical School in St. Louis, Missouri, decided to focus his studies on human sexuality. Masters had conducted groundbreaking research in hormone replacement therapy, and now he wanted to advance beyond the fallacies put forth by psychoanalyst Sigmund Freud that he felt were accepted as fact without verifiable proof. Masters used two published modern surveys of sexual behavior by Alfred C. Kinsey as springboards for his research.

Two years later, Masters decided to broaden his perspective by hiring a female research partner. He chose Virginia Eshelman Johnson, a non-degreed former student of psychology and a divorced mother of two. Rather than asking subjects questions about their sexual activities, as Kinsey did, Masters and Johnson observed sexual activity in a laboratory setting. They used surgical cameras, electrocardiographs, electroencephalograms, and serology to accurately measure the physical responses of seven hundred men and women during masturbation and intercourse. In 1964, Masters and Johnson established the Reproductive Biology Research Foundation, to treat sexual problems.

After ten years of research, Masters and Johnson published their findings in the 1966 book *Human Sexual Response*. Although intended for the medical community and written in clinical terminology, the book attracted the attention of the general public and became a runaway best seller. Masters and Johnson became the first authors to identify and describe the human sexual response cycle, present sex as a natural and healthy activity, emphasize a cooperative effort between sexual partners, and encourage each person to take responsibility for his or her own pleasure.

Despite attacks from morality groups and resistant physicians and psychologists, in 1970 Masters and Johnson published a second book, *Human Sexual Inadequacy*. The book discussed sexual dysfunction such as impotence and premature ejaculation, and how to treat them—launching the field of sex therapy.

In 1971, Masters divorced his wife Elizabeth and married his research partner Virginia Johnson.

S T R A N G E   E N C O U N T E R S

★ William Howell Masters, born on December 27, 1915, in Cleveland, Ohio, was a church-going Episcopalian and a registered Republican.

★ Virginia Eshelman Johnson, born in 1925 in Springfield, Missouri, sang with an orchestra directed by George Johnson, her first husband.

★ Masters, a graduate of Hamilton College, earned his medical degree from the University of Rochester, specializing in gynecology and obstetrics.

★ Masters' interest in studying human sexuality was fueled by Swiss researcher Simon Andre's 1758 claim that masturbation caused blindness, Elizabeth Osgood Willard's nineteenth-century assertion that an orgasm was more debilitating than a day's work in the fields, and Sigmund Freud's belief that clitorally induced pleasure probably revealed unresolved psychological problems.

★ Masters hired prostitutes to act as sexual surrogates with partners who suffered from impotence and frigidity. In 1969, he ceased using prostitutes in his studies because they failed to create appropriate sexual experiences. Masters discovered that ordinary people were willing to act as volunteer surrogates and be observed in a clinical setting.

★ In an article written for *McCall's* magazine in 1970, Masters and Johnson stated that women did not have an "equal right" to an orgasm but instead an "equal responsibility for it."

★ Masters established the American Association of Sex Education and Counselors to create strict guidelines for sex therapists and educators.

★ At a 1975 convention of the American Psychiatric Association, Masters stated that any patient seduced by a psychiatrist should charge the transgressor with rape as well as medical malpractice. The psychiatrists gave him a standing ovation.

★ In 1993, Johnson retired and divorced Masters because she wanted to spend more time with her family and friends, she said, and Masters remained too deeply absorbed in his work. A year later, Masters retired to Tucson, Arizona.

★ Masters was married three times, to Elisabeth Ellis, Virginia Johnson, and Geraldine Baker Oliver. He had two children: William and Sara (with Ellis).

★ Masters died from the complications of Parkinson's Disease in Tucson, Arizona, on February 16, 2001, at age eighty-five.

Paul McCartney and Linda Eastman

In 1967, American photographer Linda Eastman, eager to photograph the Beatles, visited the London office of the Fab Four's manager, Brian Epstein, and showed her portfolio of photographs of rock musicians to Epstein's assistant, Peter Brown, who had previously met her backstage in New York at the Fillmore East concert hall. "I let her in on the Sergeant Pepper session," recalled Brown, "which was a big thing because only fourteen photographers were allowed from the whole world's press."

Soon afterwards, Linda, a divorcée with a five-year-old daughter, ran into Brown one night when he was with Beatle Paul McCartney and other rock musicians at London's Bag O' Nails club. He introduced her to Paul, who was romantically involved with actress Jane Asher at the time. "That was it," Brown recalled. "The two of them just went off together."

On Christmas Day 1967, Paul and Asher announced their engagement at a McCartney family party. In May 1968, Paul flew to New York with fellow Beatle John Lennon to announce the launch of Apple records. Linda, attending the launch party and egged on by her journalist friend Lilian Roxon, handed her telephone number to Paul. They met at the New York apartment of Brian Epstein's assistant, Nat Weiss, and later in Los Angeles.

A few weeks after returning to London, Paul broke off his engagement to Jane Asher. He telephoned Linda and invited her to move in with him at his home on Cavenish Avenue. After meeting Linda's daughter, Heather, he invited her to live with him, too.

On March 11, 1969, Apple's Press Office issued a press release that Paul McCartney, the last eligible Beatle, planned to marry Linda Eastman the next day in London, at Marylebone Register Office.

Linda was three-months pregnant.

STRANGE ENCOUNTERS

★ James Paul McCartney was born on June 18, 1942, in Liverpool, England.

★ Linda Louise Eastman, born on September 24, 1941, in New York, New York, was raised in Scarsdale, New York.

★ Linda was not related to George Eastman, the founder of the Eastman-Kodak Company. Her father, New York lawyer Lee Eastman, changed his last name from Epstein to disguise his Jewish identity.

★ Linda's mother, Louise Linder, related to the founders of Linder's department stores, died in an airplane crash when Linda was eighteen. Paul's mother, Mary McCartney, died from breast cancer when Paul was fourteen years old.

★ Linda attended the same college as Yoko Ono: Sarah Lawrence College.

★ Linda met her first husband, geologist Mel See, Jr., while attending the University of Arizona in Tucson. Mel committed suicide in March 2000 at the age of sixty-two.

★ Linda began her photography career as an assistant on *Town and Country* magazine.

★ Linda dated Mick Jagger, Jim Morrison, Jimi Hendrix, Steve Winwood, Eric Burdon, Neil Young, and Warren Beatty.

★ In late 1968, Linda took Paul home to New York to meet her family. Linda's father Lee and brother John, partners together in the law firm Eastman & Eastman, showed Paul their elegant and efficiently run Fifth Avenue law offices. When Paul returned to London, he recommended that the Beatles hire the Eastmans as advisers to Apple. The Beatles, who had been without a manager since the death of Brian Epstein in 1967, hired the Eastmans. Then John, George, and Ringo hired the Rolling Stones' manager, Allan Klein, as an adviser as well—creating an enormous rift between themselves and Paul, who did not wish to be represented by Klein.

★ Linda inspired Paul to write the songs "I Will," "Lovely Linda," "Maybe I'm Amazed," and "My Love."

★ Linda, a member of Paul's band Wings, played on nearly all of Paul's albums and cowrote many songs.

★ Linda and Paul lived on a farm in Scotland, where Linda did the cooking and cleaning.

★ Paul played all the instruments on his 1970 album *McCartney* and his 1980 album *McCartney II*.

★ In 1980, Paul was arrested in Tokyo, Japan, for marijuana possession and spent ten days in a Japanese prison. He claimed these were the only nights he ever spent separated from Linda during their marriage.

★ An animal rights activist and outspoken vegetarian, Linda wrote best-selling vegetarian cookbooks and launched a highly successful vegetarian food business.

★ Paul and Linda had three children together: Mary, Stella, and James—whom they raised with Linda's daughter, Heather (adopted by Paul).

★ In 1997, Queen Elizabeth II knighted Paul.

★ In 1998, Linda died from breast cancer.

★ The New York Police Department made Paul an honorary detective in honor of the benefit Concert for New York he organized in April 2002 for the victims of the September 11, 2001, terrorist attack on the World Trade Center.

Marilyn Monroe and Arthur Miller

O n January 16, 1951, director Elia Kazan brought 33-year-old playwright Arthur Miller to the Twentieth Century Fox lot in Los Angeles. Kazan had directed Arthur's hit play, *Death of a Salesman*, on Broadway, and he and Arthur planned to turn the playwright's screenplay, *The Hook*, into their first film together. They visited director Harmon Jones on the set of *As Young as You Feel* to meet a 24-year-old actress named Marilyn Monroe, recommended to Kazan by Hollywood agent Charles Feldman (at whose home Kazan and Arthur were staying as houseguests).

Jones was having serious difficulties with Marilyn on the set. A month earlier, her agent, Johnny Hyde, had died from a heart attack in Palm Springs, where Marilyn had refused to join him for the weekend. The day after Hyde's funeral, Marilyn, blaming herself for her agent's death, attempted suicide by swallowing a bottle full of barbiturates. Kazan and Arthur watched a depressed Marilyn struggle through a scene. To buoy her spirits, they invited her to join them for dinner in the studio commissary. She turned them down. But then, realizing that Kazan was casting the film *Viva Zapata!*, Marilyn tracked down the director and Arthur in the commissary and joined them. Soon she was spending nights with the married Kazan in his room at Charles Feldman's house, where Arthur, a married man with two children back home in Brooklyn Heights, slept in a room down the hall.

On Friday, January 26, Feldman hosted a party at his home. Kazan, planning to be elsewhere that evening with another woman, asked Arthur to escort Marilyn to the party. Marilyn quickly realized that Kazan had passed her along to Arthur. Infatuated,

Arthur told her about his marital problems, danced intimately with her, and drove her home—yet made no attempt to sleep with her. The next day, torn by guilt over his feelings for Marilyn, Arthur insisted upon returning home to Brooklyn Heights, ostensibly to work on the script for *The Hook*. Kazan and Marilyn took Arthur to the airport. Arthur wrote frequent letters to Marilyn, but insisted he wasn't the man for her.

Four years later, after starring in the 1955 movie *The Seven Year Itch*, Marilyn left her husband, Joe DiMaggio, and moved to New York City to study acting with Lee Strasberg at the Actors Studio, determined to shed her sexpot image. Two new friends from the Studio, Eli Wallach and Anne Jackson, invited Marilyn to accompany them to a party, where she ran into Arthur Miller for the first time since January 27, 1951. Arthur, still married to Mary and still attracted to Marilyn, left the party without asking for her phone number at the Waldorf Towers.

A few days later, Marilyn convinced her friend Sam Shaw to wander around Brooklyn Heights with her to take pictures, in the hope of running into Arthur. Shaw took her to the apartment of Arthur's best friend, poet and playwright Norman Rosten. Marilyn began cultivating a friendship with Rosten and his wife Hedda. Two weeks later, Arthur called Paula Strasberg, the wife of director Lee Strasberg, to get Marilyn's telephone number. Soon after, he and Marilyn were meeting frequently at her apartment on the twenty-seventh floor of the Waldorf Towers, beginning a long love affair.

STRANGE ENCOUNTERS

★ Arthur Miller was born on October 17, 1915, in New York, New York.

★ Marilyn Monroe was born Norma Jean Mortenson on June 1, 1926, in Los Angeles, California.

★ As a journalism major at the University of Michigan, Arthur worked as a reporter and night editor on the student newspaper, *The Michigan Daily*.

★ Arthur was exempted from military service during World War II due to a football injury.

★ In 1955, Arthur's wife learned of his affair with Marilyn and threw him out of their house.

★ When Arthur took Marilyn to meet his parents, they fed her two bowls of matzah-ball soup. When she declined a third bowl, Arthur's father asked her if she liked the soup. "Oh, I just love it," Marilyn replied. "But gee, isn't there any other part of a matzah you can eat?"

★ Arthur divorced his first wife, Mary Slattery, on June 11, 1956, in Reno, Nevada, after establishing residency in Nevada for the required six weeks. While waiting for his divorce, Arthur met a group of cowboys who inspired the short story "The Misfits," which he later adapted into a screenplay for a movie starring Marilyn Monroe.

★ On June 29, 1956, Marilyn married Arthur at the Westchester County Court House in White Plains, New York. Two days later, they were married again in a Jewish ceremony at the home of Arthur's agent, Kay Brown, in South Salem, New York. Lee Strasberg gave the bride away. Marilyn had converted to Judaism.

★ When she married Arthur, Marilyn had no veil to match her beige wedding dress so she dyed a white veil in coffee.

★ In 1957, Congress found Arthur guilty of contempt for refusing to reveal to the House Un-American Activities Committee the names of members of a literary circle suspected of Communist affiliations. A year later, a U.S. Court of Appeals reversed the conviction.

★ Marilyn, suffering from endometriosis, miscarried a child in 1958 and again in 1960.

★ In November 1960, Clark Gable, Marilyn's costar in the movie *The Misfits*, written by Arthur Miller, suffered a fatal heart attack—the day after filming ended. Marilyn, undergoing psychotherapy and taking tranquilizers, blamed herself for Gable's death, for bringing her problems to the film set. Two months later, she divorced Arthur Miller in Juarez, Mexico.

★ On August 5, 1962, Marilyn's housekeeper found the 36-year-old star nude and lying face down on her bed with a phone in her hand in her Brentwood home, the victim of an overdose of sedatives.

★ In her will, Marilyn bequeathed 75 percent of her 1.6 million-dollar estate to Lee Strasberg, her acting coach, and 25 percent to Dr. Marianne Kris, her psychoanalyst. A trust fund provided her mother, Gladys Baker Eley, with five thousand dollars a year.

★ In 1995, the United States Postal Service issued a thirty-two-cent commemorative postage stamp picturing Marilyn Monroe.

★ Arthur has been married three times, to Mary Grace Slattery, Marilyn Monroe, and Inge Morath.

Demi Moore and Bruce Willis

In August 1987, actress Demi Moore attended a screening of the movie *Stakeout*, starring her boyfriend Emilio Estevez. Demi had met Emilio three years earlier on the set of the movie *St. Elmo's Fire*. "Estevez was definitely my first love," she told *Cosmopolitan*. At one point, they got engaged and sent out wedding invitations, but then Demi called off the wedding. The couple remained romantically involved.

At the *Stakeout* screening, Demi met actor Bruce Willis, then starring in the television detective series *Moonlighting*. Both Demi and Bruce had struggled to overcome self-destructive behavior. In order to play a cocaine addict, in the 1995 movie *St. Elmo's Fire*, the studio required Demi to sign a contract stipulating that she would cease using alcohol and drugs, prompting her to turn her life around. A few days after meeting Demi, Bruce threw a raucous, three-day party at his home over Memorial Day weekend, resulting in his arrest on charges of disturbing the peace and assaulting a police officer who had shown up at his door to quell the noise. Police dropped the charges after Bruce agreed to apologize to his neighbors.

Soon after meeting Bruce, Demi dumped Emilio and began seeing Bruce almost daily. Four months later on November 21, 1987, Demi Moore and Bruce Willis were married in a small ceremony in Las Vegas, Nevada, later to be married again before friends and family by singer/minister Little Richard.

STRANGE ENCOUNTERS

★ Bruce Willis, born Walter Bruce Willis on March 19, 1955, in Idar-Oberstein, West Germany, grew up in Penns Grove, New Jersey, and stammered as a child.

★ Demi Moore was born Demetria Gene Guynes on November 11, 1962 in Roswell, New Mexico. Her father left her mother before Demi was born, and her stepfather, Danny Guynes, committed suicide.

★ As a child, Demi wore a patch over her left eye following an operation to fix her crossed eyes.

★ Demi dropped out of high school at age sixteen to work as a pin-up girl.

★ In high school, Bruce was elected student council president, then expelled for three months during his senior year for his involvement in what he later called "the annual riot, the black-white anti-human-relations fest."

★ At age eighteen Demi married rock musician Freddy Moore. The marriage lasted four years.

★ Bruce attended Montclair State College in Montclair, New Jersey, and worked as a security guard at the construction site for a large nuclear plant.

★ While trying to break into acting, Bruce worked as a bartender in New York City. A casting director patronizing the bar liked Bruce's personality and cast him as a bartender in a movie.

★ In 1982, Demi made her television debut at age nineteen as Jackie Templeton on the soap opera *General Hospital*.

★ Demi was chosen as one of three finalists for the lead role in the 1983 movie *Flashdance*. The producers, unable to decide among the final three, showed the audition tapes to a focus group of some fifty men and asked them which woman they most wanted to have sex with. Actress Jennifer Beals won by a landslide.

★ In 1987, Bruce's recording of the song "Respect Yourself" reached #5 on the charts.

★ In 1991, Demi, then seven-months pregnant, posed nude for the cover of *Vanity Fair* magazine. In 1992, she again posed nude for *Vanity Fair*, this time wearing body paint that resembled a man's suit.

★ Demi hired three cameramen to videotape the birth of her first child.

★ Demi had her breasts enlarged to star in the movie *Striptease*.

★ In 1996, Bruce appeared on *Late Show with David Letterman* to promote Demi's movie *Striptease* by doing his own striptease act. Demi also took her clothes off on the show.

★ Bruce and Demi have three daughters together: Rumer, Scout, and Tallulah.

★ Bruce and Demi starred together in two movies: *Mortal Thoughts* and *Beavis and Butt-head Do America*.

★ On October 18, 2000, Bruce and Demi divorced after twelve years of marriage.

Mary Tyler Moore and Grant Tinker

In 1961, Grant Tinker, a 35-year-old advertising executive with Benton and Bowles, met 24-year-old Mary Tyler Moore during the filming of the pilot for *The Dick Van Dyke Show.* Mary has no recollection of that meeting. "I was so focused on the show, and the high it produced, I don't remember meeting anyone," she wrote in her autobiography.

Grant, handling the advertising for sponsor Procter & Gamble, occasionally visited the set of the show. When a newspaper column reported that Mary had ended her six-year marriage to Ocean Spray cranberry products salesman Richard Meeker, Grant reintroduced himself, expressed sympathy for her failed marriage, and invited her to dinner. She turned him down, saying she needed time before seeing anyone. Undaunted, Grant invited her to join him in Palm Springs for the weekend. Mary wanted to go, but again, she turned him down.

A few days later, Mary, asked by the show's publicist, agreed to go to New York City during the next hiatus from filming *The Dick Van Dyke Show* to speak with reporters. Grant, based in New York and having suggested the publicity trip, called Mary and invited her to have dinner with him when she came to New York and to accompany him to see the Broadway play *How to Succeed in Business Without Really Trying.*

"We fell in love that night," recalled Mary, "and committed ourselves to each other." Before they could get married, however, Mary had to finalize her divorce, just as Grant, separated from his wife and four children, had to finalize his. And their relationship would have to remain long distance. Grant had just been offered a job in programming for NBC on the East Coast. A few months later, Grant became Vice President of Programming for the West Coast and moved to Los Angeles. On June 1, 1962, Mary married Grant in Las Vegas.

STRANGE ENCOUNTERS

★ Grant Almerin Tinker, born on January 11, 1925, in Stamford, Connecticut, served as chairman of NBC from 1981 to 1986.

★ Mary Tyler Moore was born on December 29, 1936, in Brooklyn, New York.

★ In 1955, Mary made her first television appearance as "Happy Hotpoint," the Hotpoint Appliance elf, in commercials aired during *The Ozzie and Harriet Show.*

★ On David Letterman's show, Mary claimed that she and others on *The Dick Van Dyke Show* jokingly gave Dick Van Dyke the nickname Penis Von Lesbian, as a crude wordplay on his name.

★ In the 1969 movie *Change of Habit,* Elvis Presley stars as a doctor who runs an inner-city health clinic, aided by a nun played by Mary Tyler Moore.

★ In 1969, Mary, after experiencing a miscarriage, was diagnosed with Type 1 Diabetes, requiring that she inject herself with insulin several times a day.

★ In 1969, Mary and Grant founded MTM Enterprises and produced the television series *The Mary Tyler Moore Show, Lou Grant, Hill Street Blues, St.* *Elsewhere, The Bob Newhart Show,* and *WKRP in Cincinnati.* They sold the company in 1990.

★ Mary had one child: Richie (with her first husband Richard Meeker). Richie was born three months before Mary's forty-year-old mother gave birth to her last child. In 1980, Richie, a recovering alcoholic and cocaine addict, accidentally shot himself at age twenty-four.

★ Grant has four children: Mark, Michael, Jodie, and John (with his first wife, Ruth Byerly).

★ In her autobiography, *After All,* Mary claims that during her marriage to Grant she had an affair with a married man while shooting the 1980 movie *Ordinary People* on location in Chicago. Mary and Grant divorced in 1981.

★ In 1983, Mary Tyler Moore married her third husband, Dr. Robert Levine.

★ On May 8, 2002, the city of Minneapolis unveiled a bronze statue of Mary Richards tossing her hat into the air at the intersection where the opening of *The Mary Tyler Moore Show* was originally filmed. At the unveiling ceremony, Moore tossed her hat into the air.

Ozzie Nelson and Harriet Hilliard

In 1930, while studying law at Rutgers University, former star quarterback Ozzie Nelson formed a dance band to play for the summer season at Glen Island Casino in New Jersey. The public's enthusiasm for the band prompted Ozzie to drop out of law school and concentrate solely on his music career. Soon, saxophonist Ozzie Nelson and his orchestra were playing the best clubs on the East Coast. Two years later, Peggy Sue Snyder, having sung and danced on the vaudeville circuit in New York under the stage name Harriet Hilliard, joined the band as vocalist, becoming the second female vocalist ever featured in a big band. (Mildred Bailey, with Paul Whiteman, was the first.)

Ozzie and Harriet's musical partnership blossomed into a romantic partnership as well, and the couple got married on October 8, 1935. The couple gave birth to their first child, David, in 1936, followed by Ricky in 1940. That same year, Harriet made her movie debut as Randolph Scott's love interest in the Fred Astaire-Ginger Rogers musical *Follow the Fleet*. Although critics raved over her performance, Harriet carefully selected future film roles to avoid being separated from Ozzie.

Meanwhile, Ozzie Nelson and His Orchestra recorded many albums, appeared in several films, and performed on radio. In 1941, the Nelsons moved to Hollywood, where Ozzie became bandleader for comedian Red Skelton's radio program. Harriet sang on the show and played several roles. In 1944, CBS let Ozzie and Harriet create their own radio show, *The Adventures of Ozzie and Harriet*. Ozzie and Harriet played themselves. Child actors played the roles of their sons David and Ricky. Five years into the show, the real David and Ricky came in to play themselves. The Nelson family also starred as themselves in the 1950 movie *Here Come The Nelsons*. In 1952, the Nelson family moved to television with their own sitcom.

STRANGE ENCOUNTERS

★ Ozzie Nelson was born Oswald George Nelson on March 20, 1906, in Jersey City, New Jersey.

★ Harriet, born Peggy Lou Snyder on July 18, 1909, in Des Moines, Iowa, to Hazel and Roy Hilliard Snyder, used the alliterative stage name Harriet Hilliard when she was hired as a vocalist by bandleader Ozzie Nelson.

★ At age thirteen, Ozzie became the youngest person to become an Eagle Scout. The modern-day requirements for attaining Eagle Scout status inhibit anyone from breaking Ozzie's record.

★ After marrying Ozzie, Harriet continued using her stage name, Harriet Hilliard, throughout her film career.

★ Ozzie and Harriet starred together in the movies *Sweetheart of the Campus, Strictly in the Groove, Honeymoon Lodge, Ozzie Nelson and His Orchestra, Hi Good Lookin'!, Take It Big,* and *Here Come the Nelsons.*

★ Utilizing his legal training, Ozzie negotiated a non-cancellable ten-year contract with ABC, guaranteeing the Nelsons a base salary for ten years regardless of whether or not they worked, protecting them from sponsor or network interference.

★ On *The Adventures of Ozzie and Harriet,* Ozzie never seemed to go to work or to have a specific occupation. Ozzie believed that this vagary enabled viewers to more easily identify with his character. He also claimed that each episode took place over the weekend.

★ Ozzie and Harriet were the only couple allowed a double bed on a television show—until *The Brady Bunch* premiered in 1969.

★ As David and Ricky grew up, they became teenage heartthrobs, especially when Ricky began to sing rock 'n' roll tunes on the show. He recorded the hit singles "I'm Walkin'," "Travelin' Man," and "Poor Little Fool."

★ When David and Rick each got married in real life, their wives, June and Kris, became characters on the television show.

★ On *The Adventures of Ozzie and Harriet,* Ricky's wife Kristin gave birth to their daughter Tracy three months prematurely. In reality, Kristin was three months pregnant when she married Ricky.

★ *The Adventures of Ozzie and Harriet* holds the record as television's longest-running sitcom, lasting fourteen years and 435 episodes.

★ Ozzie acted as head writer, script supervisor, producer, and editor on all 435 episodes of *The Adventures of Ozzie and Harriet.*

★ In 1973, Ozzie and Harriet starred in the short-lived television series *Ozzie's Girls,* in which they rented out Ricky and David's room to two female college students.

★ Ricky Nelson died in a plane crash in 1985.

Paul Newman and Joanne Woodward

In 1952, 27-year-old Paul Newman went to meet with his agent Maynard Morris at the offices of MCA. While there, he got into a conversation with another agent, John Foreman, and the two men lost track of the time. When Foreman escorted Paul to the lobby to show him out, he realized he had kept one of his own clients waiting impatiently in the reception area. That person was 22-year-old model and actress Joanne Woodward, a native of Thomasville, Georgia.

Foreman apologized profusely to Joanne and, in an attempt to make amends, introduced her to the handsome Paul Newman. Neither Joanne nor Paul was particularly impressed. Paul was married to Jackie Witte, a Wisconsin native and graduate of Lawrence University whom he had met while the two were costarring in *Dark of the Moon* in stock theater in Woodstock, Illinois, in 1949. The couple had a baby boy.

Several weeks later Paul was cast as Jake (a gas station attendant with one line) and an understudy for the lead role in a new Broadway play called *Picnic*. During rehearsals he recognized the actress hired as an understudy for two of the female roles. He couldn't place where he had seen her before, until the woman—Joanne—refreshed his memory about the incident at his agent's office.

The two understudies rehearsed for the lead roles together and worked on the slow jitterbug that created the most sexual heat in the play. During this time, Joanne fell deeply in love with Paul, but never confessed her feelings. The two became close friends, and Joanne became determined to win Paul from his wife.

In an attempt to arouse Paul's feelings for her, Joanne got engaged to playwright James Costigan, but the shrewd trick failed to work. By now Paul had three children with Jackie and a home in Queens Village, Long Island. In 1956, Joanne got engaged to a second fiancé, but when Paul failed to be irked by the engagement, Joanne broke it off. Finally, Joanne confided her feelings to Paul. He cherished their relationship, he said, but would never leave his wife and children.

In 1956, after winning an Academy Award for her role in *The Three Faces of Eve*, Joanne was cast to costar with Paul in *The Long Hot Summer*. Paul's wife, outraged that her husband would be spending endless hours on the set with Joanne, took her children and moved back home to her mother's in Wisconsin. On the set, Paul tried to keep his relationship with Joanne professional, but Joanne inflamed his jealousy by dating actor Timmy Everett. After filming ended, Paul, Joanne, writer Gore Vidal, and his companion Howard Austen moved into a house in Malibu. Joanne was soon engaged to Gore Vidal and pregnant with Paul's child, prompting Paul to ask Jackie for a divorce. In January 1958, Paul and Joanne got married in Las Vegas. While honeymooning in London, Joanne had a miscarriage.

STRANGE ENCOUNTERS

★ Born on January 26, 1925, to a Jewish father and a Christian Scientist mother, Paul Leonard Newman was raised as a Christian Scientist yet visited doctors for medical checkups.

★ Despite his magnetic blue eyes, Paul is color-blind.

★ Nine-year-old Joanne convinced her mother to take her to Atlanta for the 1939 premiere of *Gone With The Wind*. During a parade to celebrate the movie, Joanne leaped into a limousine carrying the actor Laurence Olivier and sat in his lap.

★ In the Shaker Heights High School production of *Hamlet*, Paul failed to get the role of First Gravedigger and instead worked as stage manager.

★ During his years as an English major at Kenyon College, Paul rented a store in the college town and opened a laundry, offering free beer to his customers. He sold the successful business in his senior year.

★ Before he became an actor, Paul ran his family's sporting goods store in Cleveland, Ohio.

★ Paul and his first wife Jackie Witte had three children together: Scott (who died of a drug overdose in 1978), Susan, and Stephanie. With Joanne, Paul has three daughters: Nell, Clea, and Melissa.

★ Paul and Joanne have costarred in ten movies: *The Long Hot Summer, Rally 'Round the Flag, Boys!, From the Terrace, Paris Blues, A New Kind of Love, Winning, WUSA, The Drowning Pool, Harry and Son*, and *Mr. & Mrs. Bridge*.

★ Years after their divorce, Paul's first wife Jackie Witte played a bar owner in the 1966 movie *Harper*, starring her ex-husband Paul. Her name in the credits reads Jacqueline de Wit.

★ In the 1980s, Paul launched his own line of food products under the brand-name Newman's Own.

Richard M. Nixon and Thelma "Pat" Ryan

As an undergraduate at Whittier College, Richard Milhous Nixon took part in several theater productions. In 1938, after graduating from Duke University Law School and becoming a partner in Whittier's oldest law firm, Dick played a prosecuting attorney in the local amateur theater group's production of *The Night of January 16th* by Ayn Rand. A few months later, he auditioned for a part in the group's production of *The Dark Tower* by George S. Kaufman and Alexander Woollcott. That night he noticed an attractive young newcomer named Pat Ryan, a new teacher at Whittier High School. "For me," recalled Dick, "it was love at first sight."

Dick asked a friend to introduce him to Pat. He offered Pat a ride home, and before dropping her off, asked her out on a date. Pat insisted that she was too busy. "You shouldn't say that, because someday I am going to marry you," replied Dick. In his memoirs, Dick recalled, "We all laughed because it seemed so unlikely at that time. But I wonder whether it was a sixth sense that prompted me to make such an impetuous statement."

Dick and Pat began dating regularly. In May 1940, Dick sent Pat a basket of flowers with a boxed engagement ring set among the flowers. On June 21, 1940, 27-year-old Dick married 28-year-old Pat at the Mission Inn in Riverside, California. For their honeymoon, the newlywed couple drove through Mexico for two weeks, with a trunk full of canned food to keep expenses to a minimum.

STRANGE ENCOUNTERS

★ Richard Milhous Nixon was born on January 9, 1913, on his father's lemon farm in Yorba Linda, California.

★ Thelma Catherine Ryan was born on March 16, 1912, in a mining camp at Ely, Nevada. Her father nicknamed her Pat because she was born on the eve of St. Patrick's Day.

★ At age ten, Dick worked part time as a bean picker. As a teenager, he worked as a janitor at a public swimming pool.

★ When her mother died of cancer, thirteen-year-old Pat began to cook and keep house for her father and two brothers.

★ Before Pat's graduation from high school, her father contracted silicosis, compelling Pat to postpone her plans to attend college so she could stay home and take care of him.

★ After the death of Pat's father, an elderly couple hired Pat to drive them in their car across the country to New York City.

★ In New York City, Pat took a job as a secretary and enrolled in a course at Seton Hospital to become an X-ray technician.

★ As a freshman at Whittier College, Dick founded and served as the first president of a social club named the Orthogonian Society. Nicknamed the "Square Shooters," the group dedicated itself to "The Four B's: Beans, Brawn, Brain, and Bowels." Dick wrote the group's constitution and song.

★ During Prohibition, Dick visited a San Francisco speakeasy where he drank his first alcoholic beverage—a Tom Collins.

★ Dick ran for president of the student body at Whittier College on the platform that dances should be allowed on campus.

★ At Whittier College, Dick played on the football team, but "the only times I got to play were in the last few minutes of a game that was already safely won or hopelessly lost."

★ To work herself through UCLA, Pat worked as an extra in the movies *Becky Sharp* and *Small Town Girl.*

★ As a law student at Duke University, Dick lived in a primitive cabin, ate a Milky Way candy bar each morning for breakfast, shaved each morning in the men's room at the law library, and took a shower every afternoon in the gym after playing handball.

★ In 1952, in a television address defending himself against allegations that he had used an eighteen-thousand-dollar campaign fund for personal purposes, Dick said, "Pat doesn't have a mink coat. But she does have a respectable Republican cloth coat." He also vowed to keep one gift that had been given to his daughters: a cocker spaniel named Checkers.

★ In December 1970, Elvis Presley, concerned with drug abuse among young people in America, dropped in unannounced at the White House and asked to meet with President Richard M. Nixon. The President met with Elvis and made him an honorary federal marshall for the Drug Enforcement Agency. In 1977, Elvis, heavily dependent on amphetamines and barbiturates, died of a heart attack.

★ In July 1973, a Senate committee investigating the 1972 Watergate break-in learned that President Richard M. Nixon had secretly made tape recordings of conversations in the Oval Office. When the House of Representatives began steps to impeach him, the President handed over the tapes to United States District Court Judge John J. Sirica—with three key conversations erased, including an eighteen-and-a-half-minute gap that the President claimed had been accidentally erased by his secretary Rosemary Woods.

★ President Richard Nixon was not impeached. He resigned from office after the House Judiciary Committee recommended three articles of impeachment against him, but before the House of Representatives began impeachment proceedings.

Annie Oakley and Frank Butler

Born the sixth of eight children in a log cabin on the Ohio frontier, fourteen-year-old Annie Oakley used her dead father's Kentucky rifle to shoot rabbits and quail to support her family, who were on the verge of losing their farm. A self-taught marksman, Annie sold the game in the nearby town of Greenville and to hotels and restaurants in northern Ohio, earning enough money to pay off the entire mortgage on her family's farm by the time she was fifteen years old. "Oh, how my heart leaped with joy," she recalled in her autobiography, "as I handed the money to mother and told her that I had saved enough to pay it off!"

Annie achieved notoriety for her uncanny ability to shoot an animal in the head, leaving the meat untouched by shotgun pellets or bullets. In 1876, one of Annie's customers, a Cincinnati hotel owner, invited the sixteen-year-old girl to compete in a shooting contest against vaudeville sharpshooter Frank E. Butler. Frank, on tour with several other marksmen, always garnered publicity for his shows by challenging local shooters to a contest, claiming that he could outshoot "anything living, save Carver or Bogardus." Upon learning that a young woman paid the fifty-dollar entry fee, Frank reportedly laughed. In the contest, Frank fired twenty-four out of twenty-five shots into their mark. Annie hit the mark with all twenty-five of her shots, winning the contest and Frank's heart as well.

The two sharpshooters began a romantic relationship that resulted in marriage on August 23, 1876. Annie became Frank's assistant in his traveling shooting act. Recognizing Annie as a far more talented gunslinger, Frank eventually relinquished the limelight to his wife, becoming her assistant and personal manager. Annie and Frank traveled across the United States giving shooting exhibitions with their dog, George, as part of the act. In 1885, they joined Buffalo Bill's Wild West Show, run by the legendary frontiersman and showman Buffalo Bill Cody, who featured Annie as his star attraction for the next seventeen years.

★ Annie Oakley, born Phoebe Anne Oakley Moses on August 13, 1860, in a log cabin in Patterson Township, Ohio, never received a formal education.

★ After her father died of pneumonia, Annie lived at the county poor farm.

★ When Annie and Frank first appeared in a show together on May 1, 1882, Annie used the stage name Annie Oakley. In private, she remained Mrs. Frank Butler.

★ Sitting Bull adopted Annie to replace a daughter he lost after the battle of Little Big Horn.

★ Annie, nicknamed "Little Sure Shot" by Sitting Bull, stood only five feet tall and was also known as "The Peerless Lady Wing-Shot" due to her superb marksmanship.

★ Using a .22 rifle, Annie shot 4,772 glass balls out of five thousand tossed into the air in a single day.

★ Annie could shoot a gun and hit a playing card with the thin edge facing her.

★ She could also hit a falling playing card, puncturing it five or six times before it touched the ground. At ninety feet, Annie could shoot a dime tossed in midair.

★ Free tickets with holes punched in them came to be called "Annie Oakleys."

★ At the request of the German Crown Prince Wilhelm II, Annie shot a cigarette from his mouth.

★ Annie died of natural causes on November 3, 1926. Frank died less than three weeks later of natural causes on November 21.

★ The musical *Annie Get Your Gun,* with music and lyrics by Irving Berlin, portrayed the life and times of Annie Oakley and included such memorable hit songs as "There's No Business Like Show Business" and "Anything You Can Do." Ethel Merman starred as the original Annie.

★ Barbara Stanwyck starred as Annie Oakley and Preston Foster was Frank Butler in the 1935 movie *Annie Oakley*.

★ The 1950 movie version of *Annie Get Your Gun* stars Betty Hutton as Annie Oakley and Howard Keel as Frank.

★ Actress Gil Davis, having costarred in nearly twenty movies with Gene Autry, starred as Annie Oakley in the television series *Annie Oakley,* which depicted Annie living in her hometown of Diablo with her kid brother, Tagg.

Georgia O'Keeffe and Alfred Stieglitz

In 1915, while teaching art at Columbia College in Columbia, South Carolina, 28-year-old Georgia O'Keeffe, determined to develop her own unique style, created a series of abstract charcoal drawings. She mailed some of these drawings to her close friend and former classmate Anita Pollitzer in New York City, on the condition that Anita not show the drawings to anyone else.

Impressed by the drawings, Anita immediately broke her promise and, on January 1, 1916, brought the drawings to internationally renowned photographer and art impresario Alfred Stieglitz, owner of the avant-garde New York gallery 291. Alfred admired the powerful erotic imagery in the drawings and held on to them. When Anita told Georgia what she had done, Georgia expressed her gratitude and began corresponding with Alfred.

That spring, West Texas State Normal College in Canyon, Texas, hired Georgia to train future art teachers, on the condition that she first return to New York City to take a required course at Teacher's College. While living in Manhattan, Georgia, busy with classes and family problems, did not contact Alfred.

In June, while having lunch in a cafeteria at Columbia University, Georgia learned from a fellow student that a notice on a bulletin board advertised a showing of her work at the 291 gallery. Without notifying her or requesting her permission, Alfred had put ten of her charcoal drawings on exhibit in his gallery alongside the work of two other artists.

Incensed, Georgia raced downtown and stormed into the gallery to demand that Alfred take down her work immediately. Alfred, however, was not there. He was on jury duty until the following week. A week later, Georgia returned to the gallery, found 51-year-old Alfred alone in the gallery, curtly introduced herself, and demanded that he remove her drawings from the walls—unaware of the huge influence he wielded in the art world. Alfred persuaded Georgia to let the artwork stay up, beginning their long professional alliance.

In 1917, Georgia became romantically involved with Alfred, who began taking nude photographs of her. At the time, Alfred had been married for thirty-one years to Emmeline Obermeyer, the sister of his business partner, Joe Obermeyer. In 1924, Alfred divorced his wife and married Georgia on December 11 in Cliffside Park, New Jersey.

STRANGE ENCOUNTERS

★ Alfred Stieglitz, born on January 1, 1864, in Hoboken, New Jersey, was 23 years older than Georgia O'Keeffe.

★ Georgia O'Keeffe, born on November 15, 1887, in Sun Prairie, Wisconsin, was the second of seven children.

★ After studying at the Art Institute of Chicago and at the Art Students League in New York, Georgia won the 1908 William Merritt Chase prize for her untitled oil painting of a dead rabbit with a copper pot. She then quit art altogether, convinced she could never achieve any distinction in the art world.

★ In 1909, Georgia worked in Chicago, drawing advertisements for lace and embroidery.

★ Before meeting Alfred, Georgia taught art to Mexican children in public schools in Amarillo, Texas.

★ In the spring of 1918, Alfred offered to support Georgia financially if she would move to New York and paint. Shortly after she moved to New York, she moved in with Alfred. They divided their time between New York City and the Stieglitz family estate at Lake George, New York. In 1929, Georgia spent the first of many summers painting in Taos, New Mexico, whose stunning vistas and stark landscapes inspired her work.

★ From 1923 until his death in 1946, Alfred worked diligently to promote Georgia and her work, organizing annual exhibitions of her art at galleries.

★ Art critics claimed that Georgia's close-up views of skulls and flowers contained overt female sexual imagery. Georgia emphatically denied any sexual representations in her work.

★ After Alfred's death, Georgia moved to New Mexico, where she grew her own vegetables and ground wheat flour by hand for bread.

★ Georgia continued to work until the late 1970s, when failing eyesight forced her to abandon painting. She then became a three-dimensional artist, producing objects in clay until her health failed in 1984. She died two years later, at the age of ninety-eight.

Aristotle Onassis and Jacqueline Kennedy

In August 1955, Jackie and Jack Kennedy stayed at the home of Karim Aga Khan IV, the Château de l'Horison, in Antibes in the South of France, then a mecca for the jet set. Docked nearby was Greek shipping tycoon Aristotle Onassis, who often entertained world leaders and celebrities on his yacht, the *Christina*. Upon learning that Onassis' onboard guests included former British Prime Minister Winston Churchill, Jack arranged to meet his hero. One evening, Jack and Jackie went for a drink aboard the *Christina*, and Jackie met Onassis for the first time. While Jack, dressed in a white dinner jacket, spoke with Churchill, Onassis took note of Jackie's grace and beauty. "She's got a carnal soul," he purportedly told his friend Costa Gratsos.

After the death of Jackie's infant son Patrick, Jackie's younger sister Lee, then having an affair with Onassis, persuaded him to invite Jackie on a cruise on the *Christina* to help buoy her spirits. Jack agreed to let Jackie go—with his Secretary of Commerce, Franklin D. Roosevelt, Jr., and his wife Suzanne as chaperones. Jackie also invited Princess Irene Galitzine to accompany her. The cruise garnered international media attention, with pictures of Jackie and Ari walking through the streets of the island of Smyrna. She returned to America on October 17, 1963.

When Kennedy was assassinated one month later, Onassis attended the funeral, stayed as a guest in the White House, and mourned with the Kennedy family. From then on, Ari kept in contact with Jackie by telephone.

In 1967, reporters spied Jackie with Ari on the island of Skorpios.

When Bobby Kennedy was shot on June 5, 1968, Onassis flew to New York to be by Jackie's side. She took him to the Kennedy compound in Hyannisport on Cape Cod, and then took him to meet her mother and stepfather. Three months later, they were engaged to be married.

STRANGE ENCOUNTERS

★ Aristotle Socrates Onassis was born on January 20, 1900, in Smyrna (now known as Izmir), Turkey. When the Turkish army sacked Smyrna in 1922, Onassis escaped, eventually making his way to Buenos Aires, Argentina, where he worked as a telephone switchboard operator.

★ Onassis divorced his first wife, Athina "Tina" Livanos, because of his affair with Greek-born opera diva Maria Callas. Callas left her husband for Onassis, who later had an affair with Jackie's sister Lee. When that affair ended, Callas returned to Onassis.

★ Onassis made his fortune in tobacco, then entered the shipping trade. He bought several freighters at a very low price during the Depression, and built several large tankers, foreseeing the inevitable demand for these for oil trade.

★ In the 1940s, Onassis, living in Hollywood, had a brief love affair with actress Gloria Swanson, then Joe Kennedy's mistress.

★ In 1946, Onassis, then 46 years old, married seventeen-year-old Athina Livanos, daughter of Stavros Livanos, the world's largest ship owner.

★ In 1953, Onassis bought the company that owned approximately one-third of the real estate in Monaco—including the casino, the Hotel de Paris, and the yacht club.

★ Onassis upholstered the barstools on the *Christina* with fabric made from a whale's scrotum.

★ Jackie and Ari were married on the evening of October 20, 1968, in a Greek Orthodox service in the small chapel of Panayitsa on the Greek island of Skorpios.

★ Onassis had two children from his first marriage: Alexander and Christina.

★ Diagnosed with the incurable disease myasthenia gravis, Onassis died in 1975. Jackie forbid her sister Lee from attending the funeral. Onassis was buried at the church on Skorpios where he had married Jackie and next to the grave of his son, Alexander, who had died after a plane crash two years earlier. Onassis left all his money to Jackie, prompting his daughter Christina to contest the will.

★ In 1978, Jackie took a job as an editor at Doubleday. She died in 1994 of cancer.

Ozzy Osbourne and Sharon Arden

In 1976, the heavy metal band Black Sabbath, fronted by lead singer Ozzy Osbourne, hired a new manager named Don Arden. Two years later, the other three members of Black Sabbath—Terry "Geezer" Butler, Tony Iommi, and Bill Ward—kicked Ozzy out of the band because they could no longer cope with his uncontrolled drug and alcohol abuse. Ozzy continued his downward spiral. His wife Thelma threw him out after he shot her seven cats, and Ozzy moved into a hotel, sedating himself with drugs and alcohol. Don Arden sent his daughter Sharon to collect a five-hundred-dollar debt from Ozzy. Finding Ozzy surrounded by a sea of empty alcohol bottles, Sharon encouraged Ozzy to strike out as a solo musician.

Under Sharon's management, Ozzy teamed up with Quiet Riot guitarist Randy Rhoads to record a 1980 solo album, *Blizzard of Ozz*. The album went platinum. The following year Ozzy released a second album, *Diary of a Madman*. During the *Diary of a Madman* concert tour, while Ozzy performed in concert, a fan threw a live bat on stage. Ozzy, convinced the bat was a rubber toy, bit off its head, causing the bat to lash his face with its wings. Ozzy had to be rushed to the hospital for rabies shots. The resulting publicity caused his record sales to skyrocket.

On July 4, 1982, Ozzy married Sharon, who then purchased Ozzy's management contract from her father and became Ozzy's manager.

★ Ozzy Osbourne was born John Michael Osbourne on December 3, 1948, in Birmingham, England.

★ Sharon Arden was born on October 10, 1952, in London, England.

★ Ozzy dropped out of high school at age fifteen and worked as a car-horn tester.

★ While serving time in prison for petty theft, Ozzy had the letters O-Z-Z-Y tattooed across his knuckles and a smiley face tattooed on each knee.

★ Ozzy Osbourne, Terry "Geezer" Butler, Tony Iommi, and Bill Ward named their band Black Sabbath after the title of a 1963 Boris Karloff movie.

★ Ozzy has three children from his first marriage (to Thelma Mayfair): Jessica, Louis, and adopted son, Elliot Kingsley (from Thelma's previous marriage).

★ Ozzy named his 1981 solo album *Diary of a Madman* after a 1963 Vincent Price horror movie.

★ In 1982, Texas police arrested Ozzy, drunk and clad in a dress, for urinating on the Alamo in San Antonio, and threw him in jail for defacing a national monument.

★ The cover of Ozzy's 1982 album *Speak of the Devil* depicts a fang-toothed Ozzy with blood oozing from his mouth. When some record stores covered the bloody mouth with a sticker, Ozzy threatened to have the record pulled from those stores. Not wanting to lose record sales, the stores removed the stickers.

★ When one of Ozzy's fans committed suicide in the 1980s, his parents sued Ozzy, blaming the lyrics of his song "Suicide Solution" for motivating their son to take his own life. Ozzy had written "Suicide Solution" about the dangers of alcohol, in memory of former AC/DC vocalist Bon Scott, who died from alcohol abuse.

★ The cover of Ozzy's 1988 album *No Rest for the Wicked* generated controversy for depicting young children gathered around what appears to be a Satanic shrine.

★ Ozzy and Sharon have three children together: Aimee, Kelly, and Jack.

★ In 1989, police arrested a drunken Ozzy for attempting to strangle Sharon. He woke up the next day in jail without any idea why he had been imprisoned. In 1990, after undergoing extensive drug rehabilitation treatment, Ozzy rekindled his relationship with Sharon, who dropped the charges against him for attempted manslaughter.

★ In 1991, Ozzy performed three songs onstage with Black Sabbath.

★ Ozzy and Sharon's two children, Kelly and Jack, agreed to take part with their parents in the MTV reality show *The Osbournes*, but their eldest daughter Aimee refused to participate. *The Osbournes* became the highest rated show in the history of the channel, and MTV hired the foursome to do two more seasons for a reported twenty million dollars.

★ Ozzy says he sleeps with a bayonet under his bed.

Bonnie Parker and Clyde Barrow

In January 1930, nineteen-year-old Bonnie Parker, a waitress at Marco's Cafe in East Dallas, Texas, and married to an imprisoned murderer, visited a friend in West Dallas, where she met 21-year-old Clyde Barrow, a petty thief who had been arrested several times on charges of auto theft and safecracking. They fell in love. Unfortunately, the police soon arrested Clyde and took him to Waco, where, confessing to a couple of burglaries and several car thefts, he was sentenced to two years in prison.

Bonnie, who visited Clyde every day, smuggled a pistol to him, enabling Clyde to escape that night with his cellmate William Turner and a third inmate, Emory Abernathy. The police recaptured Clyde and Turner in Middletown, Ohio, and Clyde was sentenced to fourteen years in the Texas State Penitentiary. Bonnie and Clyde kept in close contact by letter.

During a prison work detail, Clyde persuaded a fellow inmate to chop off two toes of his left foot so he could avoid work in the cotton fields. Soon after, Clyde's mother helped arrange for her son to be pardoned on February 2, 1932. After holding down a job for two weeks in Massachusetts, Clyde returned to Bonnie. They took off in a stolen car, attracting the attention of the police. Clyde escaped, but Bonnie was arrested and sentenced to several months in jail in Kaufman, Texas.

Released in June, Bonnie rejoined Clyde, who had committed several

robberies and killed a police officer. Together they robbed banks and gas stations, which sometimes culminated in murder. The two lovebirds were forever on the run from the law, resulting in one of the most spectacular manhunts in police history.

STRANGE ENCOUNTERS

★ Clyde Chestnut Barrow, born on March 21, 1909, in Teleco, Texas, claimed his middle name was Champion and went by the aliases Roy Bailey, Jack Hale, and Elvin Williams.

★ Bonnie Parker, born on October 1, 1910, in Rowena, Texas, grew up in Cement City, where she won the Cement City spelling championship.

★ Clyde dropped out of school in the fifth grade and was raised in West Dallas, where his father ran a service station.

★ At age sixteen, Bonnie married Roy Thornton and got a tattoo on the inside of her thigh of two intertwined hearts with their names in the middle. A year later, Thorton left her.

★ In 1932, during her prison sentence in Kaufman, Texas, Bonnie wrote the poem "The Story of Suicide Sal."

★ In 1933, after a police gun battle with Bonnie and Clyde and their gang (seventeen-year-old petty thief W.D. Jones, Clyde's brother Buck, and his second wife Blanche), a newspaperman found some undeveloped film in the group's abandoned apartment in Joplin, Missouri. One of the developed pictures showed Bonnie smoking a cigar (borrowed

from Jones). The press called her the cigar-smoking moll of the Barrow gang. Bonnie, who smoked Lucky Strike cigarettes, hated the moniker.

★ Near Wellington, Texas, the Barrow gang's stolen Ford plunged off a bridge under construction, pinning Bonnie underneath. The farmers who helped rescue Bonnie noticed the arsenal of guns in the car, and notified the police, resulting in a gun battle. The Barrow gang escaped, but Bonnie's leg would never be the same.

★ During a shootout with the Barrow gang in Dexter, Iowa, on July 29, 1933, police fatally wounded Buck Barrow and captured his wife Blanche.

★ In November 1933, W.D. Jones left Bonnie and Clyde, but police captured him in Houston, Texas.

★ On November 22, 1933, while trying to visit Bonnie's parents in Grand Prairie, Texas, the Dallas sheriff and his deputies set up an ambush and blasted the car. Bonnie and Clyde, both hit in the legs, escaped in a stolen car.

★ In April 1934, Bonnie and Clyde kidnapped Police Chief Percy Boyd in Commerce, Oklahoma. Bonnie let Percy go free after he promised to tell the public she did not smoke cigars.

★ In 1934, Bonnie Parker wrote a poem entitled "The Story of Bonnie and Clyde," which Bonnie mailed to the newspapers.

★ Bonnie and Clyde had been traveling with Henry Methvin, whom they had sprung from the Eastham Prison Farm in Huntsville, Texas, along with Raymond Hamilton. Methvin's father, having harbored Bonnie and Clyde in the past, now feared for his son's life. He agreed to give Texas authorities information on the Barrow gang in exchange for a full pardon for his son. Before dawn on May 23, 1934, a posse composed of police officers from Louisiana and Texas, including Texas Ranger Frank Hamer, concealed themselves in bushes along the highway near Sailes, Louisiana. At 9:10 a.m., Bonnie and Clyde drove up in an automobile and were told to give up. When they reached for their guns, the officers opened fire, pumping 167 rounds into the car, killing 23-year-old Bonnie and 24-year-old Clyde.

★ Authorities believe that Bonnie and Clyde committed thirteen murders and innumerable robberies and burglaries.

★ Clyde was buried in a West Dallas cemetery next to his brother Buck. Bonnie's mother refused to bury Bonnie next to Clyde, and instead had her daughter buried at the West Dallas Fishtrap cemetery.

★ Criminal John Dillinger said Bonnie and Clyde gave bank robbing a bad name.

★ Warren Beatty and Faye Dunaway starred as Bonnie and Clyde in the 1967 movie *Bonnie and Clyde.*

Brad Pitt and Jennifer Aniston

In 1998, having crossed paths with movie star Brad Pitt at a number of celebrity functions, Jennifer Aniston, one of the stars of the hit television comedy *Friends*, decided she wanted to date the man who had been voted "The Sexiest Man Alive" in 1994 by the readers of *People* magazine.

Before contacting Brad, Jennifer did her homework. She researched his interests so that when they did meet, she could hold up her end of the conversation. She discovered that Brad had dropped out of the University of Missouri at Columbia, where he had majored in journalism and been a member of Sigma Chi fraternity. He loved the movie *Planet of the Apes*, had named his dented silver Datsun "Runaround Sue," and, when he first arrived in Los Angeles, he drove strippers around on weekends to make extra money.

Once Jennifer felt comfortable with the information she had gathered, she asked her agent to call Brad's agent to arrange a first date—a quiet dinner for two.

In 1998, while Jennifer was filming the comedy *Office Space* in Austin, Texas, Brad flew to the set to be with her. The couple spent much of their time getting to know each other at Jennifer's hotel, ordering room service and working out in the gym.

On July 30, 2000, Brad married Jennifer in a million-dollar sunset ceremony on a Malibu coastal estate owned by a television executive. The couple had never publicly admitted they were engaged.

STRANGE ENCOUNTERS

★ Born on December 18, 1963, in Shawnee, Oklahoma, William Bradley Pitt sang in the choir of the South Haven Baptist Church in Springfield, Missouri, and attended Kickapoo High School.

★ Born on February 11, 1969, in Sherman Oaks, California, Jennifer spent a year of her childhood living in Greece.

★ Jennifer's godfather is actor Telly Savalas, who starred in the television series *Kojak*.

★ While in college, Brad posed without a shirt for a campus calendar.

★ When Jennifer was eleven years old, the New York Metropolitan Museum of Art displayed one of her paintings in an exhibit.

★ While trying to break into acting in Los Angeles, Brad worked for El Pollo Loco, a fast-food chain of Mexican restaurants, greeting customers dressed in a chicken costume.

★ The popularity of *Friends* started a worldwide craze for Jennifer's "Rachel" hair style.

★ Brad rose to fame as Geena Davis's one-night stand in the 1991 movie *Thelma and Louise*.

★ Jennifer dated actor Tate Donovan, a frequent guest star on *Friends* and *Ally McBeal*, for two years.

★ Brad dated actress Robin Givens (heavyweight boxer Mike Tyson's ex-wife), had a three-year relationship with actress Juliette Lewis, and was engaged to Academy Award-winning actress Gwyneth Paltrow, who reportedly dumped him "for not setting a date."

★ Jennifer's father John Aniston starred on the soap operas *Love of Life* and *Days of Our Lives*.

★ In the summer of 1988, Brad starred in the movie *The Dark Side of the Sun*, shot in Yugoslavia, receiving roughly ten thousand dollars for his role in the film. Civil war erupted as editing neared completion and much of the footage was lost. A five-year search unearthed the lost footage in 1996, enabling producer Angelo Arandjelovic to release the film at long last, cashing in on the fact that Brad was now a major box-office draw.

★ In 1997, the People's Republic of China banned Brad from entering the country in reaction to his role in the movie *Seven Years in Tibet*.

★ In 2001, Jennifer won the People's Choice Award as Favorite Female in a Comedy Series.

★ If Jennifer's Greek ancestors had not changed the family's last name when they moved to New York, her last name would be Anastassakis.

★ Before landing the role of Rachel Green on *Friends*, Jennifer auditioned for the role of Monica Geller.

★ In 2000, Jennifer sued Man's World Publications, Inc. and Crescent Publishing Group, claiming that paparazzi scaled an eight-foot wall to photograph her as she sunbathed topless in her own backyard in February 1999. The photos appeared in the magazines *Celebrity Skin*, *Celebrity Sleuth*, *Eva Temila*, *High Society*, *Voici*, and the English newspaper *Daily Sport*.

★ After Jennifer's mother made unflattering statements about her in a tabloid, Jennifer refused to invite her to her wedding.

★ In 2001, Brad sued Damiani International, the company that made the wedding ring he gave Jennifer. Brad claimed the ring was based on his exclusive design and was never intended to be copied; the company had sold replicas of the ring. Ultimately, Brad agreed to design jewelry for Damiani, Jennifer agreed to model in ads, and Damiani agreed to stop selling copies of the original ring.

★ Jennifer and Brad have never appeared in any movie or television series together, except for Brad's one-time guest appearance on *Friends*.

Elvis Presley and Priscilla Beaulieu

In 1959, the United States Army drafted rock 'n' roll star Elvis Presley, four years into his meteoric career. Elvis joined the army as a buck private and was stationed in Bad Neuheim, West Germany.

That same year, Air Force Captain Joseph Paul Beaulieu, stationed at the Bergstrom Air Force Base in Austin, Texas, where he lived with his wife and their fourteen-year-old daughter Priscilla, was transferred to Wiesbaden, West Germany. Priscilla, having been elected Queen of Del Valley Junior High, did not want to leave her friends. Realizing that Elvis Presley was stationed in Germany, she tried to cheer herself up with the thought of actually meeting him.

One afternoon, while Priscilla was hanging out after school in the Eagles Club in Weisbaden, Air Force soldier Currie Grant introduced himself and asked her if she would like to join him and his wife for dinner with Elvis Presley. Suspicious, Priscilla insisted upon asking her parents. Her father met with Currie, verified his credentials, and agreed to let him chaperone his daughter to meet the rock 'n' roll star.

At eight o'clock on the arranged night in October, Currie and his wife picked up Priscilla at the pension in Weisbaden, where she lived with her family, and drove her to the three-story house in Bad Neuheim where Elvis lived with his father, Vernon, and his grandmother, Minnie Mae Presley. Currie introduced Priscilla to Elvis. "He was handsomer than he appeared in films, younger and more vulnerable-looking with his GI haircut," recalled Priscilla. "He was in civilian clothes, a bright red sweater and tan slacks, and he was sitting with one leg swung over the arm of a large overstuffed chair, with a cigar dangling from his lips."

After discovering that Priscilla was in the ninth grade, Elvis sat down at the piano and sang "Rags to Riches," "Are You Lonesome Tonight?," "End of the Rainbow," and then did an impression of Jerry Lee Lewis. "I noticed that the less response I showed, the more he began to sing just for me," recalled Priscilla. "I couldn't believe that Elvis was trying to impress me." Elvis's grandmother made them bacon sandwiches for dinner, and Elvis discussed his career with Priscilla, expressing his fear that fans might not accept him when he returned to the States. When Currie said it was time to go, Elvis casually suggested that Priscilla come by again. She never expected to hear from him.

A few days later, Currie telephoned Priscilla to tell her that Elvis wanted to see her that night. After dinner and singing, Elvis invited Priscilla up to his room so they could be alone. He confessed his feelings for her, held her in his arms, and told her how deeply he missed his mother, who had died one year earlier while he was in basic training. Before she left, Elvis kissed Priscilla goodnight, and soon after, Priscilla's parents insisted upon meeting her new boyfriend.

STRANGE ENCOUNTERS

★ Elvis Aron Presley, born January 8, 1935, in Tupelo, Mississippi, is a direct descendant of Abraham Lincoln's great-great grandfather, Isaiah Harrison.

★ Elvis's twin brother Jesse Garon Presley died at birth. Elvis was born thirty-five minutes later.

★ Priscilla Beaulieu was born Priscilla Wagner on May 24, 1945, in Brooklyn, New York. When she was six months old, her father, Navy pilot Lieutenant James Wagner, died in a plane crash. Two years later, her mother married Paul Beaulieu, who adopted Priscilla, keeping this information a secret from her until she was a teenager.

★ In 1947, Elvis' mother, Gladys, bought her twelve-year-old son his first guitar.

★ Elvis Presley's music teacher at L.C. Humes High School in Memphis, Tennessee, gave him a C and told him he couldn't sing.

★ Elvis was fired from his job as an usher at Loew's State Theater in Memphis, Tennessee, for punching out a fellow usher who told the manager that Presley was getting free candy from the girl at the concession stand.

★ Elvis drove a truck for Crown Electric Company.

★ Elvis made his television debut on the regionally telecast *Louisiana Hayride,* on March 5, 1955, in Shreveport, Louisiana.

★ In 1955, Elvis auditioned for a spot on *Arthur Godfrey's Talent Scouts* and was rejected.

★ Teenagers became hysterical over his sexual gesturing and particularly his "Elvis the Pelvis" gyrations. Ed Sullivan forbade television cameras from filming Elvis below his waist.

★ In 1961, Elvis convinced Priscilla's parents to let their sixteen-year-old daughter live with him in Memphis. Elvis moved Priscilla into his Graceland home until she turned twenty-one, insisting that Priscilla remain a virgin until their wedding night. After an eight-year courtship, they married on May 1, 1967, at the Aladdin Hotel in Las Vegas.

★ Elvis and Priscilla's daughter, Lisa Marie Presley, was born exactly nine months after their wedding day. Priscilla believes she and Elvis conceived Lisa Marie on their wedding night.

★ From the time they met, Elvis sent a roomful of flowers to Ann-Margret whenever she opened a show in Las Vegas.

★ Priscilla left Elvis for her karate instructor, Mike Stone. She and Elvis divorced in October 1973.

★ Elvis won three Grammy Awards, all for his Gospel music.

★ Elvis turned down the role played by Kris Kristofferson in the 1976 movie *A Star Is Born* because his manager, Colonel Tom Parker, refused to let him act in any movie unless he had top billing.

★ Elvis added gold lame jackets and jeweled white jumpsuits to his act at the advice of Liberace.

★ Elvis owned a pet chimpanzee named Scatter.

★ Elvis's autopsy detected ten different drugs in his bloodstream.

★ Elvis's body was originally placed in a family crypt in Memphis on August 18, 1977. However, when three men attempted to steal the body less than two weeks later, the Memphis Adjustment Board granted permission to Elvis's father, Vernon Presley, to bury the bodies of Elvis and his mother Gladys in the Meditation Garden behind the Graceland Estate.

★ Priscilla turned down a starring role on the television series *Charlie's Angels*.

★ Priscilla starred as Jenna Wade for five years on the television series *Dallas* and played Jane Spencer in the *Naked Gun* movies.

★ Since 1984, Priscilla has lived with Marco Garibaldi, with whom she has a son: Navarone.

★ Priscilla made an uncredited cameo appearance in the 1997 movie *Austin Powers: International Man of Mystery*.

★ Elvis has sold over one billion albums worldwide, more than any other musical act in the world, including the Beatles.

★ In June 1993, the United States Postal Service issued a twenty-nine-cent stamp featuring Elvis Presley.

William Procter and James Gamble

I n the 1830s, William Procter and his wife Martha immigrated from England to the United States and headed for the West Coast. Unfortunately, Martha got sick along the way, forcing the Procters to stop in Cincinnati, Ohio. William tried to care for ailing Martha, but despite his best efforts, she died. Heartbroken and devastated, William reluctantly settled in Cincinnati and quickly established himself as a candlemaker.

Meanwhile, James Gamble, an immigrant from Ireland on his way to the West Coast was forced to stop in Cincinnati to seek medical attention for himself. After regaining his health, James got an apprenticeship to a soapmaker, learning the trade.

William and James became brothers-in-law when they married sisters, Olivia and Elizabeth Norris. Their father-in-law, Alexander Norris, convinced them to combine their resources and go into business together.

On April 12, 1837, William and James merged their small Cincinnati businesses to make and sell soap and candles. On August 22, they each invested $3,596.47 in their new business and, on October 31, 1837, signed a formal partnership agreement, giving birth to Procter & Gamble. By 1859, Procter & Gamble had eighty employees and sales had reached one million dollars. During the Civil War, the Union Army ordered its soap and candles from Procter & Gamble, keeping the factory operating day and night. Soldiers returned home from the war with an allegiance to Procter & Gamble products, firmly establishing the company's reputation.

STRANGE ENCOUNTERS

★ In 1879, Harley Procter, son of company co-founder William Procter, decided to develop a creamy white soap to compete with imported castile soaps. He asked his cousin, chemist James Gamble, Jr., son of company co-founder James Gamble, to formulate the product. One day after the soap when into production, a factory worker (who remains anonymous) forgot to switch off the master mixing machine when he went to lunch and too much air was whipped into a batch of soap. Consumers, delighted by the floating soap, demanded more, and from then on, Procter & Gamble gave all white soap an extra-long whipping.

★ Harley, considering a long list of new names for his white soap, was inspired one Sunday morning in church when the pastor read Psalm 45: "All thy garments smell of myrrh, and aloes, and cassia, out of the ivory palaces, whereby they have made thee glad." A few years later, a chemist's analysis of Ivory soap indicated that 56/100 of the ingredients did not fall into the category of pure soap. Procter subtracted from 100, and wrote the slogan "99-44/100% Pure" which first appeared in Ivory's advertising in 1882. "It Floats" was added to Ivory's slogan in 1891.

★ In 1911, Procter & Gamble introduced Crisco, the first mass-marketed, one hundred percent vegetable shortening. The first cans of Crisco came with an eight-page circular cookbook cut to fit the lid. Starting in 1913, Procter & Gamble sent six home economists across the country to give week-long demonstrations (advertised as "cooking schools") to show homemakers how to get better results by using Crisco in their cooking. After the demonstrations, the home economists would hand out souvenir baskets of various food samples, a 1.5-pound can of Crisco, and a special Crisco cookbook to the eager audiences.

★ In the 1950s, when postwar prosperity made the automatic dishwasher popular, Procter & Gamble developed a detergent specially blended to capitalize on the new home market for these machines. In 1955, blue-green, pine-scented Cascade came in a box wrapped in gold paper, changed to green in 1958.

★ Procter & Gamble introduced Jif peanut butter in 1956, today the top-selling brand of peanut butter in America.

★ Procter & Gamble acquired Charmin Paper Mills in 1957, and in 1965, introduced Bounty, a highly absorbent, two-ply paper towel designed to satisfy the needs of consumers who wanted a better paper towel than what was currently available, including the single-ply Charmin Towel.

★ In 1968 Procter & Gamble developed stackable potato chips in a vacuum-packed can in order to deliver the chips to grocery stores through the same delivery system used to ship its other products. Pringles were made from potato flakes mixed into a dough, stamped into miniature pies, and fried on a curved screen—thus freeing Procter & Gamble from having to use cumbersome potatoes.

★ Procter & Gamble introduced Pringles potato crisps at the same time General Foods introduced Pringles pretzel snacks. Procter & Gamble ended up buying the rights to the Pringles name from General Foods for an undisclosed sum.

★ In 1970, Procter & Gamble hired model Marilyn Briggs to pose in a white terry cloth robe with her baby on the front of the Ivory Snow box. Three years later, Procter & Gamble discovered that Marilyn Briggs was porn actress Marilyn Chambers, star of the 1972 hardcore X-rated film *Behind the Green Door.*

★ In 1991, Procter & Gamble, determined to find out who leaked some of the company's proprietary information to the *Wall Street Journal,* obtained a subpoena and the help of the Cincinnati police to examine the phone records of some 800,000 people in the greater Cincinnati area. The press and the public denounced Procter & Gamble for invasion of privacy, prompting the disgraced company to end its unconstitutional search.

★ On April 30, 1998, a tanker truck flipped over on Interstate 74 in Cincinnati, Ohio, spilling four tons of inedible industrial animal fat. After workers tried unsuccessfully to clean up the spill with several industrial solvents, Cincinnati-based Procter & Gamble donated a tanker truck filled with Dawn dishwashing liquid to be sprayed over the oil slick and scrubbed with road sweeper brushes—clearly showing how well Dawn cuts through grease.

Ronald Reagan and Nancy Davis

In 1949, while the House Un-American Activities Committee hunted for communists in Hollywood, Director Mervyn LeRoy telephoned Ronald Reagan, president of the Screen Actor's Guild, on behalf of an actress starring in his new movie *East Side, West Side*. Nancy Davis, he explained, feared that she would be accused of being a communist because she shared the same name as another actress whose name appeared in the *Hollywood Reporter* on October 28, 1949. The other Nancy Davis had, along with another 207 people, signed a letter to the United States Supreme Court to reverse the conviction of Hollywood writers Dalton Trumbo and John Howard Lawson, who had taken the fifth amendment before the House Un-American Activities Committee. Ronnie researched Nancy's claim, discovered that the other Nancy Davis was the wife of agent Jerome Davis, and told Mervyn that the Screen Actor's Guild would stand behind his Nancy Davis.

Nancy, however, wanted to meet Ronnie face to face. His name topped a list she had compiled of eligible Hollywood bachelors. Nancy had previously managed to get MGM vice president Dore Schary to persuade his wife Miriam to host a small dinner party at their home so she could be introduced to Ronnie. That night, Miriam had asked Ronnie to drive Nancy home, but he could not. Nor did the recently divorced Ronnie ever telephone Nancy afterwards. Undaunted, Nancy called the Screen Actors Guild and expressed her desire to run for the board of directors. Again, Ronnie never returned the call. When Mervyn realized that Nancy had ulterior motives for wanting to meet with Ronnie, he urged Ronnie to take the young starlet out to dinner that evening to assure her that she had nothing to fear from the House Un-American Activities Committee.

When Ronnie picked up Nancy at her apartment, he walked with two canes, having shattered his right thighbone during a charity softball game. He took her to LaRue's on the Sunset Strip, and, to assuage her fear of being mistaken as a communist, suggested she change her name. Although both Ronnie and Nancy had told each other they had early calls the next morning, neither thespian wanted the evening to end. Nancy said, later, "I knew that being his wife was the role I wanted most." He suggested they go see Sophie Tucker perform at Ciro's, where they stayed for two shows, getting home around three o'clock in the morning. Ronnie invited Nancy to join him for dinner the following night at the Malibu Inn.

The couple continued dating off and on for several months. When Ronnie was about to drive down to San Diego to make a speech to the Junior League Convention at the Del Coronado Hotel, he invited Nancy to join him. (Nancy happened to be a Junior League member from Chicago.) After that trip, they began dating only each other, and one night over dinner, Ronnie proposed marriage. On March 4, 1952, they were married in a private ceremony in the Little Brown Church in the Valley. Their first child together, Patricia, was born seven months later on October 21, 1952.

STRANGE ENCOUNTERS

★ Ronald Wilson Reagan was born on February 6, 1911, in Tampico, Illinois, to a shoemaker and his homemaker wife.

★ Nancy, born Anne Frances Robbins on July 6, 1921, in New York City, took the last name of her stepfather, Dr. Loyal Davis.

★ While working as a lifeguard as a teenager, Ronnie rescued an old man's dentures from the bottom of a swimming pool, and also saved a drowning swimmer's life.

★ Ronnie graduated from Eureka College, where he was a member of Tau Kappa Epsilon fraternity.

★ When the United States entered World War II, 30-year-old Ronnie volunteered for military service. He was turned down for combat duty due to his poor eyesight.

★ In her book, *The Peter Lawford Story: Life with Monroe, the Kennedys, and the Rat Pack*, Peter Lawford's widow, Pat, wrote: "When she was single, Nancy Davis was known for giving the best head in

Hollywood." According to *Nancy Reagan: The Unauthorized Biography* by Kitty Kelley, Peter Lawford claimed that during a car trip to Phoenix, Nancy had performed oral sex with both him and actor Robert Walker.

★ Ronald Reagan and Jane Wyman (his first wife) starred in six movies together: *Brother Rat, An Angel from Texas, Brother Rat and a Baby, Tugboat Annie Sails Again, Sports Parade: Shoot Yourself Some Golf,* and *It's a Great Feeling.*

★ Nancy dated actor Robert Walker, and a few months after they broke up, Walker died from an overdose of sodium amytal administered by his doctors.

★ In 1951, 41-year-old Ronald Reagan proposed to actress Christine Larson, a devout Bahai, by giving her a diamond wristwatch. Larson turned down the offer, but kept the watch.

★ When applying for a marriage license, Nancy gave her age as twenty-eight. She was actually thirty.

★ Ronnie and Nancy Reagan spent their honeymoon in Phoenix, Arizona, with Nancy's vacationing parents.

★ Nancy and Ronnie starred in one movie together: *Hellcats of the Navy.*

★ Ronnie had four children: Michael and Maureen (with first wife, actress Jane Wyman), and Ron and Patti (with second wife Nancy Davis).

★ In 1973, Ronnie, then governor of California, became the guest of honor at the first *Dean Martin Celebrity Roast.*

★ At age sixty-nine, Ronnie became the oldest person ever elected President of the United States. He was also the first divorcé and the first union president to ever hold that office.

★ On February 15, 1980, presidential candidate Ronald Reagan said, "All the waste in a year from a nuclear power plant can be stored under a desk." The average nuclear power plant generates thirty tons of radioactive waste each year.

★ Throughout the Reagan administration, Ronnie's first wife, Jane Wyman, starred as Angela Channing on the television drama *Falcon Crest.*

★ As President, Ronnie's Secret Service codename was "Rawhide."

Debbie Reynolds and Eddie Fisher

In 1951, 22-year-old singer Eddie Fisher performed with the United States Army Band for wounded soldiers at Walter Reed Hospital in Washington, D.C. From the wings, he watched nineteen-year-old Debbie Reynolds sing and tap dance "Abba Dabba Honeymoon" from her movie *Two Weeks in Love*. The two were briefly introduced. "I don't remember what Debbie and I said to each other that

day, but I was probably too shy to flirt with her," recalled Eddie in his autobiography, *Been There, Done That*.

While serving in Korea, Eddie became infatuated with Debbie Reynolds. "One night I was sitting in a tent," he recalled. "It was pouring outside, and we were watching Gene Kelly, Donald O'Connor, and Debbie Reynolds dancing through a storm in *Singing in the Rain*. And on that sheet that was hung in the front of the tent she looked like a dream." He promised himself that he would date her when he returned to the States.

In 1953, when asked by a fan magazine which Hollywood star he would like to meet most, Eddie replied "Debbie Reynolds."

In 1954, they were formally introduced. Producer Joe Pasternak, attempting to woo Eddie to star in his movie *The Ambassador's Daughter*, gave him a tour of the MGM lot and then took him to meet America's Sweetheart, Debbie Reynolds, on the set of *Athena*. The "spontaneous" meeting had been carefully set up in the hopes that a romance would generate publicity for the studio. "The moment she opened the door of her trailer I was smitten," Eddie recalled.

Eddie obtained Debbie's home phone number from disc jockey Johnny Grant, and began calling her regularly from New York, where he was performing at Grossinger's Resort in the Catskill Mountains. When he returned to Los Angeles, he invited her to accompany him to a party at Dinah Shore's house, then to be his date for his own opening night at the Cocoanut Grove. Debbie accepted, and after sitting through his two shows, accompanied him to a party thrown in his honor. Eddie drove Debbie home and kissed her goodnight. They began seeing each other nearly every night. Eddie showered her with flowers and gifts, including a miniature poodle, a soft-drink dispenser, and a Thunderbird convertible. The romance generated huge amounts of publicity, and the couple swiftly became media darlings.

In 1954, Eddie gave Debbie a seven-carat diamond ring, and the couple set the wedding date for the following June. In the spring of 1955, Eddie, getting cold feet, postponed the wedding for several weeks. Finally, he scheduled the event to take place at Grossinger's Resort on the evening of Sunday, September 25, 1955, which he had failed to realize was Yom Kippur, the holiest Jewish holiday. When Jewish Eddie asked Debbie to postpone the wedding for one day, she threw a fit. "America's Happiest Couple" finally married on the evening of September 26, 1955— the day after Yom Kippur.

STRANGE ENCOUNTERS

★ Eddie Fisher was born Edwin Jack Fisher on August 10, 1928, in Philadelphia, Pennsylvania.

★ Debbie Reynolds was born Mary Frances Reynolds on April 1, 1932, in El Paso, Texas, to a railroad carpenter.

★ Debbie claimed that she was a virgin until her marriage to Eddie Fisher. "That I know is not true," claimed Eddie, "because I was there long before our marriage."

★ Eddie and Debbie were married in the new home of Elaine Grossinger Etess, daughter of Jennie Grossinger, owner of the famous Catskill resort Grossinger's.

★ Eddie and Debbie spent the first few days of their honeymoon at a Coca-Cola bottlers convention in Atlanta, Georgia, and ended their honeymoon with a visit to Harry and Bess Truman at their home in Independence, Missouri.

★ Six months after their wedding, Eddie and Debbie attended a Passover seder in Las Vegas in the company of the great comedians of the day. "I was the youngest Jew present," recalled Eddie, "so in keeping with tradition I asked the four questions.

Jackie Leonard did something. Milton Berle did his thing. Joe E. Lewis told a story. It was quite a group. And finally, with absolutely perfect timing, Debbie stood up and said, 'And now I'd like to say a few words on behalf of Jesus Christ . . . ' She put the best comedians in Las Vegas right on the floor with that line."

★ Eddie and Debbie had two children together: Carrie and Todd. Carrie Fisher starred as Princess Leia in the *Star Wars* movies.

★ During his marriage to Debbie, Eddie had an affair with Pat Shean, who was then Bing Crosby's girlfriend. Pat married Bing Crosby's son, Dennis.

★ By 1958, Eddie and Debbie were living apart, hadn't slept together in months, and had been to a lawyer to work out a divorce agreement. When they finalized the divorce papers, Debbie told Eddie that she was pregnant, prompting him to stick with the marriage.

★ When his close friend Michael Todd died in a plane crash, Eddie began consoling his widow, Elizabeth Taylor. The two fell in love. In 1959, Eddie divorced Debbie to marry Liz, who converted to Judaism. The media portrayed Liz as a home wrecker and Eddie as an adulterer, ruining his career.

★ Eddie has been married and divorced three times, to Debbie Reynolds, Elizabeth Taylor, and Connie Stevens.

★ Debbie has been married and divorced three times, to Eddie Fisher, Harry Karl, and Richard Hamlett.

★ Eddie and Debbie starred together in one movie: *Bundle of Joy*.

Burt Reynolds and Loni Anderson

In 1978, Burt Reynolds appeared as a guest on *The Merv Griffin Show*. While Burt was onstage with the cameras rolling, Merv introduced a second guest, Loni Anderson, who had arrived late from a rehearsal for the television comedy *WKRP in Cincinnati*, where she played receptionist Jennifer Marlowe. Burt and Loni had never met before.

"There was no sense at the time that anything would happen between us at some future date," recalled Burt. "I was heavily involved with Sally [Field], and Loni was married to actor Ross Bickell, her second husband." During the commercial break, Burt asked Loni how her husband was handling her success with *WKRP.*

Later, while dining with Ross and her daughter Deidre (from her first marriage to Bruce Hasselberg) at the Smokehouse restaurant in Hollywood, Loni noticed that her appearance on *The Merv Griffin Show* was being broadcast on the television in the bar. She also noticed Burt dining in the same restaurant. They waved to each other and pointed to the television.

Several months later, after presenting an award at the People's Choice Awards, Loni passed Burt's table. Burt, who was sitting with Sally Field, stopped Loni and asked her to introduce him to her husband. After the show, Loni brought Ross over to meet Burt, who introduced them both to Sally Field.

Years passed. In 1981, Ross confessed to an extramarital affair, prompting Loni

to divorce him. She rebounded by having a love affair with Gary Sandy, the star of *WKRP in Cincinnati*, during which time representatives for Burt starting calling on his behalf to ask Loni out on a date. Loni turned down the requests, but months later, while attending a Variety Club event honoring Burt for lifetime achievement, she decided to let him know she was now interested. After Loni rose to the podium to introduce Jim Nabors as a speaker, Burt thanked her. "Well, all right, all right," she whispered in his ear. "I'm ready to have your child." Burt, who was romantically involved with former Miss America and Los Angeles newscaster Tawny Little, replied, "When?"

In December 1981, after several lengthy phone conversations, Loni accepted Burt's invitation to join him in Florida for New Year's Eve. By the end of 1982, Burt and Loni were living together in his Beverly Hills home and engaged to be married. The wedding took place six years later, on April 29, 1988.

STRANGE ENCOUNTERS

★ When Loni was a teenager, her mother, struck by an attractive actor on television, told Loni that he was the type of man she should marry. The actor was Burt Reynolds.

★ In 1964, Loni was First Runner-up for Miss Minnesota.

★ Burt appeared as a bachelor on *The Dating Game* in 1971 and wasn't chosen.

★ Loni, famous as a platinum blond, is a natural-born brunette.

★ Burt posed nude in 1972 (with his hand covering his crotch) for the first centerfold in *Cosmopolitan* magazine.

★ In 1972, Burt became the first actor ever to guest-host *The Tonight Show Starring Johnny Carson*. His first guest was his ex-wife Judy Carne, with whom he hadn't spoken in over six years.

★ Burt turned down the opportunity to replace Sean Connery in the role of James Bond. The part went to Roger Moore, who debuted as Bond in 1973 in *Live and Let Die*.

★ Loni auditioned for the part of Chrissy on the television comedy *Three's Company*, but lost the part to Suzanne Somers.

★ Burt purportedly broke off his romantic relationship with Lucy Arnaz by telling her he was going to Hawaii and was leaving his car with her. When he failed to return for his car, Lucy went over to Burt's house only to discover him with Sally Field.

★ Loni's first husband, Ross Bickell, auditioned for the starring roll of Andy Travis on *WKRP in Cincinnati,* but lost to actor Gary Sandy.

★ Burt allegedly ended his relationship with Adrienne Barbeau by leaving a note under the windshield wiper of her car.

★ Burt supposedly ended his romance with Lorna Luft, sister of Liza Minnelli, by attending the premiere of his movie *Lucky Lady* with Dinah Shore as his date, having promised to take Lorna.

★ Burt turned down the role in the 1983 movie *Terms of Endearment* that earned Jack Nicholson an Academy Award.

★ While signing his name in cement in front of Mann's Chinese Theater on Hollywood Boulevard, Burt Reynolds misspelled his own name.

★ Burt and Loni appeared together in only two movies: *Stroker Ace* and *All Dogs Go to Heaven.* Loni guest-starred on one episode of Burt's television series *B.L. Stryker.*

★ Loni and Burt, unable to conceive a child because of Burt's low sperm count, adopted a baby boy they named Quinton, after Quint Asper, the character Burt played for three years on the television western *Gunsmoke.*

★ In her autobiography, *My Life in High Heels,* Loni claimed that during their marriage, Burt was having an affair with former waitress Pam Seals. Loni claimed that Burt had given Seals a part as an extra on *B. L. Stryker* and that everyone in their circle of friends seemed to know about the affair—except her.

★ In 1993, Burt had his lawyer and two sheriffs serve Loni with divorce papers at their home in Florida and hand her a one-way plane ticket to Los Angeles.

Nelson Rockefeller and Happy Murphy

S ometime before his 1958 campaign for governor of New York, fifty-year-old Nelson Rockefeller, a married man with four children, fell in love with 32-year-old Margaretta "Happy" Murphy, a married woman with four young children of her own. Happy and her husband James Murphy, a microbiologist at the Rockefeller Institute for Medical Research, were friends of Nelson Rockefeller and his wife, Mary Todhunter Clark.

Happy had worked on Nelson's 1958 gubernatorial campaign. Four years later, while serving as governor of New York, Nelson divorced his wife of thirty-two years. That same year, Happy divorced her husband, giving him custody of their four children.

When Nelson married Happy in May 1963, the American public viewed Happy as a home wrecker who had destroyed not one, but two families. News of the marriage provoked pubic outrage, and the scandal damaged Nelson's 1964 run for the Republican nomination for president of the United States. When he spoke before the 1964 Republican National Convention in San Francisco, the crowd jeered Nelson. "This is still a free country, ladies and gentlemen," he said, barely audible above the boos. Clearly, a good many Republicans objected to the liberties Nelson had taken in his private life.

★ Nelson Aldrich Rockefeller, born on July 8, 1908, in Bar Harbor, Maine, suffered from dyslexia, graduated from Dartmouth College, and served four terms as governor of New York.

★ Happy Murphy, born on June 9, 1926 in Lower Merion, Pennsylvania, was eighteen years younger than Nelson.

★ While Nelson emerged as the clear favorite for the 1964 Republican presidential nomination, his divorce and remarriage in 1963, however, destroyed his popularity.

★ Nelson's indecision to enter the race for the presidency in 1968 damaged his campaign and enabled his opponent, Richard Nixon, to build a strong lead in delegates.

★ Nelson's decision to suppress the Attica prison riot in 1971, resulting in the death of thirty-two inmates and eleven guards, made him the target of harsh criticism. Happy had suggested drugging the food of the inmates to quell the uprising.

★ In August 1974, President Gerald Ford nominated Nelson to be Vice President of the United States. After being confirmed by Congress, he was sworn in as the 41st vice president on December 19, 1974.

★ In 1974, Happy was diagnosed with breast cancer and underwent a mastectomy at the same time as First Lady Betty Ford.

★ Happy refused to move to Washington, D.C., while Nelson served as Vice President. Instead, he spent weekdays living at his estate on Foxhall Road in Washington, D.C., and weekends at home with Happy and their two sons in Pocantico Hills, New York. Nelson had the Vice President's mansion elaborately furnished and decorated but never lived there.

★ In 1975, at President Ford's request, Nelson withdrew from consideration as his possible running mate in his bid for reelection in 1976.

★ At a Republican rally at the State University of New York at Binghamton during the 1976 presidential campaign, a photographer captured Nelson on camera giving the finger to hippie protesters who were making similar gestures.

★ Nelson had seven children: Rodman, Anne, Steven, and twins Mary and Michael (with Mary Todhunter Clark); and Nelson, Jr., and Mark (with Happy Murphy).

★ Nelson died of a heart attack on January 26, 1979, at age seventy-one in his Manhattan townhouse while in the company of a young female staff assistant forty-five years his junior—27-year-old Megan Marshack. Marshack's delay in calling the paramedics triggered endless speculation about her relationship with the former Vice President. Nelson's longtime press secretary Hugh Morrow told reporters that Nelson had died at his office desk on the fifty-sixth floor of 30 Rockefeller Plaza.

Richard Rodgers and Oscar Hammerstein II

As a student at Columbia University, Oscar Hammerstein, the son of a theatrical manager and the grandson of an opera impresario, performed and wrote musical routines for college varsity revues. During a Saturday-morning matinee of one of those revues, he met teenager Richard Rodgers, whose older brother had brought him to the show. Rodgers, a musician who loved the works of Jerome Kern, frequently attended Saturday matinees of musicals.

At age sixteen, Rodgers teamed up with 23-year-old lyricist Lorenz Hart, a graduate of Columbia University with whom he shared a passion for Broadway musicals and clever lyrics. The duo collaborated for twenty-three years, writing more than one thousand songs together and ten Broadway musicals, including *On Your Toes, The Boys From Syracuse,* and *Pal Joey.* In 1942, when offered the opportunity to write a new Broadway musical called *Away We Go!,* based on Lynn Riggs' play *Green Grow the Lilacs,* Hart, whose health had begun to fail, passed on the project.

That summer, 39-year-old Richard Rodgers, in need of a new partner with whom to write *Away We Go!,* teamed up with 46-year-old Oscar Hammerstein II. Since Rodgers had first met Hammerstein at Columbia University, the lyricist and librettist had masterminded some of the longest-running musicals of the 1920s and 1930s, including *The Desert Song, The New Moon,* and *Show Boat.*

Rodgers and Hammerstein retitled their first collaboration *Oklahoma!* The musical dwarfed all of their previous works. Unlike other musicals, the songs in *Oklahoma!* cleverly advanced the plot. Soon after the premiere of *Oklahoma!,* the duo separated to pursue other projects. In 1944, they resumed their partnership and remained together until Hammerstein's death sixteen years later.

STRANGE ENCOUNTERS

★ Richard Rodgers was born on June 29, 1902, on Long Island, New York.

★ Oscar Greeley Clendenning Hammerstein was born on July 12, 1895, in New York City.

★ Both Rodgers and Hammerstein graduated from Columbia University, but never knew each other as students, since Hammerstein graduated three years before Rodgers enrolled.

★ Rodgers accepted a job selling children's underwear, but failed to show up for work.

★ Hammerstein wrote his first musical, *Always You*, with composer Herbert Stothart. He collaborated on other musicals with Sigmund Romberg and Jerome Kern.

★ With Lorenz Hart, Hammerstein wrote the music first, then Hart wrote the lyrics. Rodgers would write the lyrics first, then send them to Hammerstein to set to music.

★ Rodgers and Hammerstein won a Pulitzer Prize for their first collaborative work, *Oklahoma!*

★ Together, Rodgers and Hammerstein wrote eleven musicals: *Oklahoma!, Carousel, Allegro, South Pacific, The King and I, Me and Juliet, Pipe Dream, Flower Drum Song,* and *The Sound of Music;* one movie: *State Fair;* and one television musical: *Cinderella.*

★ Hammerstein's Pennsylvania estate, Highland Farms, serves as a popular bed-and-breakfast decorated with Hammerstein memorabilia.

Nicholas Romanov and Alix von Hesse

O n May 28, 1884, eleven-year-old Alix von Hesse, the daughter of the Grand Duke of Hesse-Darmstadt and a granddaughter of England's Queen Victoria, attended her sister's wedding to the brother of Czar Alexander III in St. Petersburg, Russia. At the wedding, Alix met and fell in love with the Czar's son, sixteen-year-old Nicholas Romanov. They kissed and snuck off together to write their names on the windowpane of a nearby cottage because, as Nicholas recorded in his diary, "We love each other."

Five years later in 1889, Nicholas and Alix met again at the Belossievsky Palace in St. Petersburg, rekindling their romantic relationship. They began corresponding.

Another five years passed, and on April 8, 1894, at the wedding of Alix's brother in Coburg, Germany, Nicholas and Alix announced their engagement. "A wonderful, unforgettable day in my life—the day of my betrothal to my dear beloved Alix," wrote Nicholas in his diary. "I spent the whole day in a haze, not quite knowing what had happened to me!"

While Nicholas and Alix were deeply in love, they faced one obstacle. As heir to the Russian throne, Nicholas could not marry Alix, who had been raised Lutheran, unless she converted to the Russian Orthodox faith. Ultimately, Alix's sister, Ella, who had converted to Orthodoxy of her own freewill, persuaded Alix to agree. "Oh God, what happened to me then!" wrote Nicholas in his diary. "I started to cry like a child, and so did she, only her expression immediately changed: her face brightened and took on an aura of peace."

Nicholas and Alix began writing passionate love letters to each other. On April 20, 1894, he wrote: "Oh how impatient I am for the moment when I can again press my lips to your sweet soft face!" Two days later, she replied, "Oh, if you only knew how I adore you and the years have made my affection for you grow stronger and deeper… Sweet one I cannot stop thinking of you." On July 22, Nicholas wrote, "You have got me entirely and for ever, soul and spirit, body and heart, everything is yours; I would like to scream it out loud for the world to hear it."

In the fall of 1894, when Czar Alexander III fell ill with kidney disease, 22-year-old Alix boarded a regular passenger train to be by her fiancé's side. On October 20, 1894, Alexander III died, making 26-year-old Nicholas the new ruler of Russia. The next day Alix was confirmed in the Orthodox faith and became the Grand Duchess Alexandra Feodorovna.

On November 14, Nicholas and Alix were married in a quiet ceremony in the Winter Palace. On her wedding night, Alix wrote in her husband's diary: "At last united, bound for life and when this life is ended, we meet again in the other world and remain together for eternity." The next morning, she added, "Never did I believe there could be such utter happiness in this world, such a feeling of unity between two mortal beings."

STRANGE ENCOUNTERS

★ Nicholas was born on May 6, 1868, at Tsarskoye Selo (now Pushkin), Russia.

★ Alix Victoria Helena Louise Beatrice von Hesse, born on June 6, 1872, in Darmstadt, Germany, was raised and educated by her grandmother, Queen Victoria of England.

★ In 1875, Alix's brother, Frittie, died of hemophilia and three years later, her mother and her sister died from diphtheria.

★ Eager to share her love with the Russian people, Alix worked continuously to improve living conditions for the poor, founding schools and hospitals, building workhorses, and heading the Red Cross and other charitable organizations.

★ Nicholas and Alexandra called each other "Hubby" and "Wifey."

★ Nicholas and Alexandra had five children: Maria, Tatiana, Olga, Anastasia, and Alexis.

★ On January 22, 1905, thousands of unarmed striking workers marched to Nicholas's Winter Palace in St. Petersburg to demand political reforms. Government troops fired on the workers, killing and wounding hundreds of people in a massacre—strengthening opposition to the czar's rule.

★ In October 1905, a general strike prompted Nicholas to form an elected parliament to propose and pass laws, but the revolution against the czar continued—until he ordered the army to crush an uprising in Moscow in December.

★ During World War I, Nicholas took command of the army and left the government of Russia in the hands of Czarina Alexandra Feodorovna and her meddlesome advisor Grigori Rasputin.

★ During the Russian revolution of 1917, the Bolsheviks forced Nicholas to abdicate the throne and sent him and his family into exile in the Ural Mountains city of Yekaterinburg.

★ On July 17, 1918, Bolshevik revolutionaries herded Nicholas, Alexandra, their five children, doctor, and three attendants into the cellar of a house in Yekaterinburg and lined them up against a wall, ostensibly to take a family portrait. Instead, a firing squad burst into the room and opened fire, then stabbed any survivors with bayonets.

★ The possibility that Anastasia Romanov, the youngest daughter of Nicholas and Alexandra, might have survived provided the inspiration for the 1956 movie *Anastasia*, starring Ingrid Bergman as the young woman who may be rightful heiress to the Russian throne.

★ Michael Jayston and Janet Suzman starred as Nicholas and Alexandra in the 1971 movie *Nicholas and Alexandra*.

★ Meg Ryan provides the voice of Anastasia in the 1997 animated movie *Anastasia*, featuring Christopher Lloyd as the voice of Rasputin.

Romeo and Juliet

In Verona, Italy, teenage Romeo, the son of Montague, has fallen helplessly in love with a young woman named Rosaline who does not reciprocate his amorous feelings. His cousin Benvolio urges the lovelorn Romeo to forget Rosaline and seek a girlfriend who reciprocates his affections. To cure Romeo of his heartache, Benvolio suggests that they disguise themselves in costumes and crash the Capulet family's annual masquerade party and feast so Romeo can compare Rosaline, who happens to be on the guest list, to the other beautiful women of Verona. Despite the age-old feud between his father, Montague and Capulet, the heartsick Romeo, eager to see Rosaline, agrees to the plan.

Romeo, Benvolio, and their friend Mercutio crash the party at Capulet's house. Once inside, Romeo spots fourteen-year-old Juliet from a distance, instantly falls in love with her, and forgets all about Rosaline. Romeo admires Juliet, gathers the courage to speak to her, and the two experience a profound attraction for each other. They kiss without knowing each other's names.

When Romeo discovers that Juliet is a Capulet and Juliet learns that Romeo is a Montague, they become equally upset. Mercutio, Benvolio, and Romeo leave the Capulet estate, but Romeo, unable to leave Juliet behind, leaps over the orchard wall, hides in the garden, and spots Juliet in a window above the orchard. When he overhears Juliet speaking his name, he calls out to her, and they exchange vows of love.

Romeo persuades a local cleric, Friar Laurence, to marry the young lovers in the hopes of ending the feud between Capulet and Montague. The next day, Friar

Laurence marries Romeo and Juliet, and that night Romeo uses a ladder to climb secretly into Juliet's window for their wedding night, and they consummate their love. In the morning, the lovers bid farewell, unsure when they will see each other again.

STRANGE ENCOUNTERS

★ The suicides of Romeo and Juliet closely resemble the historic deaths of Cleopatra and Mark Antony. In *Romeo and Juliet,* Romeo drinks poison and Juliet stabs herself. Antony stabbed himself with a knife, and Cleopatra killed herself by placing a poisonous snake on her body.

★ William Shakespeare based his first romantic play, *Romeo and Juliet,* written around 1595, on an Italian romance by Bandello and the poem *Romeus and Juliet* by English author Arthur Brooke.

★ In *Romeo and Juliet,* Juliet says:
"What's in a name? That which we call a rose
By any other name would smell as sweet."

★ All the moons of the Solar System are named after figures in Greek and Roman mythology, except the moons of Uranus, which are named after characters from Shakespeare.

★ William Shakespeare was born and died on the same date: April 23

★ Leslie Howard and Norma Shearer starred in the 1936 movie *Romeo and Juliet.*

★ The Broadway musical *West Side Story,* with music by Leonard Bernstein, lyrics by Steven Sondheim, and a book by Arthur Laurents, is a contemporary retelling of *Romeo and Juliet.*

★ Leonard Whiting and Olivia Hussey starred in the 1968 movie *Romeo and Juliet.*

★ Alex Hyde-White and Blanche Baker starred in the 1983 movie *Romeo and Juliet.*

★ The lyrics to the song "Mystery Dance" by Elvis Costello refer to Romeo and Juliet.

Franklin D. Roosevelt and Eleanor Roosevelt

S oon after the birth of Franklin Delano Roosevelt on January 30, 1882, his father invited his distant cousin Elliot to be the child's godfather. Four years later, Elliot and his wife Anna brought their two-year-old daughter Eleanor, born

Ann Eleanor Roosevelt on October 11, 1884, to visit their godson Franklin at his family mansion in Hyde Park, New York. "I am told that Franklin, probably under protest, crawled around the nursery… bearing me on his back," recalled Eleanor.

Neither Franklin nor Eleanor had any romantic interest in each other until the summer of 1901, when Franklin, a junior at Harvard, spotted seventeen-year-old Eleanor, who had returned home from London after three years at Allenswood finishing school, on the train to Tivoli. Franklin invited Eleanor to sit with him and his mother.

His interest in Eleanor piqued, Franklin frequently returned home from Harvard during the fall to attend debutante parties with Eleanor. The following year, they began corresponding frequently, and in October, Franklin invited Eleanor to come up to Cambridge for the forthcoming Harvard-Yale football game. She accepted. On November 22, the day after the game, they went to visit a friend of Eleanor's in Groton, where 21-year-old Franklin proposed marriage to nineteen-year-old

Eleanor. Franklin's mother, Sara, however, persuaded her son and Eleanor to keep their engagement secret for one year, during which time Sara took Franklin on a five-week winter cruise to the Caribbean to test the couple's love for one another. Before the cruise left in January, Franklin and Eleanor spent as much time together as possible, and during the cruise they corresponded almost ceaselessly.

In the fall of 1904, Franklin, who had planned to attend Harvard Law School, began at Columbia Law School instead, to be closer to Eleanor. He bought an engagement ring at Tiffany's on October 7 and gave it to Eleanor on her twentieth birthday on October 11. Yet the couple did not disclose their engagement until after Thanksgiving.

On November 29, Eleanor's uncle, President Theodore Roosevelt, sent a letter to his distant cousin Franklin. It read: "We are greatly rejoiced over the good news. I am as fond of Eleanor as if she were my daughter; and I like you, and trust you, and believe in you. No other success in life—not the Presidency, or anything else—begins to compare with the joy and happiness that come in and from the love of the true man and the true woman, the love which never sinks lover and sweetheart in man and wife. You and Eleanor are true and brave, and I believe you love each other unselfishly; and golden years open before you. May all good fortune attend you both, ever."

The engaged couple attended Theodore Roosevelt's second Presidential inauguration on March 4, 1905, and were married two weeks later on March 17. The President of the United States gave the bride away.

S T R A N G E   E N C O U N T E R S

★ Franklin and Eleanor were very distant cousins, related through Nicholas Van Roosevelt and his wife, whose name has been lost to history. They were Franklin's great-great-great-great-grandparents (one of thirty-two such couples) and Eleanor's great-great-great-great-great-grandparents (one of sixty-four such couples).

★ Eleanor was raised by her maternal grandmother.

★ In 1918, Eleanor discovered that Franklin, serving as Assistant Secretary of the Navy, was having an affair with her social secretary, Lucy Mercer.

★ After receiving his diploma from Harvard, Franklin sailed his family's sixty-foot schooner *Half Moon* from New Bedford, Massachusetts, to the family estate at Hyde Park, New York—stopping first to race her off Newport, Rhode Island.

★ In 1937, Eleanor became the first First Lady to hold a press conference.

★ Around 1937, Eleanor burned all the love letters Franklin wrote to her during their courtship, claiming they were too private.

★ In her syndicated newspaper column, "My Day," Eleanor announced her resignation from the Daughters of the American Revolution to protest the group's refusal to allow African-American singer Marian Anderson to perform at its Constitution Hall in Washington, D.C.

★ When Eleanor fell ill at the age of seventy-eight and began bleeding and bruising at the slightest touch, her doctors incorrectly diagnosed her as suffering from a fatal blood disease. The former First Lady actually had tuberculosis. Rather than performing an open bone marrow biopsy to confirm their diagnosis, doctors began treating her with prednisone—a drug that fights blood diseases. Unfortunately, prednisone also lowers the body's resistance to infection, enabling the undiagnosed tuberculosis to spread faster, killing Eleanor.

★ Franklin and Eleanor Roosevelt had six children: Anna, James, Franklin (who died in infancy), Elliott, Franklin, and John.

★ The children's television show *Sesame Street* features a muppet named Roosevelt Franklin.

Dan Rowan and Dick Martin

At a party in 1952, Dick Rowan, a failed screenwriter who worked as a car salesman for Madman Muntz, met Dick Martin, an aspiring comedy writer who had supported himself for ten years as a bartender. The two kindred spirits decided to form a comedy team. They performed together for the first time at Hymie's Barbecue in Albuquerque, New Mexico. Dan played the straight man, making a mundane statement that Dick, playing the part of the sex-crazed bird-brain, mangled into sheer lunacy.

Critic Walter Winchell discovered the duo and lauded them in his column, landing them bookings in nightclubs and theaters all over the world, including the Copacabana in New York City, the Chez Paree in Chicago, the Fountainbleu Hotel in Miami Beach, the Chevron Hilton in Sydney, and the Palladium Theater in London.

In 1958, Dan and Dick appeared briefly on the summer comedy variety television show *The Chevy Show*. When their first feature film, the 1958 Western *Once Upon a Horse*, bombed, they landed back on the nightclub circuit as a fixture at the Sahara Hotel in Las Vegas. There they were discovered by singer Dean Martin, who invited them to be guests on his NBC television show, aptly titled *The Dean Martin Show*. In the summer of 1966, Dean chose Dan and Dick as his replacements to cohost *The Dean Martin Summer Show*, bringing the comedy team to the attention of the network.

On September 9, 1967, NBC broadcast a one-hour television special called *Rowan & Martin's Laugh-In*, a zany, rapid-fire, unstructured comedy happening, cohosted by Dan and Dick. The duo attempted to orchestrate the proceedings, but seemed to be bombarded by a whirlwind of sight-gags and eccentric performances. The special became an overnight success, and in January 1968, NBC added *Rowan & Martin's Laugh-In* to its line-up. The show captured the chaotic and flamboyant irreverence of the Sixties with a pop-art sensibility, giving the age of "sit-ins," "love-ins," and "teach-ins" something new and unusual—a "laugh-in." The show quickly became the highest-rated series of the decade, turning Rowan and Martin into instant celebrities.

STRANGE ENCOUNTERS

★ Dick Martin, born on January 30, 1922, in Detroit, Michigan, starred as Harry Conners on *The Lucy Show* and appeared in the 1966 Doris Day movie *The Glass Bottom Boat*.

★ Dan Rowan was born Daniel Hale Rowan on July 22, 1922, in Beggs, Oklahoma.

★ At the peak of the popularity of *Rowan & Martin's Laugh-In*, Dan and Dick starred in the 1969 horror spoof, *The Maltese Bippy*. The movie bombed.

★ *Rowan And Martin's Laugh-In* introduced America to a new generation of comic talent, including Ruth Buzzi, Goldie Hawn, Arte Johnson, Henry Gibson, Jo Anne Worley, Alan Sues, Dave Madden, and Lily Tomlin.

★ *Rowan And Martin's Laugh-In* introduced several catch-phrases into the American vernacular, including: "Sock it to me," "Here come the judge," "You bet your sweet bippy," and "Look that up in your *Funk and Wagnalls.*"

★ On *Rowan And Martin's Laugh-In*, Dan and Dick introduced the world to Tiny Tim, who sang and played "Tiptoe Through the Tulips" on his ukulele.

★ After *Rowan And Martin's Laugh-In*, Dick directed several television series, including *The Bob Newhart Show*, *Archie Bunker's Place*, *Family Ties*, *Newhart*, and *In the Heat of the Night*.

★ Dan Rowan died from lymphatic cancer September 22, 1987, in Englewood, Florida.

Susan Sarandon and Tim Robbins

In 1988 actress Susan Sarandon, a divorcée who had starred as the sexually charged Janet in the 1975 cult classic *The Rocky Horror Picture Show* and who had been nominated for an Academy Award for her role in the 1980 movie *Atlantic City,* was cast to play a sexy schoolteacher with a fondness for younger men in the 1988 movie *Bull Durham.*

In the movie, Susan's character, the baseball-worshipping Annie Savoy, had a passionate love affair with the hot, young, dimwitted fastball pitcher "Nuke" Laloosh, portrayed by actor Tim Robbins. Tall, baby-faced Tim, twelve years younger than Susan, had played naive and obtuse characters in the movies *No Small Affair* and *Tapeheads,* and had founded the Los Angeles theater group Actors' Gang.

"I guess I met her at the audition for *Bull Durham,*" recalled Tim. "I remember thinking that she was beautiful and smart." Tim's onscreen romance with Susan soon expanded into their offscreen lives. Their long-term relationship resulted in the birth of two sons and eventually evolved into a common-law marriage.

STRANGE ENCOUNTERS

★ Susan Sarandon, born Susan Abigail Tomalin on October 4, 1946, in New York City, New York, grew up in Edison, New Jersey, where she was a cheerleader at Edison High School.

★ Tim Robbins, born Timothy Francis Robbins on October 16, 1958, in West Covina, California, studied drama at UCLA, worked his way through college by delivering pizzas and busing tables at the Hillcrest Country Club, and graduated with honors.

★ Susan majored in drama at Catholic University in Washington, D.C., where she met her first husband, Chris Sarandon. They married in 1968 and divorced eleven years later.

★ Both Susan and her first husband Chris auditioned for parts in the 1970 movie *Joe*. The producers passed on Chris, but cast Susan in a major role as the daughter of an advertising executive.

★ Tim Robbins was kicked off the Stuyvesant High School hockey team in New York City for fighting.

★ Tim made his stage debut alongside his father, Gil Robbins, a successful folk-singer in Greenwich Village with the Highwaymen, on a duet of the protest song "Ink Is Black But the Page Is White."

★ Susan has a daughter named Eva from a relationship with Italian filmmaker Franco Amurri.

★ The Actors' Gang, an experimental ensemble founded by Tim in 1981, expressed radical political observations through the European avant-garde form of theater.

★ Susan and Tim have two children together: Jack and Miles.

★ As co-presenters at the 1993 Academy Awards ceremony, Susan and Tim spoke on behalf of the hundreds of Haitians with AIDS who had been interned in Guantanamo Bay.

★ Susan keeps her Academy Award on display in her bathroom.

★ In 1999, New York police arrested Susan for disorderly conduct during a protest against four police officers who shot unarmed African immigrant Amadou Diallo.

★ In the wake of the terrorist attacks on September 11, 2001, Tim, unable to fly to New York City to be with Susan and their children, drove from Los Angeles to New York City with a friend in a 56-hour trip.

★ Susan and Tim starred together in five movies: *Bull Durham, The Player, Bob Roberts, Cradle Will Rock,* and *Last Party 2000.* Tim directed Susan in three movies: *Bob Roberts, Cradle Will Rock,* and *Dead Man Walking.*

Arnold Schwarzenegger and Maria Shriver

In 1977, NBC news anchor Tom Brokaw introduced aspiring broadcast journalist Maria Shriver to Austrian bodybuilder and three-time Mr. Universe Arnold Schwarzenegger. The meeting took place at a party on the eve of the Robert F. Kennedy Pro-Celebrity Tennis Tournament in Forest Hills, New York, a charitable event held annually in honor of Maria's late uncle.

At the time, 21-year-old Maria, a recent graduate of Georgetown University, was enrolled in the Westinghouse broadcast-training program. Her brother, Bobby, had invited thirty-year-old Arnold, the subject of the 1977 documentary film *Pumping Iron*, to compete in the tournament even though the bodybuilder was not a tennis player.

The next day on the tennis court, Arnold, teamed with former football star Rosie Grier, played a doubles game against a pair of ten-year-old boys. Hopelessly losing, Arnold and Rosie doffed their shirts and strutted for the crowd—attracting Maria's interest. "I was pretty sure when I met him that I would marry him," recalled Maria. "I admired his independence, his focus, his drive, his humor." That afternoon, she invited Arnold to join her family at their house near the Kennedy compound in Hyannisport, Massachusetts.

Maria and Arnold began dating and immediately recognized their shared determination to succeed. Before getting married, Maria wanted to become a network news anchor by age thirty. Arnold aspired to become a leading man in Hollywood movies. Both Maria and Arnold achieved their goals. Maria became an on-camera reporter for CBS and at age twenty-nine became an anchor on the *CBS Morning News*. Arnold starred in the 1982 movie *Conan the Barbarian*, followed by a sequel *Conan the Destroyer*. Two years later, he starred in *The Terminator*, a role that catapulted him to superstardom.

In the summer of 1986, Arnold took Maria home with him to Thal, Austria. While they sat in a row boat on the lake where Arnold swam as a child, Arnold proposed to Maria, giving her a diamond engagement ring. "We'd been together eight years," recalled Maria, "so naturally I said, 'Yes!'"

STRANGE ENCOUNTERS

★ Arnold Alois Schwarzenegger was born on July 30, 1947, in Thal, Austria, to a police officer and his wife. His middle name is German for "action."

★ Maria Owings Shriver was born on November 6, 1955, in Chicago Illinois, to Sargent Shriver and Eunice Kennedy Shriver, sister of John F. Kennedy.

★ Sargent Shriver served as the first director of the Peace Corps, George McGovern's vice presidential running mate in 1972, and ambassador of France. Eunice Shriver founded the Special Olympics.

★ Arnold won the title Mr. Universe at age twenty.

★ Arnold auditioned for the lead role in the television series *The Incredible Hulk*, but lost the part to his former bodybuilding competitor, Lou Ferrigno.

★ In 1979, Arnold graduated from University of Wisconsin-Superior with a major in international marketing and business administration.

★ In 1983, Arnold became a United States citizen.

★ Arnold is a staunch Republican. Maria, a niece of President John F. Kennedy, is a staunch Democrat.

★ At the rehearsal dinner for his wedding to Maria, Arnold wore traditional Tyrolean lederhosen.

★ Arnold married Maria on April 26, 1986, at St. Francis Xavier Church in Hyannisport, Massachusetts. At the ceremony, television talk-show host Oprah Winfrey read Elizabeth Barrett Browning's poem "How Do I Love Thee?"

★ A few days before her wedding, Maria broke two toes. To dance at the reception, she wore sneakers.

★ For several years, Maria commuted from her home in Los Angeles to New York and Washington, D.C., for her anchor jobs on NBC's *Sunday Today* and *Weekend Nightly News*.

★ *The Guinness Book of World Records* has called Arnold "the most perfectly developed man in the history of the world."

★ Arnold was the first private citizen in the United States to own a Humvee (High Mobility Multi-Purpose Wheeled Vehicle).

★ Arnold and Maria have four children: Katherine, Christina, Patrick, and Christopher.

Richard Sears and Alvah Roebuck

In 1886, Richard Warren Sears, a 23-year-old railroad agent at the Minneapolis and St. Louis Railway Station in North Redwood, Minnesota, received a shipment of watches for a Redwood Falls jeweler. The jeweler, however, refused to accept the watches and asked Sears to return the shipment to the manufacturer. The ambitious young Sears, recognizing an opportunity to make some extra money, bought the shipment of watches from the local jeweler at the wholesale price. He then offered the watches, which retailed for twenty-five dollars each, to other station agents along the railroad route for fourteen dollars a piece. Sears quickly sold all the watches and ordered more.

Six months later, Sears had earned more than five thousand dollars, enabling him to quit his job with the railroad and start the R. W. Sears Watch Company in Minneapolis, Minnesota. Determined to reach more customers, he moved his company to Chicago in 1887. He ran an advertisement in the April 1 edition of the *Chicago Daily News* that read: "Wanted—Watchmaker with reference who can furnish tools."

Alvah Curtis Roebuck, a watch repairman from Hammond, Indiana, answered the ad. Roebuck convinced Sears of his expertise fixing watches by bringing along a sample of his work. Sears hired him on the spot.

The next year, Sears issued his first catalog, featuring only watches and jewelry. In 1889, Sears sold the watch business, and two years later he and Roebuck formed another mail-order business. On September 16, 1893, the company became formally known as Sears, Roebuck & Co.

STRANGE ENCOUNTERS

★ In 1895, Alvah Roebuck sold his share of Sears, Roebuck & Co. for 25,000 dollars. A few years later, Roebuck's share would have been worth millions.

★ In 1906, Sears, Roebuck & Co. went public and opened a forty-acre mail-order plant, then the largest business building in the world, built at a cost of five million dollars.

★ Henry Ford reportedly visited the forty-acre Sears, Roebuck & Co. mail-order plant in Chicago to study the company's assembly-line technique.

★ The 1911 Sears, Roebuck & Co. Catalog offered blood purifiers, liver and kidney remedies, and "pink pills for pale people."

★ The Sears, Roebuck & Co. Catalog sold centrifugal cream separators for $24, men's suits for $9.95, and a "Stradivarius model violin" for $6.10.

★ When one of Sears' new partners, Julius Rosenwald, began editing the Sears, Roebuck & Co. Mail Order Catalog, he insisted that Richard Sears' fanciful advertising copy be factual. Irate, Sears left the company and Rosenwald became president.

★ With the advent of the automobile, Sears, Roebuck & Co. opened its first retail store in 1925 in the Chicago mail-order plant so farmers could drive to town to buy merchandise.

★ In the Depression, Alvah Roebuck lost all of his income. Sears, Roebuck & Co. hired him to write the history of the company and to represent the company at grand openings and press events.

★ In 1969, Sears, Roebuck & Co. began building the 110-story Sears Tower in downtown Chicago. When it opened in 1973, the 1,454-foot-tall skyscraper was the world's tallest building.

★ In 1990, Kmart surpassed Sears as the number-one retail store in the United States, only to be overtaken two year later by Wal-Mart.

★ Sears discontinued its catalog in 1993 and sold the Sears Tower in 2003.

★ A former chief of the Moscow bureau of the Associated Press claimed: "Two innocent articles of American life—the Sears, Roebuck & Co. catalog and the phonograph record—are the most powerful pieces of foreign propaganda in Russia. The catalog comes first."

★ During one twelve-month period in the late 1920s, a Sears, Roebuck & Co. store opened on the average of one every other business day.

★ Launched by Sears in 1986, the Discover card is carried by 38 million shoppers. Cardholders can use it to shop at 1.2 million stores and restaurants other than Sears, including Wal-Mart.

★ A Kenmore appliance made by Sears can be found in one out of every two American homes.

★ As of 1995, Sears employed 360,570 people. That's more than seventy-one times the population of North Redwood, Minnesota, the town where company founder Richard Sears started selling watches.

Paul Simon and Art Garfunkel

Paul Simon met Art Garfunkel at Forest Hills Elementary School during rehearsals for the sixth-grade graduation play, *Alice in Wonderland*. Paul played the White Rabbit, Art played the Cheshire Cat. The two boys walked home together after rehearsals, and became inseparable friends, sharing an interest in sports and music.

Together, Paul and Art listened to the radio shows hosted by rock 'n' roll dee-jays Alan Freed and Dick Clark, played records by Elvis Presley and Bill Haley and the Comets, and attended local rock concerts. In the mid-1950s, they stared singing together while Paul played acoustic guitar, soon entertaining at parties and school dances. Paul and Art cut a demo record, attracting the attention of an executive from a small recording company called Big Records, who renamed the duo Tom and Jerry, had them record several songs, booked them as the warm-up act for several rock 'n' roll shows, and got the boys on Dick Clark's *American Bandstand*. In 1958, the Tom and Jerry single "Hey! Schoolgirl" hit Number 54 on Billboard's Top 100. When their later singles failed to achieve similar success, "Tom Graph" (Art) and "Jerry Lindis" (Paul) parted ways.

After graduating from high school, Paul majored in English literature at Queens College. Art went to Columbia University to study architecture. The two college students rekindled their friendship and shared their growing interest in the folk music of Bob Dylan, Joan Baez, and the Kingston Trio. Paul and Art began singing together in Greenwich Village's Washington Square Park, the Gaslight Club, and Gerde's Folk City—attracting a loyal following. In 1964, after graduating from college, Paul played some of his original songs for Tom Wilson, a producer for Columbia Records, who immediately signed the duo to record an album.

Soon after the release of *Wednesday Morning, 3 A.M.* in October 1964, radio disc jockeys began receiving requests for one of the songs on the album, "Sounds of Silence," penned by Paul. Columbia quickly released the song as a single. In 1966, "The Sounds of Silence" reached #1 on the charts, earning Paul and Art their first gold record.

After two more Simon and Garfunkel albums (*Sounds of Silence* and *Parsley, Sage, Rosemary and Thyme*), director Mike Nichols hired Simon and Garfunkel to compose and perform original soundtrack music for his 1968 movie *The Graduate*. "It was Mike's concept that we would be the voice of Benjamin," Paul told the *New York Times*. "A song like 'The Sounds of Silence' is really Benjamin talking about his life and his parents and where he lives and what he sees around him."

The soundtrack album topped the charts for six months, won a Grammy Award for Record of the Year, and the single "Mrs. Robinson" won Simon and Garfunkel a second Grammy, firmly establishing the duo as a pop-music phenomenon.

STRANGE ENCOUNTERS

★ Arthur Ira Garfunkel was born on November 5, 1941, in Forest Hills, New York.

★ Paul Frederick Simon, born on October 13, 1942, in Newark, New Jersey, grew up in Forest Hills, New York.

★ After graduating from Queens College, Paul entered Brooklyn Law, but dropped out after six months to pursue a music career.

★ Although executives at Columbia Records feared that Simon and Garfunkel might be mistaken for a law firm or fashion boutique, the record company agreed to release the duo's first album under their real names.

★ Released in 1970, the album *Bridge Over Troubled Water* sold more than nine million copies in less than two years. The album won an unprecedented six Grammy Awards.

★ Rather than playing nightclubs, Paul and Art wisely heeded the advice of their agent, show business veteran Mort Lewis, and performed concerts solely before educated, young audiences at colleges and universities, or in dignified settings like Carnegie Hall and Philharmonic Hall in New York City.

★ The duo's agent restricted their television appearances to uninterrupted guest segments on variety shows like *The Ed Sullivan Show*.

★ Art appeared in the movies *Catch-22* and *Carnal Knowledge*.

★ Simon and Garfunkel broke up in 1970, but reunited to sing together at a McGovern for President rally in Madison Square Garden in 1972, on *Saturday Night Live* in 1978, for a free concert in New York's Central Park in 1981, on an international tour, and in a series of concerts in 1993.

★ Paul has been married three times, to Peggy Harper, actress Carrie Fisher, and singer Edie Brickell.

★ Art has been married twice, to Linda Grossman and Kim Cermak.

O. J. Simpson and Nicole Brown

In 1977, thirty-year-old Heisman trophy winner and former Buffalo Bills football player O. J. Simpson met eighteen-year-old Nicole Brown, a recent high school graduate, in the Daisy, a Beverly Hills nightclub where she worked as a waitress. At the time, O. J. had been married for twelve years to his high school sweetheart, Marguerite Whitley, with whom he had three children. In 1978, he separated from his wife and brought nineteen-year-old Nicole to live in his palatial home in Brentwood, on Rockingham Avenue. Seven years later, on February 2, 1985, he married Nicole, then two months pregnant with his child.

Nicole frequently complained to friends and family that O. J. beat her in jealous rages over her flirtatious associations with other men. O. J. denied ever hitting Nicole and insisted that her injuries resulted from friendly "wrassling." Whenever she called the police for help, they refused to charge the former football star with any crime—with one exception. According to Nicole's diary, O. J. began abusing her as early as 1977, physically and mentally. In 1985, while pregnant with O. J.'s first child, Nicole called the police to report that O. J. had attacked her car with a baseball bat. On New Year's Eve in 1989, police were called to the Rockingham estate and charged O. J. with spousal battery. He pleaded "no contest" and was sentenced to 120 hours of community-service work and two years' probation.

Finally, in January 1992, after two children and seven years of an abusive marriage, Nicole separated from O. J. and relocated with their children to a rented home on Gretna Green Way, a few miles from O. J.'s estate. The couple divorced on October 15, 1992, and a year later, Nicole and her children moved into a condominium on nearby South Bundy Drive.

★ O. J. Simpson was born Orenthal James Simpson on July 9, 1947 in San Francisco, California.

★ Nicole Brown was born on May 19, 1959, in West Germany.

★ At age thirteen, O. J. joined a street gang, the Persian Warriors, and at age fifteen, he spent time in custody at San Francisco's Youth Guidance Center.

★ At age eighteen O. J. married his Galileo High School sweetheart Marguerite Whitley. Together they had three children: Arnelle, Jason, and Aaren.

★ In the 1974 movie *The Klansman*, O. J. played a man framed for murder by the police.

★ In 1979, after O. J. separated from his first wife, his son Aaren drowned in the swimming pool at his Rockingham estate.

★ Simpson starred in television commercials for Hertz rental cars, leaping over luggage and other obstacles to catch an airline flight.

★ On October 25, 1993, Nicole summoned police to her home after O. J. kicked in the rear French doors.

★ While living at a rented house on Gretna Green Way, Nicole rented out a spare room to aspiring actor Kato Kaelin, who doubled as an unpaid housekeeper and babysitter. When Nicole moved into a condominium on South Bundy Drive, O. J. let Kaelin live in a bungalow at his Rockingham estate.

★ On Sunday night, June 12, 1994, Nicole and her friend, Ron Goldman, were stabbed and slashed to death at Nicole's condominium. O. J. claimed that he was in his back yard hitting golf balls at the time of the murder.

★ After Nicole's funeral, O. J. fled in his Ford Bronco, holding a gun to his own head, with his friend, Al Cowling, at the wheel. The police chased the Bronco, but let O. J. surrender voluntarily.

★ O. J. pleaded "absolutely, positively, 100 percent not guilty" to the murder charges and pledged to find the real murderer. He has yet to do so.

★ By the time of O. J.'s 1995 murder trial, the prosecution had compiled a list of sixty-two separate incidents of abuse of Nicole by O. J.

★ In 1995, after a lengthy trial, a jury found O. J. not guilty of murdering his ex-wife and her friend, Ron Goldman. However, the jury in a 1997 civil suit held O. J. liable for the deaths and awarded 8.5 million dollars in damages to the Goldman family.

★ Whoever murdered Nicole and Ronald Goldman wore a pair of expensive Bruno Magli "Lorenzo" style shoes, leaving bloody prints near the victims at the crime scene. In a February 1996 civil lawsuit deposition, O. J. claimed, "I would have never owned those ugly-ass shoes." The next month, a photographer came forth with the negatives to a series of thirty-one photos he had taken of Simpson wearing Bruno Magli "Lorenzo" style shoes at a 1993 Buffalo Bills football game.

Frank Sinatra and Mia Farrow

In October 1964, 49-year-old Frank Sinatra returned to Twentieth Century-Fox studios in Hollywood to shoot the interior scenes for the movie *Von Ryan's Express*. Every day, nineteen-year-old Mia Farrow, determined to attract Frank's attention, stood at the door to the sound stage, wearing a transparent gauzy ankle-length nightgown borrowed from the wardrobe department. Mia, the daughter of actress Maureen O'Sullivan and director John Farrow, had been cast to play Alison MacKenzie on the television series *Peyton Place*, which was shot on the Fox lot.

As Frank left the set with two friends after the first week of shooting, he told Mia, who had become a permanent fixture, that he was flying to his house in Palm Springs for the weekend in his private jet. Mia asked him to invite her along. Since the plane could only hold three passengers, Frank flew to Palm Springs with his two friends, then sent his pilot back to Los Angeles to get Mia, who was five years younger than his daughter Nancy and one year younger than his son Frank, Jr.

That weekend launched Frank and Mia's romantic relationship. They began spending many quiet weekends at Frank's Palm Springs home. He took Mia to a screening of his 1965 movie *None But the Brave* (the only film he ever directed) and called her on the set of *Peyton Place* every day.

In August 1965, Frank chartered a yacht and invited Mia and eight guests to cruise with him for a month off the coast of New England. The writers of *Peyton Place* wrote Mia's character into a coma for four weeks, figuring if she got married and left the show, the character would die; otherwise, she would awaken. When asked by reporters if the couple would be getting married, Mia's mother, Maureen O'Sullivan, replied, "If Mr. Sinatra is going to marry anyone, he ought to marry me!"

On July 4, 1966, while staying at the summer home of Random House publisher Bennett Cerf in Mt. Kisco, New York, Frank gave Mia a nine-carat diamond engagement ring. Two weeks later, on July 19, Frank and Mia were married in Las Vegas, in the living room of Frank's friend, Jack Entratter, president of the Sands Hotel. The newlywed couple flew to Los Angeles for a wedding dinner at the home of Edie Goetz, where they spent the night to avoid being hounded by the media.

STRANGE ENCOUNTERS

★ Frank Sinatra was born on December 12, 1915, in Hoboken, New Jersey.

★ Mia Farrow was born on February 9, 1945, in Los Angeles, California, to director John Farrow and actress Maureen O'Sullivan.

★ Mia made her screen debut in the 1959 movie *John Paul Jones*, directed by her father John Farrow.

★ When Mia and Frank were dating, Dean Martin said, "I've got Scotch older than Mia Farrow."

★ During their courtship, Mia called Frank "Charlie Brown," while he called her "doll face."

★ Mia was the first American actress to be accepted as a member of London's prestigious Royal Shakespeare Company.

★ During his honeymoon with Mia in New York City, Frank punched a photographer who was trying to take a picture of the newlyweds outside the 21 Club, where Bennett Cerf was hosting a party for the couple.

★ In November 1966, during opening night of Frank's engagement in Las Vegas at the Sands Hotel, he introduced his new wife to the audience. "Yeah, I got married," he told the crowd. "Well, you see I had to.... I finally found a broad I can cheat on...." The audience gasped and Mia bowed her head in shame.

★ In 1967, while married to Frank, Mia went to India with the Beatles to study Transcendental Meditation with the Maharishi Mahesh Yogi. Beatle John Lennon wrote the song "Dear Prudence" for her younger sister Prudence Farrow.

★ While Mia was filming *Rosemary's Baby* in 1967, Frank ordered her to leave the set and start work with him in the movie *The Detective*. When Mia refused, he sent his lawyer to Mia's trailer on the Paramount lot to serve notice that he was filing for divorce.

★ Frank and Mia were divorced quickly in Juarez, Mexico. She refused to accept any alimony and gave up the house he had bought for her in Bel Air, insisting only that they remain friends.

★ On the *Tonight Show*, on the night Frank and Mia were divorced, Johnny Carson said, "Hear about the trouble at Frank Sinatra's house? Mia Farrow dropped her Silly Putty in Frank's Poligrip."

★ Mia lives with her children in a large rent-controlled apartment in the building next door to Manhattan's legendary Dakota building, the scene of her 1968 movie *Rosemary's Baby*. The Dakota was also home to her friend John Lennon.

★ The cover of the first issue of *People* magazine featured a photograph of Mia Farrow.

★ Frank was married four times, to Nancy Barbato, Ava Gardner, Mia Farrow, and Barbara Marx. He had three children: Nancy, Tina, and Frank (all with first wife, Nancy).

★ The epitaph on Frank's headstone reads: "The best is yet to come."

Gene Siskel and Roger Ebert

In 1974, CBS news director Van Gordon Sauter hired Gene Siskel, the film critic at the *Chicago Tribune*, to deliver movie reviews during local newscasts at Channel 2, the CBS affiliate in Chicago. The following year, WTTW-Channel 11 paired Siskel with his rival Roger Ebert, film critic at the *Chicago Sun-Times*, in a show called *Opening Soon at a Theater Near You.* The show's producer, Thea Flaum, had Siskel and Ebert wear casual clothes and sit in a row of movie theater seats, as if they were typical movie patrons. The brutally honest film critics spontaneously discussed and debated the merits of newly released movies with the passion of two competitive and fiercely opposite newspapermen. Audiences loved watching the combative yet intelligent arguments between two critics who clearly loved movies. "We've always wanted viewers to feel as if they were just eavesdropping on a couple of guys who loved movies and were having a spontaneous discussion that we'd be doing even if they weren't watching," explained Siskel.

The show became an immediate hit, and, in 1977, PBS syndicated the show (renamed *Sneak Previews*) nationwide, turning Siskel and Ebert into national celebrities. In 1982, the duo, who had become the most popular film critics in the United States, moved their show to commercial television, renaming it *At the Movies.* Four years later, they switched to Buena Vista Television and renamed the show *Siskel & Ebert.*

Audiences could not tell whether Siskel and Ebert feigned their mutual antagonism onscreen or whether they truly despised each other offscreen. In truth, Siskel and Ebert, while frequently holding opposing points of view, deeply respected each other.

STRANGE ENCOUNTERS

★ Roger Ebert was born on June 18, 1942, in Urbana, Illinois.

★ Eugene Kal Siskel was born on January 26, 1946, in Chicago, Illinois.

★ At age fifteen, Ebert worked as a sportswriter.

★ Ebert and actor David Ogden Stiers (best known as Major Charles Winchester on the television comedy M*A*S*H) were high school classmates.

★ As a student at the University of Illinois, Ebert won a national college award for his campus newspaper columns.

★ At age twenty-six, Ebert was drafted into the Army to serve in the Vietnam War, but was rejected from military service for being overweight. He weighed 206 pounds.

★ In 1969, Siskel, hired by the *Chicago Tribune* as a local news reporter, convinced his editors to let him critique films.

★ While doing movie reviews at the CBS-affiliate television station in Chicago, Siskel met producer Marlene Iglitzen, whom he later married.

★ Siskel claimed that his favorite movie was *Saturday Night Fever*. At a charity auction, he purchased the white suit John Travolta wore in the movie.

★ When asked by David Letterman what one film he would want if stranded on a desert island, Siskel chose *2001: A Space Odyssey*. Ebert picked *Citizen Kane*.

★ Ebert is the only person ever to win a Pulitzer Prize for film commentary.

★ In 1995, the city of Chicago changed the name of the street Erie Way to Siskel & Ebert Way.

★ Ebert owns a life-sized statue of Oliver Hardy.

★ Siskel died on February 20, 1999, at age fifty-three, from complications during brain surgery.

★ In 2002, Ebert slipped on a wet floor and broke his left shoulder in two places, preventing him from attending the Cannes Film Festival for the first time in twenty-five years.

★ In 2002, the fourth annual "EbertFest of Overlooked Films" in Champaign, Illinois, attracted some twenty thousand people.

Horace Smith and Daniel B. Wesson

In 1852, two former gunsmith apprentices, Horace Smith and Daniel B. Wesson, teamed up in Springfield, Massachusetts, to manufacture a lever-action pistol with a tubular magazine that fired a self-contained cartridge. Smith and Wesson opened up their first factory in Norwich, Connecticut, and began producing the lever-action pistol. *Scientific American* nicknamed the rapid-fire pistol "The Volcanic."

In 1854, Smith and Wesson encountered financial difficulties—until an investor, shirt manufacturer Oliver Winchester, pumped money into the company and moved the factory to New Haven, Connecticut, where he had some of his holdings. Smith and Wesson sold their majority interest in the company and Smith returned to Springfield. Wesson supervised the Winchester plant and designed a small revolver that could shoot the self-contained cartridge he and Smith had patented earlier that year.

In 1856, Smith and Wesson rekindled their partnership in Springfield and began producing the newly designed revolver and accompanying cartridge. The overwhelming demand for the handguns and cartridges forced Smith and Wesson to build a new factory, turning the two men into major firearms manufacturers and two of the wealthiest industrialists in the world.

STRANGE ENCOUNTERS

★ Horace Smith was born on October 28, 1808, in Chester, Massachusetts.

★ Daniel Wesson, born on May 18, 1825, in Worcester, Massachusetts, worked as an apprentice at a shoe manufacturing company run by his two older brothers.

★ By 1862, the Civil War created such a huge demand for Smith & Wesson firearms that the company had to stop taking new orders and concentrate solely on fulfilling its heavy backlog of existing orders.

★ After the Civil War, gun sales plummeted and Smith & Wesson sold only a few guns each month.

★ The Russian Grand Duke, Alexis, purchased several Smith & Wesson pistols.

★ In 1871, the Russian government ordered twenty thousand Smith & Wesson Model 3 revolvers.

★ In 1914, Smith & Wesson supplied its new mass-produced N-Frame revolver to the British government to fight World War I.

★ During the Depression, Smith & Wesson produced the .357 Magnum, the world's first Magnum handgun, designed for law enforcement officers. The company sent one of the first .357 Magnums to FBI director J. Edgar Hoover.

★ During World War II, Smith & Wesson supplied the Allied Forces with 1,110,392 revolvers.

★ In the 1950s, Smith & Wesson introduced the .44 Magnum.

★ In the *Dirty Harry* movies, Clint Eastwood carries a Smith & Wesson .44 Magnum.

★ In the 1980s, Smith & Wesson developed its L-Frame line of .357 Magnums, the most popular revolvers ever made.

★ In 1998, Smith & Wesson introduced AirLite Ti revolvers, made from a combination of aluminum, titanium, and stainless steel—creating the lightest full-feature revolvers in history.

★ Each Smith & Wesson handgun is test fired.

Sonny and Cher

In November 1962, sixteen-year-old Cherilyn Sarkisian LaPiere, a high school dropout who had moved to Hollywood to take acting lessons, was introduced to 27-year-old Salvatore Philip "Sonny" Bono by a mutual friend in a coffee shop on Hollywood Boulevard. In her autobiography *The First Time*, Cher recalled seeing Sonny and the world going into soft-focus "like Tony and Maria at the dance" in the 1961 movie musical *West Side Story*. Sonny and Cher went out on a group date that night and continued dating after that, but Sonny, who worked as a recording artist and record promoter for Phil Spector, was more interested in Cher's roommate. Undaunted, Cher pursued Sonny relentlessly. "I was crazy about him in the beginning," she remembered.

When her roommate moved out, Cher, unable to afford the apartment on her own, convinced Sonny to let her live with him as a cleaning lady. The relationship was strictly platonic. Sonny was still married, though separated from his first wife (she divorced him in 1963). When Cher's mother discovered that her sixteen-year-old daughter was sharing an apartment with Sonny, she threatened to press charges against him unless Cher moved back home. "When Sonny started to help me pack my meager belongings," recalled Cher, "he just looked at me, and we both started to cry." Cher soon returned to live with Sonny again, and when she turned eighteen, she told her mother that she had married Sonny in Tijuana. In reality, Sonny and Cher had pledged themselves to one another with their own vows and souvenir rings in a hotel bathroom. They were not legally married until 1969.

In 1964, Sonny, who worked as an assistant and occasional percussionist for Phil Spector, dragged Cher into Spector's Gold Star studio to sing backup when one of the Ronnettes failed to show up for a recording session. Impressed, Spector invited Cher back to the studio for more backup work over the next few months. Terrified of singing solo, Cher recorded a few duets with Sonny, which evolved into a singing act they performed in bowling alleys, calling themselves Caesar and Cleo. As Caesar and Cleo, they released two forgettable records, "The Letter" and "Love Is Strange."

When Spector fired Sonny in 1965, Sonny and Cher released the record "Baby, Don't Go" under their own names, followed by "I Got You, Babe," which became an instant hit, launching the duo's musical career.

STRANGE ENCOUNTERS

★ Born in Detroit on February 16, 1935, Sonny dropped out of high school in Los Angeles, married Donna Rankin, had a daughter named Christy, and drove a meat delivery truck, squeezing in trips to record companies to drop off songs he had written —all before meeting Cher.

★ Cher was born on May 20, 1946, in El Centro, California, to part-Cherokee actress Georgia Holt and Armenian farmer John Sarkasian. Her parents divorced during the pregnancy, and Cher was raised primarily by her mother and Gilbert LaPiere, one of several stepfathers.

★ In 1949, director John Huston cast Cher's mother, Georgia Holt, in a small role in the movie *The Asphalt Jungle*. At the last minute, Huston fired Holt, replacing her with Marilyn Monroe.

★ Cher told *Playboy* that she got into a fender-bender in 1962 with established actor Warren Beatty, resulting in a one-night fling. "What a disappointment," she recalled. "Not that he wasn't technically good, or couldn't be good, but I didn't feel anything!"

★ Sonny started his career in the music business by screening song submissions for Phil Spector at Specialty Records in Hollywood. He was soon singing background vocals for some of Spector's classic hits and then began writing and recording songs under the pseudonyms Sonny Christie, Ronny Sommers, and Prince Carter.

★ Cher's very first recording was the 1963 novelty record "I Love You Ringo," released under the name Bonnie Jo Mason.

★ Sonny acknowledged an illegitimate son, Sean, born in 1964 from an affair with actress Mimi Machu. Machu became Jack Nicholson's longtime girlfriend and appeared in the B-movies *Hells Angels on Wheels, Psych-Out,* the Monkees' *Head,* and *Drive, He Said.*

★ Sonny and Cher starred in only one movie together, the 1967 film *Good Times,* in which they spoofed scenes from several classic movies. Sonny wrote the 1969 movie *Chastity,* starring Cher as a lonely young girl hitchhiking across the country in hopes of finding a lover to help her forget her disturbed past. Sonny and Cher named their daughter Chastity, born on March 4, 1969, after Cher's character in the film. Today Chastity is a gay rights activist.

★ As Sonny and Cher's musical career began dwindling at the end of the sixties, Sonny developed their act into a musical nightclub routine, making himself the brunt of jokes about their marriage. In 1971, CBS gave Sonny and Cher their own show, *The Sonny and Cher Comedy Hour,* as a summer replacement. The show's success prompted CBS to bring the program back in December as a regular series. When Sonny and Cher divorced in 1974, the show fell apart.

★ In 1975, Cher married guitarist Greg Allman, divorced him within a week, and the following year gave birth to a son, Elijah Blue Allman (now frontman for the synth-rock band Deadsy).

★ Cher was diagnosed with dyslexia at the age of thirty.

★ Cher lived with rock musician Gene Simmons of Kiss for several years.

★ Sonny married Mary Whitaker in 1986 and opened Bono's, an Italian restaurant in Los Angeles, then moved the business to Palm Springs. In 1988, frustrated by the red tape he encountered trying to remodel his restaurant, Sonny ran for Mayor as a Republican, won the election, and served until 1992.

★ In 1989, Cher's music video "If I Could Turn Back Time" became the first video banned by MTV. Network executives objected to scenes in which Cher's skimpy outfit revealed her tattooedderriere.

★ Cher legally changed her name from "Cherilyn Sarkisian LaPiere Bono Allman" to "Cher."

★ In 1992, when Fox-TV announced plans to produce an autobiographical movie about Sonny and Cher, Sonny suggested that his part be played by Kevin Costner and the role of Cher be played by Roseanne.

★ In 1995, Sonny ran for a seat in the House of Representatives and was elected to Congress.

★ Sonny died in a skiing accident on January 5, 1998, at the age of sixty-two.

Steven Spielberg and Kate Capshaw

Director Steven Spielberg met actress Kate Capshaw when she walked into his office to audition for a leading role in the movie *Indiana Jones and the Temple of Doom*. When he sent her audition tape to the screenwriters, he asked them to kindly put in a good word for Kate with his coproducer on the project, director George Lucas.

Thirty-year-old Kate, however, had gone into the audition with the hopes of striking up a relationship with 37-year-old Steven. "I'd often thought how much I'd like to meet him because I admire him so much," Kate told the *Los Angeles Times*. "But when I realized it was actually going to happen, I thought, 'What can I say to him that he hasn't heard before? Gee, I loved *E.T.*?' That would be ridiculous. So when we finally met I said nothing. When the meeting was over, he got up and said, 'Thanks for not saying anything about *E.T.*'"

Kate, then living with director Armyan Bernstein, who had directed her in the 1984 movie *Windy City*, felt an instinctive attraction to Steven. "What attracted me was the way he smelled," she recalled. "Like babies when they are born, like he was mine."

Kate won the role of nightclub singer Willie Scott, a whiny, spoiled, and squeamish woman easily tormented and humiliated by the harrowing adventures she experiences alongside Indiana Jones. Despite the tortures to which Steven subjected her character, Kate later said, "I fell in love with him watching him direct a movie." She flirted aggressively with Steven throughout the shooting of the movie, but his romantic interests lay elsewhere.

A few months earlier, while scouting locations in India for *Temple of Doom*, Steven had reunited with his former fiancée, actress Amy Irving, after a five-year hiatus from their long-term relationship. Irving, shooting a television miniseries in India, had surprised Steven by meeting him at the airport when he first landed on the subcontinent. On June 13, 1985, she gave birth to his son Max, and five months later, on November 27, 1985, Steven and Amy got married in a civil ceremony in the courthouse in Santa Fe, New Mexico. The marriage lasted less than four years.

After Amy and Steven announced their divorce in April 1989, Steven invited Kate to London for the premiere of *Indiana Jones and the Last Crusade.* He finally responded to Kate's advances, and on May 14, 1990, Kate gave birth to her first child with Steven. Soon afterwards, she converted to Judaism, and on October 12, 1991, Kate married Steven in a traditional Jewish ceremony at his estate in East Hampton, New York.

STRANGE ENCOUNTERS

★ Steven Allan Spielberg, born December 18, 1946, in Cincinnati, Ohio, was raised in Phoenix, Arizona.

★ Kate Capshaw, born Kathleen Sue Nail on November 3, 1953, in Fort Worth, Texas, to a beautician and an airline operations manager, was raised in St. Louis, Missouri.

★ Steven majored in English at California State University in Long Beach, but his mediocre grades and failure to complete his degree prevented him from getting into film school. He applied to University of Southern California Film School twice and was rejected both times.

★ In 1966, Steven found an empty office at Universal Studios, made up a name plate for himself, and pretended he belonged there—literally breaking his way into Hollywood.

★ Kate's first acting role was on the soap opera *The Edge of Night*, where her character died of an undisclosed disease.

★ Steven met his first wife, actress Amy Irving, at a casting call for his 1977 movie *Close Encounters of the Third Kind.*

★ Steven produced four of the top ten films of all time: *Jaws, E.T., Indiana Jones and the Last Crusade,* and *Jurassic Park.*

★ As an Eagle Scout, Steven sat on the advisory board for the Boy Scouts of America, but resigned to protest against the Boy Scouts' policy of discriminating against homosexuals.

★ On May 31, 2002, Steven graduated from California State University at Long Beach with a bachelor's degree in film and electronic arts. Having finished his degree by completing independent projects, Steven wore a cap and gown and marched in the commencement ceremony. When he stepped up to the dais to receive his diploma, the band played the theme song from the *Indiana Jones* movies.

★ Kate has a daughter named Jessica from her first marriage to former high school principal Robert Capshaw.

★ Together, Steven and Kate have six children: Theo (adopted), Sasha, Sawyer, Jessica, Mikaela (adopted), and Destry.

Henry Morton Stanley and David Livingstone

In 1866, Dr. David Livingstone, having received a grant from the British government, went to Africa to lead an expedition to find the source of the Nile River. An ordained missionary, Livingstone had previously made two lengthy expeditions into the African interior, becoming the first European to see the Zambezi River and Victoria Falls. As the first European to cross the African continent from west to east, Livingstone claimed large portions of Africa for Great Britain and returned to England to be hailed as a national hero.

When Livingstone failed to return from his search for the source of the Nile after two years, rumors reached Britain that the great explorer was dead. In 1869, James Gordon Bennett, publisher of the *New York Herald*, decided to send one of his reporters to find Livingstone. That reporter was Henry Morton Stanley. Having previously covered Britain's attack on Ethiopia and other stories in the Middle East, Stanley spent the next two years searching the African continent for Livingstone.

On November 10, 1871, thirty-year-old Stanley found 58-year-old Livingstone, sick and short on supplies, in the town of Ujiji on Lake Tanganyika in present-day Tanzania. Stanley greeted the explorer with the famous words, "Dr. Livingstone, I presume?"

Instead of returning home immediately with the news of Livingstone's whereabouts, Stanley, inspired by his newfound friend's dream of finding the source of the Nile River south of Lake Victoria, stayed with him until March 1872. Livingstone continued his explorations and died of malaria on May 1, 1873, at Chitambo in present-day Zambia. His servants buried his heart at the spot where he died, and shipped his embalmed body back to England, where it was buried at Westminster Abbey. After Livingstone's death, Stanley returned to Africa to continue his friend's work.

★ David Livingstone, born on March 19, 1813, in Blantyre, Scotland, worked in a cotton mill at age ten.

★ Henry Morton Stanley, born John Rowlands on January 28, 1841, in Denbigh, Wales, sailed for New Orleans at age sixteen as a cabin boy. In 1859, a cotton broker named Henry Hope Stanley adopted him.

★ In 1841, the London Missionary Society, having rejected Livingstone for missionary work in China, sent him to Kuruman, South Africa.

★ In 1849, Livingstone, dissatisfied with the routine of missionary life, guided the first successful European crossing of the Kalahari Desert to Lake Ngami.

★ During his first expedition into the African interior, from 1853 to 1856, Livingston traveled from the Chobe River (in modern-day Botswana) up the Zambezi River, followed African trade paths across the Cuango River into Portuguese Angola, and arrived at Luanda on the Atlantic coast. Livingstone then followed the Zambezi River downstream to Victoria Falls and continued east across what is now Zimbabwe and Mozambique until he emerged at Quelimane, on the Indian Ocean.

★ On his second expedition into the African interior, from 1858 to 1863, Livingstone became the first Briton to describe Lake Nyasa and the Shire Highlands of what is now Malawi.

★ In 1859, Livingstone reached what is currently known as Lake Malawi and asked the local people what it was called. When they told him *nyasa,* he named the huge body of water Lake Nyasa. Unbeknownst to Livingstone, the Chichewa word *nyasa* means "mass of waters," so the explorer actually named the body of water "Lake Lake." In 1964, the newly independent Malawi government renamed the mass of water Lake Malawi.

★ During the Civil War, Stanley served in the Confederate Army until 1862, when he was captured by the Union Army. He switched sides to get out of prison.

★ Livingstone wrote two best-selling books recounting his African travels—*Missionary Travels* and *The Zambezi and Its Tributaries*—catapulting him to worldwide fame.

★ On his third expedition, from 1866 to 1873, Livingston searched for the source of the Nile and Congo rivers and investigated how the great African lakes connected to one another and by which great rivers. Along the way, he discovered Lake Mweru and Lake Bangweulu and reached the Lualaba tributary of the Congo River.

★ In 1868, a year after becoming a reporter for the *St. Louis Weekly Missouri Democrat*, Stanley persuaded the *New York Herald* to send him to Africa to cover Britain's attack on Ethiopia.

★ Spencer Tracy starred as Henry Stanley in the 1939 movie *Stanley and Livingstone* and delivers the historic line "Dr. Livingstone, I presume" to actor Cedric Hardwicke.

Ringo Starr and Barbara Bach

In February 1980, former Beatle Ringo Starr, cast to play Atouk in the comedy movie *Caveman*, met actress Barbara Bach on the set near Puerto Vallarta, Mexico. Barbara had been cast to play Lana, Atouk's love interest. Atouk and Lana's romance, Ringo later told *Weekend*, "just spilled over nicely into real life."

Barbara admitted that "it wasn't love at first sight," but "it began to grow within days of meeting each other."

Ringo's willingness to play ball with local kids warmed Barbara's heart. He, in turn, had admired her willingness to be repeatedly hurled into a river until the director was satisfied with the take. During the last week of shooting, Ringo escorted Barbara to a Saint Valentine's dance and on a trip to see the Mexican Grand Prix. When he invited her to his home in Monte Carlo to watch the Monaco Grand Prix, Barbara immediately accepted. "I didn't hesitate a second," she recalled. "It seemed totally natural."

At the time, however, Ringo was engaged to model Nancy Andrews, and Barbara, awaiting a divorce from Italian industrialist Augusto Gregorini, was dating cinematographer Roberto Quezada. Roberto gracefully bowed out of his relationship with Barbara. The spurned Nancy, however, hired renowned attorney Marvin Mitchelson to sue Ringo for palimony. (Mitchelson, having represented Michelle Triola against her ex-lover, actor Lee Marvin, had established the right of palimony for unmarried couples in California.)

Ringo and Barbara announced that they planned to be married as soon as her divorce was finalized, and, in the meantime, they lived in a rented house off Sunset Boulevard while waiting to buy a new home in the two-million-dollar price range.

On April 27, 1981, Barbara became the second Mrs. Richard Starkey at a ceremony in Marylebone Register Office performed by Joseph Jevons, who twelve years earlier had married Paul and Linda McCartney in the exact same building. The McCartneys, Harrisons, and John Lennon's widow Yoko Ono attended the wedding and reception. Photographer Terry O'Neill captured the first reunion after the death of John Lennon of the surviving three Beatles, their American wives, and Yoko.

STRANGE ENCOUNTERS

★ Ringo Starr was born Richard Starkey on July 7, 1940, in Liverpool, England, making him seven years older than Barbara and the eldest Beatle.

★ Barbara was born Barbara Goldbach on August 27, 1947, in Queens, New York, to an Irish Catholic mother and an Austrian Jewish father who worked as a policeman. She changed her last name to Bach.

★ In 1955, fifteen-year-old Ringo Starr worked for British Railways.

★ On February 11, 1965, Ringo married eighteen-year-old Maureen Cox, who was two months pregnant. Beatles manager Brian Epstein served as best man. Maureen gave birth to their first son, Zak, on September 14, 1965. The couple had two more children: Jason and Lee.

★ In 1963, Beatle Ringo Starr told reporters, "I want to be a hairdresser or two." His first wife, Maureen, was a former Liverpool hairdresser. In 1985, his son Zak Starkey married the daughter of a hairdresser.

★ At age seventeen, Barbara, sent to Rome to model for *Seventeen* magazine, fell in love with 28-year-old Italian businessman Augusto Gregorini. A year later, she married Augusto and moved with him to Rome. Together, they had two children: Francesca and Gianni. Barbara left Augusto in 1975 and moved back to the United States.

★ Barbara attended the Beatles' historic Shea Stadium concert in 1965 as a chaperone to her younger sister Marjorie. Barbara said she was not really a fan of the Beatles but instead preferred the music of Ray Charles, Bob Dylan, and Aretha Franklin.

★ Ringo's first wife Maureen can be heard singing on the Beatles song "The Continuing Story of Bungalow Bill" on *The White Album*.

★ On the Beatles album *Let It Be,* at the end of the song "Get Back," Paul says "thanks, Mo." He is referring to Maureen, who can be heard cheering the loudest.

★ Ringo had three children with Maureen. The eldest, Zak, has played drums with Ringo's All Starr Band and the Who.

★ Barbara auditioned for a starring role in the television series *Charlie's Angels,* but failed to get the part.

★ Maureen divorced Ringo in 1976 on the grounds of Ringo's extramarital affair with American model Nancy Andrews.

★ Barbara starred as Major Anya Amasova in the 1977 James Bond movie *The Spy Who Loved Me,* leading to her exclusive pictorial feature in the June 1977 issue of *Playboy.*

★ Barbara posed nude in the December 1980 issue of *Playboy* that contained John Lennon's last magazine interview.

★ When John Lennon was shot on December 8, 1980, Ringo and Barbara interrupted their vacation to fly to New York to console Yoko Ono and Sean Lennon.

★ Fashion designers David and Elizabeth Emmanuel, creators of Princess Diana's wedding gown, designed Barbara's wedding dress.

★ At Barbara and Ringo's wedding party, Paul McCartney, George Harrison, Ringo, and Harry Nilsson played piano and guitar together.

Jerry Stiller and Anne Meara

In 1953, struggling actor Jerry Stiller and his friend, aspiring actress Bea Mortensen, went to a casting call at an agent's office in New York City. Jerry tagged along with Bea in the hopes that their relationship might bloom into something more amorous. He also hoped they might form a comedy act together.

As they sat in the waiting room, Bea recognized a friend, Anne Meara, sitting among the other actors. She introduced Jerry to Anne.

When Anne was beckoned inside to audition, Bea told Jerry that he might like Anne. When Anne emerged from the audition, crying because the agent had chased her around his desk, Jerry confronted the agent—only to get chased around the desk himself. Back in the waiting room, Bea excused herself to go to another appointment, urging Jerry to console Anne over a cup of coffee. Jerry took Anne to Longley's Cafeteria, where she asked him to help her steal the silverware from their table to replace the silverware her roommates had lost.

A few weeks later, Jerry bumped into Anne on West 40th Street. She brought him into a nearby building, to the offices of the American Radiator Company, to meet her father. Afterward, while walking up Broadway together, Jerry noticed Anne's comedic talents and began wondering if she might make a good partner for a comedy act. A few days later, while Jerry was having a cup of coffee at Cromwell's drugstore, he ran into Anne again. Soon after, she invited him to her apartment for dinner, and before long, Jerry and Anne were spending all their time together.

Uneasy about their interfaith relationship, Jerry suggested they break up on the grounds that he was penniless. Anne responded by proposing marriage. She recommended that they live together in her apartment and demanded to meet Jerry's mother. Anne told Jerry's mother that she loved her son and wanted to marry him, promising to make a good wife. "Will you come to the wedding?" Anne asked. Jerry's mother said yes and kissed her future daughter-in-law.

On the morning of September 14, 1953, Jerry and Anne got married in a civil ceremony at City Hall, then celebrated with a wedding breakfast hosted by Anne's father at the Republican Club.

STRANGE ENCOUNTERS

★ Jerry Stiller, born on June 8, 1929, in Brooklyn, New York, graduated from Syracuse University.

★ Anne Meara, born Catholic on September 20, 1929, in New York City, converted to Judaism early in her marriage to Jerry Stiller.

★ Three years after getting married, Jerry and Anne joined the Compass Players (an improvisational group that later became Second City), then left to develop their own comedy act at David Gordon's Phase II in Greenwich Village. Cleverly mining their different ethnic backgrounds (Jewish and Irish Catholic) to create their famous "Hershey Horowitz/Mary Elizabeth Doyle" routines, Stiller and Meara played record-breaking engagements at Max Gordon's Blue Angel and the Village Vanguard, then toured nightclubs across the country, appearing at the Hungry i, the Flamingo, and the Sands, and working with Count Basie, the Supremes, and Diahnn Carroll.

★ Stiller and Meara appeared thirty-six times on *The Ed Sullivan Show.*

★ Jerry and Anne appeared together in the movies *Lovers and Other Strangers, Nasty Habits, The Other Woman, In Our Hands, That's Adequate, The Sunset Gang, Highway to Hell, So You Want to Be an Actor, Heavyweights, A Fish in the Bathtub, Chump Change, Amy Stiller's Breast, The Independent, Keeping It Real,* and *Zoolander.*

★ Jerry and Anne starred together in the award-winning play, *After-Play,* written by Anne.

★ On television, Jerry and Anne starred as regulars on *The Paul Lynde Show* and hosted the short-lived *The Stiller & Meara Show.* They appeared together as guest stars on *Love, American Style, The Courtship of Eddie's Father,* and *The Love Boat.*

★ Without Jerry, Anne appeared in many movies, including *The Out-of-Towners, The Boys from Brazil, Fame, Reality Bites,* and *Day Trippers.* She starred in the television series *Kate McShane* (the first series to feature a woman lawyer), and costarred as tavern owner Mae on *The Corner Bar,* airline stewardess Sally Gallagher on *Rhoda,* cook Veronica

Rooney on *Archie Bunker's Place*, Dorothy Halligan on *Alf*, and as a regular on *All My Children*.

★ Jerry and Anne wrote, performed, and produced award-winning radio commercials for Blue Nun Wine, United Van Lines, and Amalgamated Bank.

★ Jerry and Anne have two children: actor Ben Stiller and actress Amy Stiller.

★ Without Anne, Jerry appeared in the movies *The Taking of Pelham One-Two-Three, Airport '75, Nadine, The Ritz, Hairspray, The Pickle*, and *The Independent*. On television, he played Frank Costanza on *Seinfeld* and Arthur on *King of Queens*.

★ In 1999, the New York Friars Club honored Jerry with a televised roast that received the highest ratings of any program in the history of Comedy Central.

Barbra Streisand and James Brolin

On July 1, 1996, Barbra Streisand met actor James Brolin at a dinner party hosted by mutual friends, who fixed them up by inviting thirty guests to their home to disguise the blind date.

Both Barbra and Jim tried to cancel at the last minute. The unnamed hosts sat Barbra and Jim next to each other. "I looked at him," Barbra recalled in an interview with Barbara Walters on *20/20*, "and I said—because his hair really looked awful, I thought, you know, so I said 'Who screwed up your hair?'"

Jim immediately warmed to Barbra's honesty. "I feel like we were married from the moment we sat down there," recalled Jim. They monopolized each other all evening at the party, then left together. "We were smitten with each other from the first moment," Jim told *Entertainment Tonight*. "She's one of the sweetest little girls I've ever met."

They talked until three o'clock in the morning, then got very shy. Jim went home. "I remember going to sleep with a smile on my face," recalled Barbra.

Two weeks later, Jim traveled to the Philippines. He called Barbra every day. "We were on the phone sometimes eight hours a day," he recalled. Jim proposed several times, but each time Barbra thought he was joking. "He said, 'I really mean it' each time," admitted Barbra, who still refused to believe him—until May 1997, when Jim showed up with a ring that he later described as "kind of overkill."

Not wanting such a big ring, Barbra told Jim that she preferred a high school solitaire. Jim returned the ring and told Barbra to pick something on her own, prompting the tabloids to incorrectly report that Barbra had paid for her own engagement ring. That summer, Jim appeared on *The Rosie O'Donnell Show* and confirmed the rumors that he and Barbra were engaged.

The couple got married on July 1, 1998—the second anniversary of their first date.

STRANGE ENCOUNTERS

★ Barbra Streisand, born Barbara Joan Streisand on April 24, 1942, in Brooklyn, New York, changed the spelling of her first name to Barbra.

★ James Brolin was born on July 18, 1940, in Los Angeles, California.

★ As a child, Barbra attended the Jewish Beis Yakov School in Brooklyn, New York.

★ Barbra attended Erasmus High School in New York City and sang in the school choir with fellow Jewish singer and songwriter Neil Diamond. In 1978 she sang a duet with Neil on the hit song, "You Don't Bring Me Flowers."

★ Barbra worked as a switchboard operator and theater usherette while trying to break into show business as a singer in Greenwich Village coffeehouses.

★ Barbra made her stage debut at age nineteen on October 21, 1961, in the off-Broadway revue *Another Evening with Harry Stoones,* which opened and closed in one night.

★ Mary Martin, Anne Bancroft, Carol Burnett, and Edie Gormé all turned down the role of Fanny Brice in the Broadway production of *Funny Girl,* before Barbra landed the part.

★ Barbra has one son, Jason Gould (with her first husband, actor Elliott Gould). Jason played Barbra's son in the movie *Prince of Tides.*

★ Jim costarred as Dr. Steven Kiley for seven years on the television medical drama *Marcus Welby, M.D.,* starring Robert Young. He starred as Peter McDermott for five years on the dramatic series *Hotel* opposite Connie Selleca.

★ Jim has designed and built several homes, is a licensed pilot, has trained horses, and was a professional race-car driver.

★ Jim has been married three times, to Jane Cameron Agee, Jan Smithers, and Barbra Streisand.

★ Barbra was the first person ever to receive a Grammy Award, Emmy Award, Academy Award, and Tony Award.

★ Barbra and actress Shirley MacLaine celebrate their joint birthday (April 24) together every year.

★ Barbra dated former Canadian Prime Minister, Pierre Trudeau, and newscaster Peter Jennings.

★ With the 1983 movie *Yentl*, Barbra became the first woman since the silent era to direct, produce, write, and star in a feature film.

★ Barbra and Jim declined an invitation to stay at the White House for the 1997 inauguration of President Bill Clinton because unmarried couples are forbidden to sleep together in the White House.

★ At Barbra and Jim's wedding, composer Marvin Hamlisch conducted a sixteen-piece orchestra.

★ Barbra was named the best-selling female singer of the twentieth century, having sold more than 68 million records.

★ Barbra earned forty-seven gold albums, second only to Elvis Presley.

Spencer Tracy and Katharine Hepburn

In 1937, actress Katharine Hepburn, having won an Academy Award for her role in the 1933 movie *Morning Glory*, saw the 1937 movie *Captains Courageous*, starring Spencer Tracy. "I think it is just the best goddamned performance I've ever seen," she said. Overwhelmed by the actor's talent, she ran out to see his previous film, *Fury*. Kate told her friend, Garson Kanin, "I don't know the man, but gosh, I would love to do a picture with him!"

Spence seemed to feel the same way about Kate. Cast to play the lead in the 1941 remake of *Dr. Jekyll and Mr. Hyde*, Spence suggested that director Victor Fleming cast Katharine Hepburn to play the role of the leading female character. Instead, Fleming hired Ingrid Bergman for the part.

Meanwhile, screenwriters Ring Lardner, Jr., and Michael Kanin wrote the script for *Woman of the Year* specifically for Katharine Hepburn and Spencer Tracy. Kate sold the script to MGM on the condition that her costar be Spencer. Producer Joseph Mankiewicz convinced Spence to costar in the movie, after arranging a private screening for him of the latest movie he had produced with Kate—*The Philadelphia Story*. In 1942, after selling the script to MGM, 33-year-old Kate met 41-year-old Spence, walking with Mankiewicz, as she emerged from the side entrance of the Thalberg Building on the MGM lot. Kate, wearing four-inch-heels, stood two inches taller than Spence. She shook his hand, apologized for wearing the heels, and promised that on the set, she'd wear shoes that made her shorter than he. After Kate disappeared, Spence turned to Mankiewicz and expressed his second thoughts about working with such a forceful woman.

On the set of *Woman of the Year*, Kate and Spence, playing a political journalist who falls in love with a sports writer, began a secret life-long off-screen romance. Spence—a devout Catholic—refused to divorce his wife, Louise, even though they lived apart for decades.

★ Spencer Tracy was born Spencer Bonaventure Tracy on April 5, 1900, in Milwaukee, Wisconsin, to a truck salesman and his wife.

★ Katharine Hepburn was born Katharine Houghton Hepburn on May 12, 1907, in Hartford, Connecticut. Until her eighty-fourth birthday, she told the world that her birthday was November 8, in memory of her brother Tom, who committed suicide in 1921.

★ Kate is a direct descendant of King John of England through one of his illegitimate children.

★ Spence, a former Jesuit prep-school student, originally intended to become a priest.

★ Spence and future actor Pat O'Brien dropped out of Marquette Academy to join the Navy at the start of World War I. After dropping out of Ripon College, Spence and Pat attended the Academy of Dramatic Arts. In 1923, both Spencer and Pat were cast as non-speaking robots in *R.U.R.*

★ Kate, educated at the Oxford School for Girls, nearly flunked out of Bryn Mawr College.

★ In 1928, Kate married Ludlow Ogden Smith, who changed his legal name to Ogden Ludlow so Kate would not share the same name with singer Kate Smith. After divorcing Ludlow in 1934, Kate had long-running affairs with agent Leland Hayward and billionaire Howard Hughes.

★ Spence had two children with his wife, actress Louise Treadwell: John and Susie.

★ In 1933, Spence separated from his wife, Louise, after ten years of marriage. A devout Catholic, he refused to divorce her and remarry—to avoid being excommunicated from the church or putting his children through the trauma of a divorce.

★ Before meeting Kate, Spence had extramarital affairs with actresses Joan Crawford, Myrna Loy, Lorretta Young, and Ingrid Bergman.

★ Tracy and Hepburn starred together in ten movies: *Woman of the Year, Keeper of the Flame, Without Love, The Sea of Grass, State of the Union, Adam's Rib, Pat and Mike, Desk Set, The Big Parade of Comedy*, and *Guess Who's Coming to Dinner.*

★ Spence refused to accept the role of the Penguin in the television series *Batman* unless he was allowed to kill Batman.

★ Kate's niece, actress Katharine Houghton, played her daughter in the 1967 movie *Guess Who's Coming to Dinner?*

★ On June 10, 1967, a few weeks after completing the filming of *Guess Who's Coming to Dinner?* Spence died of a heart attack in the Beverly Hills home he shared with Kate. She immediately called her secretary, Phyllis Wilbourn, and the two women cleared all of Kate's belongings out of the house— to protect Spence's wife, Louise, from knowing about their relationship. Then, realizing that the love of her life was dead, she dropped her concern for Louise and returned all her belongings to the house.

Harry S. Truman and Bess Wallace

In 1890, six-year-old Harry S. Truman and five-year-old Elizabeth "Bess" Virginia Wallace attended Sunday school kindergarten together at First Presbyterian Church, in Independence, Missouri. For five years, Harry, intimidated by Bess's beauty, did not have the courage to speak to the little girl who would one day become his wife. The two children attended separate elementary schools. When the Truman family moved to a new house, Harry began attending the Columbian School only to find Bess in his class. Reunited, the two became childhood sweethearts, although they never dated.

Recalled Truman's cousin Ethel Noland, who went through school with Harry and Bess: "There never was but one girl in the world for Harry Truman, from the first time he ever saw her at the Presbyterian kindergarten."

In 1901, the Trumans moved to Kansas City, Missouri. While Harry and Bess occasionally saw each other during their high school years, after graduation, their lives drifted apart. Harry worked as a bank clerk for several years until 1906, when he moved to Grandview, Missouri, to help run the family farm. One weekend afternoon, while visiting the home of his cousin Ethel Noland, Harry eagerly volunteered to return a cake plate that belonged to the Wallace family, in the hopes of seeing Bess. When he knocked at the door to the Wallace home, Bess answered. They were soon courting.

★ Harry S. Truman was born on May 8, 1884, in Lamar, Missouri. His parents gave him the middle initial "S," without a middle name so that both his grandfathers, Solomon Young and Anderson Shippe Truman, could say the child was named for them.

★ Harry was rejected from both West Point and Annapolis due to his poor eyesight.

★ Harry worked as a timekeeper for a construction crew with the Santa Fe Railroad, a clerk in the mailroom of the *Kansas City Star*, a bank clerk in a Kansas City bank, and a movie theater usher.

★ As a bank clerk, Harry worked alongside Arthur Eisenhower, whose younger brother Ike attended high school in Abilene, Kansas.

★ In 1917, Harry, age thirty-four, proposed to Bess, age thirty-three. They became engaged shortly before he left to fight in World War I.

★ Before Harry left for the war, Bess gave him a photograph of herself. Inscribed on the back was: "Dear Harry, May this photograph bring you safely home again from France — Bess." Harry carried the picture throughout the war. The framed photograph stood on his desk in the White House and today stands on his desk in the Truman Library.

★ On June 28, 1919, six weeks after he returned from overseas, Harry married Bess.

★ After World War I, Harry went into business with his Army buddy Eddie Jacobson, as the co-owners of a haberdashery in Kansas City. When the farm depression of 1921 forced them out of business, Harry refused to go into bankruptcy, choosing instead to spend the next fifteen years paying off some twelve thousand dollars in debt.

★ Harry and Bess Truman had one child, Mary Margaret, whom they called Margaret. Harry referred to Bess as "the boss" and to their daughter Margaret as "the one who bosses her."

★ On April 12, 1945, when First Lady Eleanor Roosevelt informed Vice President Harry Truman that the President was dead, Truman replied, "Is there anything I can do for you?" Eleanor replied, "Is there anything *we* can do for *you?* For you are the one in trouble now."

★ In 1948, the headline on the front page of an edition of the *Chicago Daily Tribune* declared "Dewey Defeats Truman." President Harry Truman actually won that election, winning 303 electoral votes, while New York Governor Thomas E. Dewey received only 189.

Ike Turner and Anna Mae Bullock

In 1957, Ike Turner, a rhythm-and-blues guitarist and piano player touring the South playing small nightclubs with the Rhythm Kings, met seventeen-year-old high school student Anna Mae Bullock at the Club Manhattan in East St. Louis, Missouri. One night while Ike played the B.B. King song "You Know I Love You" on the organ, drummer Gene Washington handed a microphone to Anna Mae, who, eager to join the group, began belting out the song. Recognizing Anna Mae's extraordinary talent as a singer, Ike immediately asked her to join his band as the lead singer. As a child Anna Mae had been a gospel singer at the Baptist Church in Nutbush, Tennessee, where her father served as deacon.

Later that year, Tina became pregnant by Ike's saxophone player, Raymond Hill, and moved into Ike's house. In 1958, she gave birth to a son named Craig. The Rhythm Kings recorded the hit record "Little Ann" on Sun Records, followed in 1960 by "A Fool in Love," which rose to #2 on the rhythm-and-blues charts. They followed up with four more Top Ten rhythm-and-blues hit songs: "I Idolize You," "It's Gonna Work Out Fine," "Poor Fool," and "Tra La La La La."

Living and working closely with Ike, Anna Mae became romantically involved with him. They were married in Tijuana in 1962 (which turned out to be illegal, since Ike had never bothered to divorce his first wife, Lorainne Taylor, with whom he had two children). In 1964, Tina gave birth to a son by Ike. Ike decided that the name Tina Turner sounded better as a stage name than Anna Mae Turner, and he renamed his group the Ike and Tina Turner Revue. Tina's gyrating and prancing, and her thrilling voice transformed the group from rhythm-and-blues to a solid, high-energy touring act, powered by hit singles like "River Deep, Mountain High," "Want To Take You Higher," "Nutbush City Limits," and "The Midnight Special." In 1969, Ike and Tina achieved worldwide fame as the opening act for the Rolling Stones and solidified their popularity in 1971 with the hit single "Proud Mary," which became the signature song of the Ike and Tina Turner Revue.

STRANGE ENCOUNTERS

★ Ike Turner, born Izear Luster Turner on November 5, 1931, in Clarksdale, Mississippi, began his musical career at age eleven as a piano accompanist to Sonny Boy Williamson and Robert Nighthawk.

★ Tina Turner was born Anna Mae Bullock on November 26, 1939, in Nutbush, Tennessee.

★ As a teenager, Ike worked as a disc jockey on radio station WROX in Clarksdale, Mississippi.

★ Ike worked at Sun Records as a session musician, playing guitar and piano on records by blues legends Elmore James, Howlin' Wolf, and Otis Rush.

★ While working as a talent scout and producer for Modern Records, Ike ostensibly discovered B.B. King and Howlin' Wolf.

★ In 1976, Tina—describing her husband as a violent, drug-addicted wife beater—left Ike (and the Revue), taking only 36 cents and a Mobil gasoline credit card.

★ The frequent beatings she received from Ike compelled Tina to have reconstructive surgery on her nose.

★ Tina refused to accept any money as part of her divorce from Ike.

★ Tina starred as the Acid Queen in the 1975 movie *Tommy*.

★ In 1984, Tina made an enormously successful comeback with the album *Private Dancer*, featuring the chart-topping hit single, "What's Love Got to Do With It?"

★ Tina turned down the role of Celie in the 1985 movie *The Color Purple*. The part went to Whoopi Goldberg.

★ Tina has lived with German recording executive Erwin Bach since 1986.

★ Tina turned down a role in the 1991 movie *Thelma & Louise*.

★ Actress Angela Bassett starred as Tina in the 1993 biographical movie, *What's Love Got to Do With It?* Laurence Fishburne played Ike.

★ Tina, winner of seven Grammy Awards, has sold more concert tickets than any other female performer in history.

James Watson and Francis Crick

During his third year studying ornithology at the University of Chicago, James Watson read a book that changed his life. In *What Is Life?*, quantum physics founder Erwin Schrödinger asserts that the genetic code transferred from parent to child could only exist at the molecular level since it had to fit inside a single cell. After graduating from the University of Chicago at age nineteen, Watson proceeded to Indiana University to study viruses in the hopes of finding the code in the simplest life form on earth.

In 1951, after receiving his doctorate at age twenty-two, Watson attended a conference in Naples, Italy, sat in on lecture by biophysicist Maurice Wilkins of King's College, London, and saw a molecule of deoxyribonucleic acid (better known as DNA) rendered by X-ray crystallography. Realizing that DNA might hold the key to genetic information, Watson obtained a fellowship at the Cavendish Laboratory at Cambridge University (where X-ray crystallography had been developed), determined to unleash the secret of DNA.

In the fall, Watson showed up at the Cavendish Laboratory, where he met Francis Crick, a physicist who, having studied at London and Cambridge universities, helped develop radar during World War II. Crick, similarly influenced by Schrödinger's *What Is Life?*, had crossed over into biology and chemistry, and in 1949, began research work in molecular biology at Cambridge University to earn his doctorate in protein structure.

Watson and Crick recognized each other as kindred spirits and joined forces to understand the structure of DNA. "We immediately discovered that we thought alike," Watson told an audience in Monterey, California, in 2003. Crick concurs.

"Jim and I hit it off immediately," he recalls in his book, *What Mad Pursuit.*

Based on research by Maurice Wilkins and the X-ray pictures of DNA crystals by chemist Rosalind Franklin, Watson and Crick used big 3-D molecular models to build a model of the molecular structure of DNA. On February 28, 1953, 24-year-old Watson and 36-year-old Crick figured out that the structure of DNA is a double helix that looks like a twisted ladder. Watson and Crick realized that the double helix could "unzip" to reproduce itself, confirming suspicions that DNA carries hereditary information. The sequence of certain chemicals on the successive rungs of the ladder forms a code that determines the size, structure, and function in an organism. The two scientists adjourned to the Eagle Pub in Cambridge to toast their discovery, and Crick proclaimed to the patrons that he and his colleague had just unearthed "the secret of life."

STRANGE ENCOUNTERS

★ Francis H. C. Crick was born on June 8, 1916, in Northampton, England, to a shoe manufacturer.

★ James Dewey Watson was born on April 6, 1928, in Chicago, Illinois.

★ In 1869, Swiss biochemist Johann Friedrich Miescher accidentally discovered DNA while studying the chemistry of the cell nucleus in pus collected from bandages used by soldiers wounded in the Crimean War.

★ Before Watson and Crick's discovery, scientists believed that complex cell proteins—not DNA—carried genetic information. They dismissed DNA—comprised of only sugars, phosphates, adenine, cytosine, guanine, and thymine—as being too simple to encode genetic information.

★ After attending a lecture by Rosalind Franklin in November 1951, Watson failed to take notes and incorrectly remembered the amount of water in the DNA samples. Based on this erroneous information, Crick and Watson built an incorrect molecular model of DNA as a triple helix.

★ Before sending a one-page report on their discovery to the scientific journal *Nature,* Watson and Crick flipped a coin to see whose name would go first on the byline. Watson won.

★ In 1962, Watson, Crick, and Maurice Wilkins won the Nobel Prize for their discovery. Rosalind Franklin, having died four years earlier could not be awarded the prize posthumously.

★ Scientists frequently refer to the two strands of the double helix as Crick and Watson in honor of the two biologists.

★ A human being has roughly three times as many genes as a fruit fly.

★ In the late 1950s, Crick insisted that DNA makes RNA, but not vice versa. He was wrong. In 1983, Pasteur Institute researcher Françoise Barré-Sinoussi discovered that the genetic material of the HIV virus is RNA, which makes DNA.

★ After discovering the structure of DNA, Crick did brain research at the Salk Institute for Biological Studies in La Jolla, California. Watson became a professor of biology at Harvard University, director of the molecular-biology lab at Cold Spring Harbor, New York, and served as head of the Human Genome Project.

★ Watson campaigned to get Congress to fund the Human Genome Project, a successful attempt to map the roughly three billion letters of the human genome.

Andrew Lloyd Webber and Tim Rice

On April 21, 1965, seventeen-year-old musical prodigy Andrew Lloyd Webber, living with his parents in South Kensington, England, received a letter from a 21-year-old law student named Tim Rice. "I've been told you're looking for a 'with it' writer of lyrics for your songs," wrote Tim, "and as I've been writing pop songs for a while and particularly enjoy writing the lyrics I wonder if you consider it worth your while meeting me."

Andrew and Tim met, and recognizing each other as kindred spirits, collaborated on their first musical, entitled *The Likes of Us.* It was never performed.

After Andrew and Tim wrote a few unsuccessful pop songs together, Alan Doggett, choir master at Colet Court preparatory school in London, telephoned Andrew and asked his former student to write a musical piece with a religious theme for the school's spring 1967 end-of-term concert. Andrew and Tim looked through the Bible, came across the story of Jacob and his son Joseph, and, over the next two months, wrote a fifteen-minute rock 'n' roll version of the story, entitled *Joseph and the Amazing Technicolor Dreamcoat.* When the contemporary cantata, one of the first to feature a full orchestra and pop choir, received strong praise from British newspapers and critics, Andrew and Tim wrote another piece together, the rock opera *Jesus Christ Superstar,* which rose to become a #1 album in the United States, launching Andrew and Tim as an international sensation.

★ Tim Rice, born on November 10, 1944, in Amersham, England, sang lead vocals with the pop group the Aardvarks.

★ Andrew Lloyd Webber, born on March 22, 1948, in London, and raised in South Kensington, began playing the violin at age three, began composing music at age six, and had his first composition published in the magazine *Music Teacher* at age nine.

★ Andrew's father, William Southcombe Lloyd Webber, was professor of theory and composition at the Royal College of Music in England, where Andrew's mother, Jean, was a singer and violinist.

★ Tim published his first song, "That's My Story," in 1965, the same year he met Andrew.

★ The success of *Jesus Christ Superstar* prompted Andrew and Tim to expand *Joseph and the Amazing Technicolor Dreamcoat* into a two-hour stage show.

★ Together, Andrew and Tim wrote only three musicals: *Joseph and the Amazing Technicolor Dreamcoat*, *Jesus Christ Superstar*, and *Evita*.

★ Tim and Andrew wrote the song "It's Easy For You," recorded by Elvis Presley in 1976.

★ Andrew wrote the musical *Cats* based on poet T.S. Eliot's *Old Possum's Book of Practical Cats* and his unpublished poems about an unhappy cat named Grizabella, given to Andrew by the poet's widow, Valery Eliot. When Andrew needed help with the lyrics, he chose to work with director Trevor Nunn, spurning Tim Rice and creating a huge rift with his former partner.

★ Andrew composed the musicals *Song & Dance* (lyrics by Don Black), *Cats, Starlight Express, Requiem, The Phantom of the Opera, Aspects of Love, Sunset Boulevard, By Jeeves* (lyrics by Alan Ayckbourn), *Whistle Down the Wind* (lyrics by Jim Steinman), and *The Big Game*.

★ Tim wrote the lyrics to the musicals *Blondel* (music by Stephen Oliver), *Chess* (music by Abba's Bjorn Ulvaeus and Benny Anderson), *Aida,* and *The Lion King* (music by Elton John), and *Heathcliff* (music by John Farrar). He also wrote the lyrics to three songs for Disney's animated movie *Aladdin* (music by Alan Menken), including the Academy Award-winning "A Whole New World," and the lyrics for all of the songs in Disney's animated movie *The Lion King*, including the Academy Award-winning song, "Can You Feel The Love Tonight?" (music by Elton John).

★ Andrew is the first person to have three musicals running simultaneously in New York and three in London, a record he achieved three times.

★ Andrew was knighted in 1992. Tim was knighted in 1994. Three years later, Queen Elizabeth elevated Andrew to Lord Lloyd-Webber of Sydmonton.

★ Andrew has been married three times, to Sarah Hugill, Sarah Brightman, and Madeleine Gurdon.

Henry Wells and William Fargo

In 1841, 23-year-old William Fargo became the first freight agent in Auburn, New York, for the Auburn & Syracuse Railroad. His business acumen attracted the attention of 36-year-old Henry Wells, an owner of the Pomeroy & Company express service. Wells hired Fargo in 1842 as a messenger to carry valuables on the 24-hour train journey between Albany and Buffalo, New York.

Wells had begun working as a freight agent in 1836 on the Erie Canal between Albany and Buffalo, forwarding parcels onward by land to Pennsylvania and Ohio. Five years later, he began working for Pomeroy & Company as a courier on the Albany to Buffalo run—a journey that took four days using a combination of railroads and stagecoaches. In 1841, Henry Wells began Wells & Co. in Buffalo, to compete against the United States Post Office.

On April 1, 1845, Wells made Fargo a partner in his new company, offering express service from Buffalo to Detroit and Chicago. The following year, Wells moved to New York City to concentrate his energies on the express business to Buffalo, turning over the express business west of Buffalo to Fargo and William A. Livingston, who formed their own company. Livingston & Fargo served as a connection to send Wells' shipments further west—with Livingston based in Buffalo and Fargo based in Detroit.

On March 18, 1850, Wells & Co. merged with Livingston & Fargo and a third delivery company, Butterfield, Wasson & Co., to form American Express Company, with Henry Wells as president. Wells and Fargo recognized the desperate need for expanded banking and express facilities in California, created by the

1848 discovery of gold. On March 18, 1852, unable to persuade American Express to expand beyond St. Louis, Missouri, Wells and Fargo formed Wells Fargo & Co.—to buy gold dust, sell drafts, and conduct general banking and express services, building a stagecoaching empire that spanned the American West.

STRANGE ENCOUNTERS

★ William Fargo, born on May 20, 1818, in Pompey, New York, was the eldest of twelve children.

★ Henry Wells, born on December 12, 1805, in Thetford, Vermont, to a Presbyterian minister, was raised in Crown Point and Seneca Falls, New York.

★ At age thirteen, Fargo worked as a mail carrier on a 43-mile circuit around Pompey, New York.

★ At age sixteen, Wells worked as an apprentice tanner and shoemaker.

★ At age twenty-two, Wells, a stutterer, opened several schools to treat speech defects.

★ Wells campaigned for inexpensive mail delivery and built the first commercial telegraph lines in the United States.

★ In 1863, Fargo traveled by stagecoach to California, worked with the Sacramento Valley Railroad in an attempt to build a railroad across the Sierra Nevada, and laid the foundation for the Grand Consolidation of 1866 that gave Wells Fargo responsibility for all overland stagecoaching west of the Missouri River.

★ In 1868, American Express founder Henry Wells founded Wells College, an all-woman's school in Aurora, New York. A popular bar in Aurora among Wells students is named The Fargo.

★ Fargo served as president of American Express from 1868 until his death.

★ Fargo owned the *Buffalo Courier*, was elected the Democratic mayor of Buffalo, New York, during the Civil War, and served as a director of the Northern Pacific Railroad, which named one of its railroad towns in his honor—Fargo, North Dakota.

★ Fargo married Anna H. Williams and had eight children, only three of whom lived to adulthood.

★ Wells was married twice, to Sarah Daggett and Mary Prentice. He had four children with his first wife.

Gene Wilder and Gilda Radner

In 1973, aspiring comedic actress Gilda Radner, having performed and written for the Second City improvisational troupe in Toronto, Canada and appeared briefly in the Jack Nicholson movie *The Last Detail*, landed a bit part in the Mel Brooks comedy *Blazing Saddles*. On the set, Gilda met the film's star, Gene Wilder, eleven years her senior. At the time, Gene, married to Mary Jane Schutz, took little interest in Gilda.

In 1975, Gilda became the first cast member hired for a new late-night television variety show called *Saturday Night Live*, where, over the next five years,

she would create the characters Emily Litella, Roseanne Roseannadanna, Lisa Loopner, and Baba Wawa. In 1980, Gilda married the guitarist and musical director of the Saturday Night Live Band, G. E. Smith, and left *Saturday Night Live* to star in *Gilda Live*, a one-woman show on Broadway.

The following year, when comedian Richard Pryor, having costarred with Gene Wilder in the hit movies *Silver Streak* and *Stir Crazy*, was unavailable to costar in the movie *Hanky Panky* due to other film commitments, director Sidney Portier cast Gilda to costar opposite Gene. Portier had the script for the buddy film rewritten for Gilda, making her Gene's sidekick and romantic interest.

During filming, Gilda, whose marriage to guitarist G.E. Smith had been deteriorating, and Gene, whose first marriage had ended in divorce seven years earlier, became romantically involved both on and off screen. Gilda and Smith ended their marriage amicably, and in 1984, 51-year-old Gene married 38-year-old Gilda.

★ Gene Wilder was born Jerome Silberman on June 11, 1933, in Milwaukee, Wisconsin. Unable to envision anyone named Jerry Silberman playing Hamlet, he changed his name to Gene Wilder. He later admitted that he could not see Gene Wilder playing Hamlet either.

★ Gilda Radner was born on June 28, 1946, in Detroit, Michigan, to the owner of the upscale Seville hotel, where prominent entertainers of the day—including Milton Berle, George Burns, and Frank Sinatra—frequently stayed.

★ Gilda's mother named her after the title character played by Rita Hayworth in the 1944 movie *Gilda*.

★ Gilda grew up with a nanny called Dibby, on whom she based her famous *Saturday Night Live* character, hard-of-hearing news correspondent Emily Litella.

★ Gene Wilder, a graduate of the University of Iowa, taught fencing for a living and worked as a chauffeur and a toy salesman.

★ An overweight child, Gilda, whose father died when she was twelve years old, suffered from anorexia and bulimia, which she overcame by age sixteen.

★ In 1963, while appearing in the Broadway production of *Mother Courage and Her Children*, starring Anne Bancroft, Gene struck up a friendship with Bancroft's boyfriend, Mel Brooks. Mel later cast Gene as the frantic Leo Bloom in his 1967 movie *The Producers*, garnering Gene an Academy Award nomination as Best Supporting Actor.

★ In 1967, Gene made his film debut in the movie *Bonnie and Clyde*, playing a frightened young undertaker abducted for a joy ride by the legendary bank robbers.

★ Gilda dropped out of the University of Michigan in Ann Arbor to follow her sculptor boyfriend to Toronto, where she landed a job playing a clown on a children's television show.

★ Gilda made her stage debut in Toronto in the musical *Godspell*, which also starred John Belushi.

★ Gene starred as the ingenious candy magnate in the 1971 movie *Willy Wonka and the Chocolate Factory* and as a doctor who has a love affair with a sheep in the 1972 Woody Allen movie *Everything You Always Wanted to Know about Sex*.

★ Gene met comedian Richard Pryor on the set of the 1973 Mel Brooks movie *Blazing Saddles*. Pryor, having cowritten the screenplay, hoped to costar with Gene, but lost the role to actor Cleavon Little.

★ Gilda dated Martin Short and Bill Murray.

★ In 1974, Second City alumnus John Belushi convinced Gilda to move to New York to work on the *National Lampoon Radio Hour*.

★ On *Saturday Night Live*, Gilda introduced several catch phrases into the American vernacular, including "Never mind," "That was so funny I almost forgot to laugh," and "It just goes to show you, it's always something."

★ Gene starred with Richard Pryor in four movies: *Silver Streak*; *Stir Crazy*; *See No Evil, Hear No Evil*; and *Another You*.

★ Gilda and Gene costarred in three movies together: *Hanky Panky*, *The Woman in Red*, and *Haunted Honeymoon*.

★ In 1986, Gilda was diagnosed with ovarian cancer. When she lost her hair during chemotherapy and radiation treatment, Gilda wore her frizzy, gravity-defying Rosanne Rosannadanna wig. She died on May 20, 1989, at age forty-two.

★ Gene and medical therapist Joanna Ball founded "Gilda's Club" in 1994 to honor Gilda's wish that homey, nationwide centers be established where people of all ages diagnosed with cancer could gather to give one another emotional support and participate in recuperative activities.

★ Gene has been married three times, to Mary Joan Schutz, Gilda Radner, and Karen Boyer.

★ In 2000, Gene, diagnosed with non-Hodgkin's lymphoma, underwent chemotherapy and recovered.

John Young and Ray Rubicam

In 1916, high school dropout Ray Rubicam got a job as an advertising copywriter at the F. Wallis Armstrong agency in Philadelphia. There he met account executive John Orr Young and the two men became close friends. Ray worked for Armstrong for three years, which, he later said, left him convinced "that a simple formula for a sound agency would be to reverse practically everything Armstrong did."

Having written advertisements for Girard cigars, Blabon linoleum, and Victor Talking Machines, Ray joined N. W. Ayer & Son, then the largest advertising agency in the United States. Ray had helped his friend John Young get a job as an account executive at Ayer and wrote some highly successful advertising campaigns for Steinway, Squibb, and Rolls-Royce.

In 1922, company founder Wayland Ayer died and control of the advertising agency went to Ayer's son-in-law, a man in whom Ray had little faith. In 1923, the agency passed over Ray Rubicam and George Cecil, its two best copywriters, and named an older, better-connected, less proficient man as copy chief.

Incensed, Ray decided to team up with John Young to start his own advertising agency, Young & Rubicam. "We had no angel, no banker behind us, nor even one big client," recalled John. "We had no wealthy kin or influential friends socially. We had to build our business the hard way."

With a mere five thousand dollars in startup capital, the two men left Ayer and started Young & Rubicam in Philadelphia on a shoestring budget, building one of the most successful advertising agencies in history. "When I first met Rubicam in the F. Wallis Armstrong office before we moved on to N. W. Ayer & Son," recalled John, "I was impressed with the way the sickly young copywriter weighed his words and thoughts for the cigar account that was his baby at the Armstrong agency. I recognized not only a skill and talent but also a conscientious, workmanlike approach to the job. Here would be a partner to be relied upon, I concluded. And how right I was! What Rubicam saw in me, I haven't any idea."

STRANGE ENCOUNTERS

★ Ray Rubicam, born on June 16, 1892, in Brooklyn, New York, the youngest of eight children, dropped out of school at age fifteen and worked as a bellhop, movie projectionist, door-to-door salesman, and newspaper reporter.

★ Young & Rubicam was the first advertising agency founded by a person on the creative end of the industry.

★ A few years after going into business together in Philadelphia, Ray and John moved their advertising agency to a one-room office of a new building at 285 Madison Avenue in New York City. Today, Young & Rubicam owns the entire 26-story building.

★ Ray coined the aphorism "Resist the usual," a phrase used to inspire copywriters at Young & Rubicam to this very day.

★ In 1927, Ray succeeded John as president of Young & Rubicam. Tired of the hectic pace and long hours of running an advertising agency, John retired from the agency in 1934 to spend more time with his family and pursue his hobbies.

★ In 1932, Ray hired Dr. George Gallup of Northwestern University to start the first advertising agency research department and measure how thoroughly consumers read advertisements.

★ In 1946, Ray wrote an article in *McCall's* magazine condemning the United States for dropping atomic bombs on Japan during World War II. He insisted that a simple demonstration of the bomb's horrific force would have compelled the Japanese to surrender.

★ In 1951, Young & Rubicam produced the world's first color television commercial—for Jell-O Pudding and Pie Filling.

★ In 1958, Young & Rubicam became the first advertising agency to organize sponsorship of a daytime serial drama on television. These, of course, became known as soap operas.

An Affair to Remember by Christopher Andersen (New York: William Morrow and Company, 1997)

After All by Mary Tyler Moore (New York: G. P. Putnam's Sons, 1995)

"After 40 Years, Anne Bancroft Can Still Take the Heat, Keep Her Cool" by K. C. Baker, *New York Daily News*, May 5, 2000

All the President's Men by Carl Bernstein and Bob Woodward (New York: Simon and Schuster, 1974)

All Too Human: The Love Story of Jack and Jackie Kennedy by Edward Klein (New York: Pocket Books, 1996)

America's Queen: The Life of Jacqueline Kennedy Onassis by Sarah Bradford (New York: Viking, 2000)

An American Life by Ronald Reagan (New York: Simon and Shuster, 1990)

The Autobiography of Henry M. Stanley by Henry M. Stanley (London: Sampson, Low, Marston and Company, 1909)

The Autobiography of Martin Luther King, Jr. by Martin Luther King Jr. (New York: Warner Books, 1998)

"Ballad of Jerry and Linda" by Tom Mathews with Martin Kasindorf and Janet Huck, *Newsweek*, April 23, 1979

The Beatles Forever by Nicholas Schaffner (New York: McGraw-Hill, 1977)

Been There, Done That by Eddie Fisher with David Fisher (New York: St. Martin's Press, 1999)

Bogart: A Life in Hollywood by Jeffrey Meyers (New York: Houghton Mifflin, 1997)

A Charge to Keep by George W. Bush (New York: William Morrow and Company, 1999)

The Complete Directory to Prime Time Network and Cable TV Shows (1946—Present) by Tim Brooks and Earle Marsh (New York: Ballantine, 1999)

Dangerous Dances by Nick Tosches (New York: St. Martin's Press, 1984)

David Brinkley: A Memoir by David Brinkley (New York: Knopf, 1995)

"The Day DNA Met Its Match" by Rosie Mestel in the *Los Angeles Times*, February 28, 2003

Diana: Her True Story by Andrew Morton (New York: Simon & Schuster, 1992)

The Day John Met Paul by Jim O'Donnell (New York: Penguin, 1996)

The Double Helix by James Watson (New York: Touchstone Books, 2001)

Easy to Remember: The Great American Songwriters and Their Songs by William Zinsser (Jaffrey, New Hampshire: David R. Godine, 2001)

Eisenhower by Geoffrey Perret (New York: Random House, 1999)

Eleanor and Franklin by Joseph P. Lash (New York: Norton, 1971)

Elton John by Philip Norman (New York: Fireside, 1991)

Elvis and Me by Priscilla Beaulieu Presley with Sandra Harmon (New York: G. P. Putnam's Sons, 1985)

The Encyclopedia of Superheroes by Jeff Rovin (New York: Facts on File, 1985)

First Lady from Plains by Rosalynn Carter (New York: Houghton Mifflin, 1984)

The First Time by Cher, with Jeff Coplan (New York: Pocket Books, 1999)

For the Hell of It: The Life and Times of Abbie Hoffman by Jonah Raskin (Berkeley: University of California Press, 1996)

George W. Bush by John F. Wukovits (San Diego, California: Lucent Books, 2000)

The Generous Years: Remembrances of a Frontier Boyhood (New York: Random House, 1964)

Ginger: My Story by Ginger Rogers (New York: Harper & Row, 1992)

The Great Comic Book Heroes by Jules Feiffer (New York: Bonanza, 1965)

The Great One: The Life and Legend of Jackie Gleason by William A. Henry III (New York: Doubleday, 1992)

Hanna-Barbera Cartoons by Michael Mallory (Beaux Arts Editions, 1998)

Harry S. Truman by Margaret Truman (New York: William Morrow & Company, 1973)

Heavier Than Heaven: A Biography of Kurt Cobain by Charles R. Cross (New York: Hyperion, 2001)

"Henry Wells" by Robert J. Chandler in *The Encyclopedia of American Business History and Biography.*

Hillary Rodham Clinton: A First Lady for Our Time by Donnie Radcliffe (New York: Warner Books, 1993)

His Way: The Unauthorized Biography of Frank Sinatra by Kitty Kelley (New York: Bantam, 1986)

http://www.yesterdayland.com/features/interviews/mcmahon_e_4.php

Hunting Game in the Eighties by Eleanor Roosevelt (New York, 1933)

I, Tina by Tina Turner with Kurt Loder (New York: Avon, 1986).

It's Always Something by Gilda Radner (New York: Avon, 2000)

Joe Franklin's Encyclopedia of Comedians by Joe Franklin (Secaucus, New Jersey: Citadel Press, 1979)

Leading with My Chin by Jay Leno with Bill Zehme (New York: HarperCollins, 1996)

Lennon Remembers: The Rolling Stone Interviews by Jann Wenner (New York: Popular Library, 1971)

Lewis & Clark: Voyage of Discovery by Stephen E. Ambrose (Washington, D.C.: National Geographic, 1998)

Liz: An Intimate Biography of Elizabeth Taylor by C. David Heymann (New York: Carol, 1995)

"The Lost Tycoon" by Ken Auletta in *The New Yorker*, April 23, 2001

Love, Lucy by Lucille Ball with Betty Hannah Hoffman (New York: G. P. Putnam's Sons, 1996)

"Love Thee Tender" by Karen S. Schneider in *People*, October 8, 2001

Lucky Man by Michael J. Fox (New York: Hyperion, 2002)

Lyndon Johnson and the American Dream by Doris Kearns Goodwin (New York: St. Martin's Press, 1976)

Madonna: An Intimate Biography by J. Randy Taraborrelli (New York: Simon and Schuster, 2001)

Majesty: Elizabeth II and the House of Windsor by Robert Lacey (New York: Harcourt Brace Jovanovich, 1977)

Mandela: The Authorized Biography by Anthony Sampson (New York: Knopf, 1999)

Marilyn Monroe by Barbara Leaming (New York: Three Rivers Press, 1998)

Married to Laughter by Jerry Stiller (New York: Simon and Schuster, 2000)

Mick Jagger: The Story Behind the Rolling Stone by Davin Seay (New York: Birch Lane Press, 1993)

"Midnight's Mayor" by Richard Stengel in *Time*, March 16, 1992, p. 58

"Mike Stoller Remembers Elvis" by Ken Sharp in *Goldmine*, March 2, 2003

My Lives by Roseanne Arnold (New York: Ballantine, 1994)

Nancy Reagan: The Unauthorized Biography by Kitty Kelley (New York: Pocket Books, 1991)

Napoleon by Frank McLynn (New York: Arcade, 1997)

O'Keeffe & Stieglitz: An American Romance by Benita Eisler (New York: Doubleday, 1991)

The Official Batman Batbook by Joel Eisner (New York: Contemporary, 1986)

Ogilvy on Advertising by David Ogilvy (New York: Crown, 1983)

The 100 Most Influential Women of All Time by Deborah G. Felder (New York: Citadel Press, 1996)

Our Vice-Presidents and Second Ladies by Leslie W. Dunlap (Metuchen, New Jersey: Scarecrow Press, 1988)

Overdrive: Bill Gates and the Race to Control Cyberspace by James Wallace (New York, John Wiley & Sons, 1997)

"Paul Simon" in *Current Biography; World Musicians* (H. W. Wilson Company, 1975)

People Almanac 2003 (New York: Cader Books, 2002)

A People's Tragedy: A History of the Russian Revolution by Orlando Figes (New York: Viking, 1996)

Portnoy's Complaint by Philip Roth (New York: Random House, 1967)

Pure Goldie: The Life and Career of Goldie Hawn by Marc Shapiro (Secaucus, New Jersey: Carol, 1998)

Ringo Starr: Straight Man or Joker? by Alan Clayson (New York: Paragon Books, 1991)

Rock Movers & Shakers by Dafydd Rees and Luke Crampton (Santa Barbara, California: ABC-CLIO, 1991)

RN: The Memoirs of Richard Nixon by Richard M. Nixon (New York: Grosset & Dunlap, 1978)

Rock: The Rough Guide, edited by Jonathan Buckley and Mark Ellingham (London: The Rough Guides, 1996)

Rudy: An Investigative Biography of Rudolph Giuliani by Wayne Barrete, assisted by Adam Fifield (New York: Basic Books, 2000)

The Seduction of Hillary Clinton by David Brock (New York: The Free Press, 1996)

Shout! The Beatles in their Generation by Philip Norman (New York: Warner Books, 1981)

Soon to Be a Major Motion Picture by Abbie Hoffman (New York: Perigee, 1980)

Steven Spielberg: A Biography by Joseph McBride (New York: Simon & Schuster, 1997)

The Story of My Life by Helen Keller (New York: Bantam, 1991)

Stranger in Two Worlds by Jean Harris (New York: Macmillan, 1986)

A Study in Scarlet by Arthur Conan Doyle (New York: J. B. Lippincott Co., 1890)

There Really Was a Hollywood by Janet Leigh (New York: Jove, 1986)

Time 100, edited by Kelly Knauer (New York: Time Books, 1998)

The Times of My Life by Betty Ford with Chris Chase (New York: Harper & Row/Reader's Digest, 1978)

The Tragedy of Lyndon Johnson by Eric Goldman (New York: Knopf, 1969)

"A Twist of Fate" by Michael D. Lemonick in *Time*, February 17, 2003

The Unruly Life of Woody Allen: A Biography by Marion Meade (New York: Scribner, 2000)

"Walter Matthau" by Alex Lewin, *Premiere*, September 2000

What Falls Away by Mia Farrow (New York: Bantam, 1998)

What Mad Pursuit by James Crick (New York: Basic Books, 1990)

"William George Fargo" by Robert J. Chandler in *The Encyclopedia of American Business History and Biography*.

"William H. Masters, a Pioneer in Studying and Demystifying Sex, Dies at 85" by Richard Severo in the *New York Times*, February 19, 2001

Zelda: A Biography by Nancy Milford (New York: Harper & Row, 1970)

Index

Acknowledgments

My heartfelt thanks to my editor, Laura Ross, for making this book a labor of love. Her enthusiasm, editorial savvy, and wonderful sense of humor made working on this book a joy. At Black Dog & Leventhal, I am also deeply grateful to J.P. Leventhal for his wise counsel, Cindy LaBreacht for her expert designing skills, Dara Lazar for her adept photo research assistance, Sara Cameron for her copyediting, Michael Driscoll for proofreading this massive manuscript, Carol Darwin Deason for indexing, and True Sims for overseeing the production.

I am also thankful to my agent, Jeremy Solomon, for helping to breathe life into yet another book idea through his persistence and exuberence, to Peter Workman for helping this book find the perfect home, and to Anna Cutino for planting the seeds of the idea in my head at Jacqueline Bruder's second birthday party.

For their generous help in unearthing the photos for this book, my deep thanks to Heather Marsh-Rumion at Corbis, Jorge Jaramillo at AP World Wide Photos, Chris Spear at Robert Barnes Archives, the gracious Stephen Cox, Dace Taube at Doheny Library at the University of Southern California, Mark Leaf at Baskin Robbins, Stacey Gabrielle at Binney & Smith, Lee Holden at Ben & Jerry's, Mary Finch at the George Bush Presidential Library, David Stanhope at the Jimmy Carter Library, Kenneth Hafeli at the Gerald R. Ford Library, Alan Goodrich at the John F. Kennedy Library, Mike Stoller, Amie Treuer at the Texas History Division of the Dallas Public Library, Marianne Babal at Wells Fargo Historical Services, and Jemma Gould at Young & Rubicam.

Above all, all my love to Debbie, Ashley, and Julia.

Photography Credits

12: Steve Cox Collection; 14: © Lawrence Schwartzwald/Corbis Sygma; 17: Robert Barnes Archives; 20: Steve Cox Collection; 23: © Photo B.D.V./Corbis; 25: Robert Barnes Archives; 28: courtesy of Baskin Robbins; 30: © Bettmann/Corbis; 33: courtesy of Binney & Smith; 35: Robert Barnes Archives; 38-39: *Napoleon in His Study* by Jacques Louis David [1810], National Gallery of Art, Washington, D.C.; *The Empress Josephine* by Pierre-Paul Prud'hoe [1908], Musée du Louvre, Paris; 41: Robert Barnes Archives; 43: © AP Wide World Photos, photograph by Walt Zeboski; 45: Robert Barnes Archives; 47: © Bettmann/Corbis; 50: courtesy of George Bush Presidential Library; 53: © AFP Photo/Corbis, photograph by Lucy Nicholson; 55: Steve Cox Collection; 58: courtesy of Jimmy Carter Library; 61: © Bryn Colton/Assignments Photographers/Corbis; 66: © AP Wide World Photos/Doug Mills; 69: © Steve Pyke/Retna UK; 72: courtesy of Ben & Jerry's; 75: Robert Barnes Archives; 78: Robert Barnes Archives; 80: © Jay Dickman/Corbis; 82: © Mitchell Gerber/Corbis; 84: © Rufus F. Folkks/Corbis; 86: © Bettmann/Corbis; 89: © Reuters NewMedia Inc./Corbis; 91: courtesy of Dwight D. Eisenhower Library; 94: © Bettmann/Corbis; 96: © Minnesota Historical Society/Corbis; 99: © Dusko Despotovic/ Corbis Sygma; 103: courtesy of Gerald R. Ford Library; 108: © Doug Wilson/ Corbis; 111: © David Burns/Corbis Sygma; 113: Steve Cox Collection; 115: Lynn Goldsmith/Corbis; 117: © Wally McNamee/ Corbis; 119: Steve Cox Collection; 121: Robert Barnes Archives; 124: © Bettmann/Corbis; 127: © Bettmann/Corbis; 130: Robert Barnes Archives; 133: © Bettmann/Corbis; 135: © Norman Parkinson Limited/Fiona Cowan/Corbis; 137: © Photo B.D.V./Corbis, photograph by Laszlo Veres; 140: © Hulton-Deutsch Collection/Corbis; 142: Robert Barnes Archives; 144: © Bettmann/Corbis; 146: © Retna Ltd./Michael Putland; 148: Courtesy of LBJ Library; 150: Robert Barnes Archives; 152: © Corbis; 154: © Bettmann/Corbis; 156: courtesy of John F. Kennedy Library; 159: © AP Wide World Photos/Luca Bruno; 161: Robert Barnes Archives; 163: courtesy of Jerry Leiber and Mike Stoller; 165: Robert Barnes Archives; 168: © Bettmann/Corbis; 171: © Hulton-Deutsch Collection/Corbis; 175: Corbis; 177: Steve Cox Collection; 180: portraits by Charles Willson Peale, courtesy of Independence National Historic Park; 183: Robert Barnes Archives; 186: © Bettmann/Corbis; 188: Robert Barnes Archives; 190: © Reuters NewMedia Inc./Corbis; 192: © Peter Turnley/Corbis; 194: Robert Barnes Archives; 196: © Bettmann/Corbis; 198: © Hulton-Deutsch Collection/Corbis; 201: © Bettmann/Corbis; 204: © Mitchell Gerber/Corbis; 206: Robert Barnes Archives; 208: Robert Barnes Archives; 210: Robert Barnes Archives; 212: courtesy of Richard M. Nixon Library; 215: © Bettmann/Corbis; 217: © Bettmann/ Corbis; 219: © AP Wide World Photos/Jim Pringle; 221: © Neal Preston/Corbis; 223: from the collection of the Texas/Dallas History and Archives Division, Dallas Public Library; 226: © Reuters NewMedia Inc./Corbis; 229: © Bettmann/Corbis; 232: courtesy of Procter & Gamble; 235: courtesy of University of Southern California Regional History Collection—Los Angeles Examiner Collection; 238: Robert Barnes Archives; 241: Robert Barnes Archives; 244: © Bettmann/Corbis; 246: © Bettmann/Corbis; 248: Central State Archive of Cinematic & Photographic Documents, St. Petersburg; 253: courtesy of Franklin D. Roosevelt Presidential Library; 256: Robert Barnes Archives; 258: Robert Barnes Archives; 260: © Bettmann/Corbis; 262: Robert Barnes Archives; 264: © Bettmann/Corbis; 267: © Neil Ricklen/Corbis Sygma; 269: © Bettmann/Corbis; 272: © AP Wide World Photos/Douglas C. Pizac; 274: courtesy of Smith and Wesson; 276: © Bettmann/Corbis; 279: © AP Wide World Photos/Michael Caulfield; 282: © Corbis; 284: Robert Barnes Archives; 287: © Bettmann/Corbis; 290: © Richard Ellis/Corbis Sygma; 293: Robert Barnes Archives; 295: courtesy of the Harry S. Truman Library; 297: © Hulton-Deutsch Collection/Corbis; 299: © Bettmann/Corbis; 302: © Hulton-Deutsch Collection/ Corbis; 304: courtesy of Wells Fargo Bank; 306: Robert Barnes Archives; 309: courtesy of Young & Rubicam.

About the Author

On December 13, 1984, Ric Wylie, an art director at J. Walter Thompson advertising agency, introduced Joey Green to his future wife, Debbie White, at the company Christmas party in the Puck Building in New York City. Both Joey and Debbie worked on the seventh floor of the Park Avenue Atrium, but had never met. Joey kissed Debbie's hand and disappeared into the crowd.

One month later, Joey met Debbie again in the halls of the company, looked into her eyes, and instantly knew he was going to marry her. He raced to the office

of a friend, Mindy Zepp, and, panic-stricken, told her that he had just met the woman he was going to marry and asked her what he should do. Mindy, who knew Debbie, suggested that before he started worrying about the wedding plans, he might consider asking Debbie out on a date. One month later, after Debbie left an invitation to a party at her apartment on his desk, Joey, encouraged by his colleague Michelle Lowe, finally got up the courage to ask Debbie out. On their first date, they went to Theresa's restaurant in Little Italy and then to the Comedy Cellar in Greenwich Village. The next night, Joey went to the party at Debbie's apartment in Queens. They began seeing each other frequently.

One Saturday afternoon, Joey treated Debbie to a cruise on the Staten Island ferry. As they passed the Statue of Liberty, the *QE2* came into view, her passengers standing on deck throwing streamers and popping champagne bottles.

Joey turned to Debbie. "What's your idea of the perfect honeymoon?" he asked.

"A trip around the world," she replied. "What's *your* idea of the perfect honeymoon?"

"A trip around the world," Joey admitted.

On September 7, 1987, Joey and Debbie got married at the Rosyln Country Club in Roslyn, New York, and immediately after the reception, flew to Caracas, Venezuela, to begin a two-year honeymoon, backpacking around the world.

"People always ask me, 'What was the best part of that trip?' said Joey. "The best part of that trip was that I got to spend twenty-four hours a day with Debbie for two years."